D1559375

A STUDY OF
CASSIUS DIO

A STUDY OF

CASSIUS DIO

BY

FERGUS MILLAR

FELLOW OF ALL SOULS COLLEGE

OXFORD

AT THE CLARENDON PRESS

© *Oxford University Press 1964*

FIRST PUBLISHED 1964
REPRINTED LITHOGRAPHICALLY IN GREAT BRITAIN
AT THE UNIVERSITY PRESS, OXFORD
BY VIVIAN RIDLER
PRINTER TO THE UNIVERSITY
1966

TO
SUSANNA

PREFACE

A BOOK must be its own justification and must stand or fall on its own merits. But a preface (which, like most prefaces, is in reality a postscript) may serve some purpose if it allows the author to stand back for a moment from the book as he has written it and say something about its context and purpose and about the methods adopted in it.

As the subject of a book, Dio stands in no need of apology. His work, the fullest surviving history of classical Rome, is not the object of any study with the slightest claims to comprehensiveness; almost all that has been written about it has been concerned with style and language, with particular books or passages or with the ever-recurrent subject of source-criticism. In a word, while the Roman History has received considerable attention as a text and a source of facts, it has very rarely been treated as a historical work in its own right. That is the gap which this book sets out to fill.

The approach I have adopted has been, in essence, that of presenting the History in terms of its author's reaction to the world in which he lived. Hence this book is intended not least as a contribution to our understanding of the Severan period. It is, indeed, not too much to say that there is no pagan of that vital period of whom we may know as much as we can of Dio. History must include not only 'what happened', but how those happenings appeared to those who lived through them. In Dio we can see not only the perspective of Roman history available to a man who was born in the reign of Marcus Aurelius and lived into that of Severus Alexander, but also, not in his contemporary history alone, the reactions of a conservative observer to an age full of stress and change. Moreover, as a Greek who was a Roman consul, Dio can represent in a unique way a fairly advanced stage in that fusion between two historical and cultural traditions which found its full expression in Byzantium. To trace from scattered passages in the History Dio's position within the complex cultural patterns of his day is to reveal something at least of the roots from which East Rome arose.

The emphasis, therefore, falls on Dio himself and on those aspects of his History which are original to him. What is said about the composition of the work has the aim merely of making clear the time and manner of writing, and the fact that Dio evolved his own structure for the narrative and cannot be assumed, at any point, to have slavishly followed some predecessor. This is inevitably merely a sketch; I have not attempted to give a full account of the literary character of the History.

In particular, little space has been devoted to source-criticism. Some might regard a work which claims to deal with a historian, and yet largely ignores the question of his sources, as *Hamlet* without the Prince. Yet the procedure can, I think, be justified. It is not merely that a large proportion of the work on Dio, including the major part of the standard article on him, that of Schwartz in Pauly–Wissowa, has concentrated on this aspect (though no man who had been through much of this type of work on Dio could feel very inclined to add to it), but that it seems to me that no satisfactory terms of reference in source-criticism have been yet evolved. In plain terms, we do not know enough about how ancient historians worked. We have no grounds for general assumptions about what an ancient historian would do when using one or more existing works as sources of material, or how he would redeploy that material in composing his own narrative. For the fact remains that, although there are many books on individual historians, and some others on what historians *say* about their methods, there is not a single general work which analyses in detail the techniques of ancient historiography. Without some such technical guidance, source-criticism is mere speculation, and its results often no more than the product of the assumptions with which the examination of a text was begun.

Such are the intentions with which this book has been written. It does no more than give a provisional definition of some aspects of Dio's enormous text. Much more could be done; in particular this book might provoke some scholar to attempt a full analysis of the intellectual and literary procedures involved when a man composed, from many different sources, a continuous narrative covering the entire history of Rome.

It will hardly escape notice that this book could not have

been what it is without the influence of Professor Syme's
Tacitus. No other work can set before one with such vigour and
clarity that range of techniques by which an historical work can
be analysed, and illuminated in detail as the product of a man
writing in a certain political and cultural environment. I have
been doubly fortunate, however, in having the influence not
only of *Tacitus*, but of Professor Syme himself, who supervised
the thesis of which this book is a partially expanded version
and took a vital and enlivening interest in it at all stages. Syme
stands in no need of praise; but one thing must be mentioned,
his capacity for inspiring confidence—confidence that out of
material which seemed at first burdensome and unmanageable
something alive and significant could be made. To that *vivida
vis animi* of his I owe a debt which I can never hope to repay.

My thanks are due also to Mr. P. M. Fraser, who has never
grudged time or trouble on any of the very frequent occasions
on which I asked him for assistance; to Mr. E. W. Gray and
Mr. R. Browning, who examined this work as a thesis and made
many valuable corrections and suggestions; and to Mr.
J. P. V. D. Balsdon, who very kindly read it for me and made
a number of suggestions for expansion and clarification to
which the present form of the book owes a great deal.

A considerable part of the material in Chapter II. 6 ('Cicero')
and Chapter III. 2 ('The Speeches') was used in an article
which appeared in *Museum Helveticum*, 1961. I am very grateful
to the editors for allowing me to include a revised version of it
in this book.

My work has been made possible by the tenure of a Fellow-
ship at All Souls, and I must record my gratitude to the Warden
and Fellows for an opportunity to pursue my studies in circumstances which could nowhere be bettered.

My greatest debt, none the less, is to my wife, without whom
I should hardly have had the courage to begin, much less to
complete, this contribution to the study of Dio and of the age
in which he lived.

F. M.

All Souls College, Oxford
15 February 1963

CONTENTS

xiiCONTENTS

ABBREVIATIONS

1. SPECIAL ABBREVIATIONS

Albo G. Barbieri, *L'Albo senatorio da Settimio Severo a Carino (193–285)* (Rome, 1952).

Boissevain *Cassii Dionis Cocceiani Historiarum Romanarum Quae Supersunt*, ed. U. P. Boissevain, vols. 1–3 (text), 4 (*index historicus*, ed. Smilda), 5 (*index Graecitatis*, ed. Nawijn), Berlin, 1898–1931. Photo-reprint of 1–4, Berlin, 1955. Where necessary for clarity, references are given with the page number of the relevant volume in brackets, e.g. 72. 23. 5 (305).

Magie, *Roman Rule* D. Magie, *Roman Rule in Asia Minor to the End of the Third Century after Christ*, 1–2 (Princeton, 1950).

Pflaum, *Carrières* H. G. Pflaum, *Les Carrières procuratoriennes équestres sous le Haut-Empire romain*, 1–3: Inst. franç. d'arch. de Beyrouth, Biblioth. arch. et hist. 57 (Paris, 1960–1).

Rostovtzeff, *SEHRE*² M. Rostovtzeff, *Social and Economic History of the Roman Empire*², ed. P. M. Fraser (Oxford, 1957).

Schwartz *RE* 3, 'Cassius' (40), reprinted in Ed. Schwartz, *Griechische Geschichtschreiber* (Leipzig, 1957), 394–450. References are given by the column numbers in *RE*, which are marked in the new edition.

2. PERIODICALS, COLLECTIONS OF DOCUMENTS, REFERENCE WORKS

A. Arch. Hung. *Acta Archaeologica Academiae Scientiarum Hungaricae.*

AE *L'Année épigraphique.*

AJA *American Journal of Archaeology.*

AJPh *American Journal of Philology.*

Arch. Ért. *Archaeológiai Értesítő.*

Ath. Mitt. *Mitteilungen des Deutschen Archaeologischen Instituts, Athenische Abteilung.*

BCH *Bulletin de Correspondance Hellénique.*

BE Robert, *Bulletin épigraphique*, published in *REG*.

BICS *Bulletin of the Institute of Classical Studies, London.*

BSNAF *Bulletin de la Société nationale des Antiquaires de France.*

CAH *Cambridge Ancient History.*

CE *Chronique d'Égypte.*

CIG *Corpus Inscriptionum Graecarum.*

CIL	Corpus Inscriptionum Latinarum.
CQ	Classical Quarterly.
CRAI	Comptes rendus de l'Académie des Inscriptions et Belles-Lettres, Paris.
FGrH	F. Jacoby, Die Fragmente der griechischen Historiker.
HRR	H. Peter, Historicorum Romanorum Reliquiae.
HSCPh	Harvard Studies in Classical Philology.
IG	Inscriptiones Graecae.
IGLS	L. Jalabert and R. Mouterde, Inscriptions grecques et latines de la Syrie.
IGR	Inscriptiones Graecae ad Res Romanas pertinentes.
ILS	Inscriptiones Latinae Selectae.
Ist. Mitt.	Mitteilungen des Deutschen Archaeologischen Instituts, Istanbuler Abteilung.
JDAI	Jahrbuch des Deutschen Archäologischen Instituts.
JEA	Journal of Egyptian Archaeology.
JÖAI	Jahreshefte des Österreichischen Archäologischen Instituts.
JRS	Journal of Roman Studies.
MEFR	Mélanges d'archéologie et d'histoire de l'École française de Rome.
MH	Museum Helveticum.
MSNAF	Mémoires de la Société nationale des Antiquaires de France.
NC	Numismatic Chronicle.
PBSR	Papers of the British School at Rome.
PCPhS	Proceedings of the Cambridge Philological Society.
PIR	Prosopographia Imperii Romani.
RE	Pauly–Wissowa, Real-Encyclopädie der classischen Altertumswissenschaft.
REA	Revue des études anciennes.
REG	Revue des études grecques.
REL	Revue des études latines.
RFIC	Rivista di filologia e d'istruzione classica.
RhM	Rheinisches Museum für Philologie.
RSI	Rivista storica italiana.
SBAW	Sitzungsberichte der Bayerischen Akademie der Wissenschaften.
SCIV	Studi şi cercetări di istorie veche.
SDAW	Sitzungsberichte der Deutschen Akademie der Wissenschaften zu Berlin.
TAPhA	Transactions and Proceedings of the American Philological Association.
YCS	Yale Classical Studies.

INTRODUCTION

The Byzantine Excerpts, Xiphilinus and Zonaras

THE text of Dio's Roman History is preserved only in Books 36–54 (68–10 B.C.), in substantial fragments of Books 55–60 (9 B.C.–A.D. 46), and in a section covering part of Books 79–80 (from the death of Caracalla to the middle of the reign of Elagabal). It may be useful, therefore, to give a guide here to the three main sources from which the rest of the text has to be restored, and a brief discussion of their reliability.[1]

The earliest of the three sources is the excerpts from historical works made on the instructions of the Emperor Constantine Porphyrogenitus (912–59).[2] The excerpts, from a large number of classical and Byzantine Greek historians, are arranged in books according to theme—Περὶ γνωμῶν or Περὶ ἐπιβουλῶν κατὰ βασιλέων γεγονυιῶν for example.[3] Excerpts from Dio appear in the books Περὶ πρεσβειῶν, Περὶ ἀρετῆς καὶ κακίας, and Περὶ γνωμῶν. They are of considerable value where the text of Dio is missing, in that, in the nature of the case, they very largely preserve Dio's own words. The types of textual change which the excerpts introduce can be conveniently surveyed in Boissevain, vol. 3, pp. 767–75, where a number of them are printed in parallel with the relevant passages of Dio. In brief, the following alterations are common: (1) All the excerpts begin with the word ὅτι. (2) The opening sentence is sometimes expanded to make the context intelligible. (3) In the body of each excerpt minor grammatical changes are fairly frequent and whole clauses or sentences are sometimes cut. Where Dio uses the first person the excerpts tend to have the sentence corrected into the third. (4) The text may break off in mid-sentence, or occasionally end with a summary of the following passage in Dio where

---

[1] For a full discussion of the elements of the restored text of Dio, and all textual questions, see Boissevain's edition.

[2] See K. Krumbacher, *Geschichte der byzantinischen Literatur* (Munich, 1897), 252 f., especially 258 f.

[3] They are edited by Boissevain, de Boor, and Büttner–Wobst, *Excerpta Historica iussu Imp. Constantini Porphyrogeniti confecta* (Berlin, 1903–6).

it is too long to excerpt in full.[1] Alternatively a passage
may be given in two successive excerpts, both beginning with
ὅτι.[2]

Such minor changes apart, the excerpts, which cover the whole
range of Dio's History, can be taken as reliable evidence for his
text.

In the second half of the eleventh century the monk Ioannes
Xiphilinus of Trapezus made an Epitome of Books 36–80 of the
History, dividing it by reigns—beginning with those of Pompey
and Julius Caesar.[3] It is this Epitome which provides the bulk of
the work as we have it from Book 61 to the end, as well as filling
gaps in the preceding six books. Xiphilinus' work is not so much
a précis of Dio as a rather erratic selection from his material,
substantially, but not invariably, in Dio's order and often keep-
ing very close to Dio's wording.[4] Thus a large amount of material
is omitted without trace, some is given in brief, and some, especially where there is a coherent narrative or anecdote of some
special interest, is reproduced almost in full. Occasionally he adds
material or comments of his own, mostly concerned with the
history of Christianity.

Read as a work in its own right, the Epitome provides only
a spasmodic and often barely intelligible narrative. Xiphilinus'
inability to digest and condense Dio's material is, however, the
source of the most valuable feature of his work, his reproduction
in the first person of many statements by Dio about both his own
career and the writing of his History. Without this we should
know little of Dio as a man and could hardly attempt to analyse
the structure of his later books, covering the years from A.D. 47
to 229.

Half a century later Ioannes Zonaras composed his Ἐπιτομὴ
ἱστοριῶν, from the Creation to 1118.[5] He used Dio, firstly, for his
Books 7–9, the history of Rome from the arrival of Aeneas in

---

[1] See, for example, Περὶ πρεσβειῶν Ῥωμαίων 11—Dio 49. 27. 3–4.

[2] e.g. Περὶ ἀρετῆς καὶ κακίας 142 and 143—Dio 47. 10. 2–11. 1.

[3] The work is headed Ἐπιτομὴ τῆς Δίωνος τοῦ Νικαέως Ῥωμαϊκῆς Ἱστορίας ἣν
συνέτεμεν Ἰωάννης ὁ Ξιφιλῖνος περιέχουσα μοναρχίας Καισάρων εἰκοσιπέντε ἀπὸ
Πομπηΐου μάγνου μεχρὶς Ἀλεξάνδρου τοῦ Μαμαίας. On Xiphilinus see Krumbacher,
op. cit. 369 f.

[4] I can find no grounds for the view, as in Krumbacher, op. cit. 370, and Wachsmuth, Einleitung in das Studium der alten Geschichte (Leipzig, 1895), 598, n. 3, that
Xiphilinus was using an earlier epitome of Dio.

[5] See Krumbacher, op. cit. 370 f.

Italy to 146 B.C., where he states that his authorities failed him
(9. 31). This Epitome is thus the most important source for the
reconstruction of the first quarter of Dio's History.[1] He returns
to Dio with the death of Julius Caesar (10. 12—Dio 44. 3 f.) and
from that point until the reign of Nerva (11. 20) follows Dio and
combines with him large amounts of material from Plutarch
and later some from Eusebius (for instance 10. 39 on the birth of
Christ), Josephus (11. 11), and Appian (11. 16). He may have
used Xiphilinus' Epitome as an aid, since there are a few mistakes
which occur in both of them, but it is clear that he also read Dio
in the original and can be used as a supplement to Xiphilinus.[2]
From the reign of Trajan onwards he seems to have given up
direct use of Dio, and to have excerpted Xiphilinus. From that
point he thus provides no independent material for the study
of Dio.[3]

As a literary work Zonaras' Epitome is rather more coherent
and intelligible than that of Xiphilinus. He is less prone to
transcribe sections of Dio almost literally and, although he too
inevitably omits much material altogether, he is more successful
in abbreviating passages while retaining the sense. Appendix I
gives a comparative table of Xiphilinus' and Zonaras' treatment
of Dio Book 54 as an example of their technique.

Zonaras' chief usefulness with regard to Dio is that he pre-
serves the structure of the first twenty books.[4] Dio's treatment of
the history of Rome to 146 B.C. has never been discussed except in
terms of source-criticism[5] and is not analysed in the present work.
The task would repay anyone who attempted it.

The limitations which beset any discussion of those books of
Dio in which the original text is not preserved are thus severe.
They must be remembered particularly in connexion with the

[1] It is printed alongside the fragments of Dio 1–20 in Boissevain, vol. 1.
[2] See the detailed discussion by Th. Büttner–Wobst, 'Die Abhängigkeit des
Geschichtschreibers Zonaras von den erhaltenen Quellen', *Commentationes Fleckeisenianae* (Leipzig, 1890), 121, pp. 151 f.
[3] This is demonstrated, as against Büttner–Wobst, op. cit. 163 f., by U. P.
Boissevain, 'Zonaras' Quelle für die römische Kaisergeschichte von Nerva bis
Severus Alexander', *Hermes* 26 (1891), 440. See also Boissevain, vol. 3, p. 187.
[4] Though he includes also some material from Plutarch. See Büttner-Wobst,
op. cit. 142 f.
[5] See Schwarz 1692 f.; A. Klotz, 'Über die Stellung des Cassius Dio unter den
Quellen zur Geschichte des zweiten punischen Krieges', *RhM* 85 (1936), 68 and 97,
and the works listed by Boissevain, vol. 1, pp. cii–ciii.

analysis of Dio's history of his own time, where, for reasons of style, it has clearly been impossible to insert repeated warnings about the state of the text. But even here it is, I believe, possible to arrive, by a close examination of the existing text, at a true and reliable conception of how Dio wrote history.

I

THE MAN AND HIS CAREER

WITH Cassius Dio, the writing of full histories of Rome ended, as it had begun, with a work written in Greek by a Roman senator. Half a millennium of change within the Roman governing class is exemplified in the contrast between Q. Fabius Pictor, the contemporary of Hannibal, who chose Greek as the only language for a prose work—and perhaps as a vehicle for putting Rome's political standpoint before a Greek audience[1]—and Dio, from Bithynia in Asia Minor, for whom it was his native tongue. Yet more significant perhaps than this contrast is the similarity of their social standing, for the writing of history at Rome was almost the exclusive preserve of senators, from those who followed Fabius Pictor in using Greek[2] to Cato the Elder who established the fashion for Latin; to Sallust, Asinius Pollio, Velleius Paterculus, Tacitus, and the little-known senatorial historians of the early Empire;[3] and in the second century Flavius Arrianus, the friend of Hadrian,[4] and the wealthy senator from Pergamum, Claudius Charax.[5] For those who were not senators some official position was better than none. Appian carefully informs the reader in his preface that he had been prominent in his native Alexandria, had appeared as an advocate before the Emperors in Rome, and had been an imperial

---

[1] See K. Hanell, 'Zur Problematik der älteren römischen Geschichtsschreibung', *Fondation Hardt: Entretiens sur l'antiquité classique IV, Histoire et historiens dans l'antiquité* (Geneva, 1956), 147.

[2] L. Cincius Alimentus (*FGrH* 810), P. Cornelius Scipio (*FGrH* 811), A. Postumius Albinus (*FGrH* 812), C. Acilius (*FGrH* 813), Cn. Aufidius (*FGrH* 814), P. Rutilius Rufus (*FGrH* 815).

[3] e.g. C. Clodius Licinus (*HRR* 2. cvii f.; *PIR*² C 1167), A. Cremutius Cordus (*HRR* 2. cxiii f.), Bruttedius Niger (*HRR* 2. cxvi), Cn. Cornelius Lentulus Gaetulicus (*HRR* 2. cxvii), M. Servilius Nonianus (*HRR* 2. cxxviii f.).

[4] See Ed. Schwartz, *Griechische Geschichtschreiber* (Leipzig, 1957), 130 f. He is a partial exception in that of his historical works only that on the Parthian wars dealt with Roman history.

[5] See Chr. Habicht, 'Zwei neue Inschriften aus Pergamon', *Ist. Mitt.* 9–10 (1959–60), 109. He wrote Ἑλληνικῶν τε καὶ ⟨Ἰταλικῶν (or Ῥωμαϊκῶν)⟩ βιβλία μ'. See the Suda s.v. Χάραξ (ed. Adler 4. 787–8) and *FGrH* 103.

procurator,[1] while Herodian gives the posts he had held as his
qualification for writing the history of his own time, from Commodus to Maximinus.[2] Of those historians at Rome who were
neither senators nor *equites* many were in some way attached to
prominent senators or to Emperors, as freedmen, secretaries,
or protégés;[3] in this class come two considerable figures of the
Augustan age, Strabo and Dionysius of Halicarnassus.[4]

This pattern must in part be merely a reflection of the nature
of Roman society—few Roman exponents of any branch of
literature stood outside the circles where power and patronage
were exercised.[5] But there was also a theoretical justification for
the predominance of senators, for a long-established convention,
which took Thucydides as its model and which was formally
expressed by Polybius, laid down that history could only properly
be written by men of affairs. The historian, Polybius states, must
have political and military experience[6] and one of the chief aims
of his work must be the interpretation of political action for the
benefit of statesmen in the present and the future.[7] This conception of history is reflected by the Roman historian Sempronius
Asellio early in the following century, who lays down that history
should not merely record what happened but make clear the
reasons and purposes for which men had acted.[8] The underlying

---

[1] *Prooim.* 62. H. G. Pflaum, *Les Procurateurs équestres sous le Haut-Empire romain*
(Paris, 1950), 204–5 shows, as against *PIR*[2] A 943, that Appian was not *advocatus
fisci* in Rome, but gained a procuratorship by the intercession of Fronto.

[2] 1. 2. 5. ἔστι δ' ὧν καὶ πείρᾳ μετέσχον ἐν βασιλικαῖς ἢ δημοσίαις ὑπηρεσίαις
γενόμενος.

[3] For instance Theophanes of Mitylene (*FGrH* 188), the friend and historian of
Pompey, Empylus, the companion of Brutus (*FGrH* 191), C. Julius Hyginus,
a freedman of Augustus (*HRR* 2. ci f.), Potamon of Mitylene, a friend of Tiberius
(*FGrH* 147), Kriton, Trajan's doctor and historian of the Dacian wars (*FGrH* 200),
Phlegon of Tralles, a freedman of Hadrian (*FGrH* 257), and Chryserus, a freedman
of Marcus Aurelius, who wrote a chronicle of Roman history to A.D. 180 (*FGrH* 96).

[4] Strabo travelled in Egypt with the Prefect, Aelius Gallus, in 25–24 B.C. (Str.
2. 5. 12) and was a friend of Athenodorus, the sophist and teacher of Augustus
(16. 4. 21). Dionysius was the protégé of the senator and historian, Q. Aelius
Tubero, to whom he addressed his work on Thucydides.

[5] On the role of dedication and patronage in the publication of literary works
see Th. Birt, *Kritik und Hermeneutik: nebst Abriß des antiken Buchwesens* (Munich,
1913), 312 f.   [6] Polyb. 12. 25g. 1.

[7] See the concise sketch of Polybius' views on history in F. W. Walbank, *A Historical Commentary on Polybius*, 1 (Oxford, 1957), 6 f.

[8] *HRR* 1, p. 179, fr. 1. See R. Till, 'Sempronius Asellio', *Würzburger Jahrbücher* 4
(1949–50), 330 and J. P. V. D. Balsdon, 'Some Questions about Historical Writing
in the Second Century B.C.', *CQ*, N.S. 3 (1953), 158.

assumption that the task could be performed only by a man of the right social standing is fully brought out by Lucian in his work on the writing of history: the bare record of a campaign which some soldier or artisan or trader might compose could be no more than material for a real historian.[1]

For Polybius the most satisfactory type of history was that confined to events within one's own lifetime or at least to events recent enough for eyewitnesses and participants to survive.[2] It is conspicuous that the majority of the most famous historians in antiquity, Thucydides, Polybius himself, Sallust, and Tacitus, kept within these limits. But even when a man dealt with long periods of the past, where he had necessarily to rely on written accounts, political judgement and experience were still relevant, and it is noteworthy that a number of men, for instance Velleius Paterculus—or, for that matter, Nicolaus of Damascus or Josephus—Arrian, and Dio himself, wrote histories which began in the distant past but came up to and included their own time.

The well-established tradition of how history should be written by men of standing had lost none of its force by the turn of the second and third centuries—and it is no accident that Dio took Thucydides as the model for his style and to some degree for his thought. As a consequence, even if Dio could not impose his personality on the eighty books of his Roman History with the intensity of a Tacitus surveying the evils of his own age, the examination of his political experience must be highly important for the study of his work. Moreover, his background is of especial complexity and interest simply because he was a Greek and a Roman consul, a member of two societies and the heir of two very different social traditions.

It is fortunate that in recording the history of his own time Dio tells us much about himself, his experiences in Rome, his movements, offices, and governorships. It is thus possible to reconstruct his life in considerable detail over a period of nearly fifty years, from the accession of Commodus to his own second consulship in 229 with Severus Alexander, a time of no little importance in the history of Rome. Indeed, it could be said that we have for Dio a more valuable record of personal experience than for any other ancient historian, even Polybius.

[1] Lucian πῶς δεῖ ἱστορίαν συγγράφειν 15.
[2] Polyb. 4. 2. 2.

Dio's native city was Nicaea in Bithynia, a Hellenistic foundation and now a prosperous city of the second rank and a vital
cross-roads in the military system of the Empire.[1] Little remains
of the ancient site except an imposing town wall. It has never been
excavated and our information is largely limited to inscriptions
showing on the surface.[2] But it is clear that Roman rule brought
the city an importance which it had not enjoyed previously, for
Strabo calls Nicaea the metropolis of Bithynia[3] (though in fact
Nicomedia retained the title), and local coinage shows the city's
rivalry with Nicomedia which had been the capital of the Bithynian dynasty.[4] The literary evidence, Pliny's correspondence with
Trajan and the orations of Dio of Prusa[5]—exceptionally rich for
a provincial city and dating to slightly over half a century before
Dio's birth—shows not only inter-city rivalries but a province
beset by social conflicts: a sign, probably, of increasing prosperity
rather than decline.[6] It is not without significance that Dio regarded the struggles of cities for primacy and honorific titles with
profound scorn—city titles, he notes in a passing comment, used
to be awarded by the Senate, while now cities appropriate whole
lists of titles as they please.[7] In the speech he puts into the mouth
of Maecenas he even recommends the abolition of local coinage,
a right possessed by both Nicaea and Nicomedia.[8]

Dio's father, Cassius Apronianus, was himself a senator and
consul, who governed Lycia–Pamphylia, Cilicia (where Dio accompanied him), and Dalmatia.[9] It is not unlikely that he was
descended from a rich Nicaean of the Julio–Claudian period,
Cassius Asclepiodotus, who, as Tacitus and Dio himself record,
was the friend of Barea Soranus and had his property confiscated

---

[1] See E. Gren, *Kleinasien und der Ostbalkan in der wirtschaftlichen Entwicklung der
römischen Kaiserzeit* (Uppsala, 1941), especially 52 f.

[2] See especially A. M. Schneider and W. Karnapp, *Die Stadtmauer von Iznik
(Nicaea)*, Istanbuler Forschungen, Bd. 9 (Berlin, 1938); W. Ruge, *RE* 17 (1936),
'Nikaia' (7), 226.

[3] Strabo 12. 4. 7.

[4] See Ruge, art. cit. 229–31. On the coinage of Nicomedia see C. Bosch, *Die
kleinasiatischen Münzen der römischen Kaiserzeit II. 1. Bithynien 1.* (Stuttgart, 1935),
200 f., especially 220 f.

[5] For Nicaea, Pliny, *Ep.* 10. 31, 39, 40, 81, 83, 84; Dio, *Or.* 38, 39 (and *Or.* 47.
13).

[6] So Gren, op. cit. 20.   [7] 54. 23. 8.   [8] 52. 30. 9.

[9] *PIR²* C 485; W. Jagenteufel, *Die Statthalter der römischen Provinz Dalmatia von
Augustus bis Diokletian*, Öst. Akad. der Wiss., Schr. der Balkan-Kom. Ant. Abt. 12.
(Wien, 1958), 84–85.

by Nero and restored by Galba.[1] The obelisk of Asclepiodotus' son, Cassius Philiscus, stands outside the city.[2] How this family gained the Roman citizenship is not clear: no Cassius is known to have governed Bithynia, or served there, in its first century as a province.[3] From the same family may come the Cassius Chrestus who supervised the construction of a tower in the town wall in 78/79,[4] and another Nicaean Cassius was perhaps consul in 130.[5] Other Cassii from Bithynia are known,[6] but the evidence suggests that there was a single wealthy family in Nicaea whose links with Roman society were already close in the first century A.D. By contrast, there is little to show that they had close connexions with their native city. This may be important, for it is a predominant characteristic of Greek senators in the second and third centuries that they came from families which played, and continued to play, an important part in the official life of their homelands.[7] The same families could include magistrates of Greek cities, provincial High Priests, Roman equestrian officials and senators.[8] A striking example from Bithynia, of a family with strong local connexions and members in the service of Rome and in the Senate itself, is afforded by the Domitii of Prusias ad Hypium. There were many Domitii and Domitiani in Bithynia, whose name went back probably to grants of citizenship by Cn. Domitius Ahenobarbus, the legate of Antonius,[9] but the

---

[1] Tac. *Ann.* 16. 33: 'magnitudine opum praecipuus inter Bithynos.' Dio 62. 26. 2 mentions Asclepiodotus' restoration under Galba. See *PIR²* C 486.

[2] See *PIR²* C 515.   [3] See Magie, *Roman Rule*, 1590–3.

[4] *IGR* 3. 37 = Schneider and Karnapp, op. cit., no. 11 (p. 45).

[5] [Ca]ssius Agri[ppa?], suffect consul in A.D. 130 (*PIR²* C 481), may be identical with the [Γάϊον? Κάσ]σιον [Ἀγρίππαν, Γαΐου? Κασσίου Ἀγρί]ππου υἱόν who appears in A. M. Schneider, *Die römischen und byzantinischen Denkmäler von Iznik-Nicaea* (Berlin, 1943), ins. no. 2. See *BE* 1947, no. 189.

[6] See *BCH* 24 (1900), 383, 407–8; 25 (1901), 67, no. 208; L. Robert, *Études anatoliennes* (Paris, 1937), 245.

[7] The term 'Oriental', which is largely used, is entirely invalid (see the remarks of L. Robert, *Hellenica* 9 (Paris, 1950), 51 n. 3). 'Greek' has the advantage of a clear reference to language and culture. Even this term, however, has its ambiguities (see the discussion on pp. 182 f.).

[8] The evidence has not yet been put together in convenient form. The best illustration is A. Stein, 'Zur sozialen Stellung der provinzialen Oberpriester', Ἐπιτύμβιον *H. Swoboda* (Reichenberg, 1927), 300.

[9] Domitii—*IGR* 3. 73, *BCH* 24 (1900), 418 no. 119, 419 no. 120, 426 no. 141; F. K. Dörner, *Bericht über eine Reise in Bithynien*, Öst. Akad. der Wiss., Phil.-hist. Klasse, 75. 1 (1952), ins. nos. 106, 112, 149, *BCH* 25 (1901), 87 no. 218. Domitiani— *BCH* 25 (1901), 65 no. 208, 80 no. 211; 27 (1903), 316 no. 5. See *BE* 1953, no. 194 ad fin. and *BE* 1958, no. 476 (T. Flavius Domitianus Nestor).

most numerous and prominent seem to have derived from a
family or group of families in Prusias.[1] From here came M.
Domitius Candidus, a consul and imperial legate, and probably
a younger contemporary of Dio.[2]

The evidence suggests, however vaguely, that the Cassii were
attached as much to Rome as to Nicaea. Dio himself appears to
be divided in his local loyalties: in the first fragment of his
History he refers to Italy as 'this land in which we dwell', but at
the very end he speaks of going home to Bithynia—'I set off home
to pass the remaining part of my life in my native land.'[3] In
theory, as Trajan laid down, all senators were supposed to own
property in Italy and to regard it as more than a place of business.[4] There is some evidence of Greek senators owning property
in Italy, but not perhaps as much as could be expected if the
regulations were in fact observed.[5] A certain change of emphasis
can be detected in a passage of the *Digest* where Paulus states
that a senator has a double *domicilium*—Rome in addition to his
patria.[6] Cassius Apronianus himself may have had Italian property. An inscription, now lost, bearing his name, was found in
Portus Augusti, but it is not clear whether it was on a tile (which
would indicate property) or merely on a bronze clasp.[7] Dio says
that when free of public business he used to retire to Capua to

---

[1] See *BCH* 25 (1901), 65 no. 208 (three examples), 76 no. 209, 78 no. 210,
83 no. 214 (an equestrian military career), 87 no. 218. Dörner, *Bericht*, nos. 5, 18.
A. Körte, *Ath. Mitt.* 24 (1899), 435–6.

[2] M. Domitius Candidus is known from Dörner, *Bericht*, no. 4 and *BE* 1958, no.
476 (p. 326) and can be identified with M. Domitius Valerianus, legate of Arabia
in 238–9 (*PIR*² D 168).

[3] Fr. 1. 3. τήνδε τὴν γῆν, ἥν κατοικοῦμεν. 80. 5. 2 (476) ἀπῆρα οἴκαδε ... ὥστε
πάντα τὸν λοιπὸν τοῦ βίου χρόνον ἐν τῇ πατρίδι ζῆσαι. See J. Palm, *Rom, Römertum
und Imperium in der griechischen Literatur der Kaiserzeit* (Lund, 1959), 82.

[4] Pliny, *Ep.* 6. 19. One-third of their property should be invested in Italian land.
It was shameful that 'honorem petituros urbem Italiamque non pro patria sed pro
hospitio aut stabulo quasi peregrinantes habere'. Marcus Aurelius lowered the re-
quirement to a quarter, SHA *vita M. A.* 11. 8.

[5] M. Ulpius Arabianus from Amastris, Pontus (*PIR*¹ U 540—*Albo* no. 532)—
a house in Rome; Ti. Claudius Telemachus (*PIR*² C 1037—*Albo* no. 175) bought
the *Fundus Rutilianus—Dig.* 4. 4. 38 *praef.* (Paulus); C. Asinius Nicomachus
Julianus (*PIR*² A 1237), not certainly of Greek origin, had property at Drepanum;
L. Calpurnius Proculus (*PIR*² C 303) had property near Volsinii. The Julii Frugi
(father and son, *RE* 10 (1917), 252–3) had a house in Rome and property at
Alba Fucens, but the view that they came from north-west Asia Minor is not secure.
T. Flavius (Claudius?) Sulpicianus (*PIR*² F 373), who may have originated from
Crete, had property near Praeneste.

[6] *Dig.* 1. 9. 11.

[7] *CIL* 14. 4089, 26 = 15. 2164.

write in peace. He clearly knew and liked the area (τοῦτο γὰρ τὸ χωρίον ἐξειλόμην τῶν τε ἄλλων ἕνεκα καὶ τῆς ἡσυχίας ὅτι μάλιστα).[1] He also records elsewhere that the inhabitants took pride in the aqueduct and enjoyed the fruits of the territory of Knossos which Octavian had given them,[2] and devotes a lengthy and enthusiastic excursus to Agrippa's constructions at Baiae, which, he says, he had seen himself.[3] The possession of property at Nicaea, more (presumably a villa) at Capua, and, it can be inferred, at least a *pied-à-terre* in Rome indicates a comfortable level of wealth. It is clear, however, from some remarks of his about Pertinax that Dio did not identify himself with the richest members of the Senate; the Emperor, he says, was assiduous in hospitality and when not giving a dinner would send round choice dishes to his friends—the rich and arrogant laughed, but the others approved.[4]

It is generally inferred from Dio's full name, Cassius Dio Cocceianus, that he must have been a descendant of the rhetor, Cocceianus Dio of Prusa. Some have even given the relationship—grandson[5] (which is, in fact, impossible on chronological grounds). Dio himself gives no help, for, although he makes one reference to the rhetor, he does not actually name him (in the extant text) or claim any connexion.[6] It remains possible that the names 'Dio Cocceianus' were given to him in honour of a famous local figure and do not indicate any connexion; one L. Valerius Cocceianus Callicles is attested at the Bithynian town of Prusias ad Hypium, for example.[7] But Dio of Prusa himself happens to mention marriages between citizens of different cities in Bithynia,[8] and it is probable that Dio's name does indeed arise from a marriage-connexion between the Cassii of Nicaea and the family of Cocceianus Dio of Prusa. If so, the marriage was probably that of Dio's father, for his own name, Cassius Apronianus, shows no trace of the connexion. He will have made

---

[1] 76. 2. 1 (358). Capua seems to have been relatively in decline in this period and very little is known about it. See J. Beloch, *Campanien* (Berlin, 1879), 295 f. and the remarks of M. W. Frederiksen, 'Republican Capua; a Social and Economic Study', *PBSR*, n.s. 14 (1959), 80, on p. 124.

[2] 49. 14. 5.

[3] 48. 50–51.   [4] 73. 3. 4 (308).

[5] e.g. H. Peter, *Die geschichtliche Literatur über die römische Kaiserzeit*, I (Leipzig, 1897), 431, and A. von Gutschmid, *Kleine Schriften* 5 (Leipzig, 1894), 547.

[6] 69. 3. 6 (225). Philos. *VS* 1. 8 (Teubner ed. 9) shows that Dio of Prusa is referred to.

[7] Robert, *BE* 1953, no. 193 *init.*   [8] *Or.* 38. 22.

a good match, for Dio of Prusa's speeches show that his family was rich, and influential in the area.[1]

Such a marriage between wealthy families in the Greek provinces would have followed a well-established pattern. For, with all due caution (since the inscriptional evidence, for obvious reasons, tends to relate to local dynasts and benefactors), it can be said at least that there is evidence to show that Greek families could retain their local position and connexions after some members had become Roman senators, and that there are only a few known cases of their marrying into Italian senatorial families. Marcus Aurelius, for instance, endeavoured to marry his daughters to the most virtuous members of the Senate;[2] one of those selected was Cn. Claudius Severus, consul for the second time in 173. This seems a clear example of a family from Phrygia or Paphlagonia whose connexion with Rome is attested from Trajan to 235 (Cn. Claudius Severus, consul II) and perhaps to Diocletian; the inscriptions do not, however, make clear whether they abandoned their original connexions and possessions.[3] Another was Ti. Claudius Pompeianus from Antioch, also consul for the second time in 173; his descendants certainly stayed in Rome.[4] Apart from these political alliances put through by Marcus Aurelius the evidence is fairly sparse: the most notable cases are Herodes Atticus, married to Appia Annia Regilla Atilia Caucidia Tertulla, the sister of a consul and probably the descendant of an Italian family whose citizenship went back to Marius,[5] and Pompeia Agrippinilla, sister of M. Pompeius Macrinus the consul of 164, who was married to M. Gavius Squilla Gallicanus consul of 150; both families are represented in the famous Bacchic inscription from Tusculum.[6] Since the connexions of the Mytilenean family of the Pompeii with Rome went back to the last age of the Republic they are not perhaps a true exception to the

---

[1] Evidence in H. von Arnim, *Leben und Werke des Dio von Prusa* (Berlin, 1898), 122 f.

[2] Herodian 1. 2. 2. See J. Keil, 'Kaiser Marcus und die Thronfolge', *Klio* 31 (1938), 293.

[3] See *PIR²* C 1023-8.   [4] *PIR²* C 973, 970-2, 1177.

[5] Herodes *PIR²* C 802; Annia, A 720; citizenship, A 653.

[6] A. Vogliano, 'La grande iscrizione bacchica del Metropolitan Museum', *AJA* 37 (1933), 215, M. P. Nilsson, *The Dionysiac Mysteries of the Hellenistic and Roman Age*, Skrift. Svenska Institut. Athen 8°, 5 (Lund, 1957), 46 f. On the family of the Pompeii, H. G. Pflaum, 'La Chronologie de la carrière de M. Pompeius Macrinus Theophanes *legatus leg. VI Victrix*', *Germania* 37 (1959), 150.

pattern. There are few other known cases of Greek senators who married into Italian families.[1]

Dio too was married, or so one may justifiably assume from the appearance of a Cassius Dion, consul of 291 and *Praefectus Urbi* in 296/7[2]—probably a great-grandson. He managed, it may be noted, to write a speech of some individuality and conviction on the delights of marriage, which he puts into the mouth of Augustus addressing the equestrian order in A.D. 9.[3] It would be of some interest to know to whom he was married, but amid all that he tells us of his own life, this detail is not recorded.

Dio must have been born about 163 or 164.[4] We know nothing of his life until he came to Rome about 180, but these years, and the first two stages of his education, were presumably spent in Nicaea. If he followed the established pattern of Graeco-Roman education he will have gone first to a γραμματιστής or *primus magister* at the age of seven, then to a *grammaticus*, and finally, at eighteen or so, to a rhetor.[5] The traces of rhetorical training are obvious throughout his work, while a reference to the teachers of Marcus Aurelius makes clear his approval of sophists and dislike of philosophers.[6] Moreover, an important passage shows that he read Atticist writers with the conscious aim of

---

[1] T. Flavius Sulpicianus, who may have originated from Crete (see p. 10, n. 5, and *Albo* no. 243), was the father-in-law of Helvius Pertinax. It is significant that, for instance, in the lines descended from C. Julius Demosthenes, *procurator Augusti*, Licinius Musaeus and Marcus Titianus, Lyciarch (stemmata in *PIR*[2] 2, pp. 166 and 230), no Italian appears until Q. Pompeius Sosius Falco, the consul of 193, husband of Sulpicia Agrippina—five generations from the procurator.

[2] *PIR*[2] C 491.

[3] 56. 2–9.

[4] The date has been disputed and many have preferred to place Dio's birth about 155—see the opinions assembled by G. Vrind, *De Cassii Dionis vocabulis quae ad ius publicum pertinent* (The Hague, 1923), 164–5. This view depends on the belief that Dio was a senator as early as 180. The pattern of Dio's career as set out below shows that such a view is untenable. In particular, Dio, as the son of an imperial legate, would expect to have his praetorship (in 194) at thirty or soon after; and it is difficult to imagine that he could have governed Pannonia (226–28) in his seventies. Recently J. F. Gilliam, 'The plague under Marcus Aurelius', *AJPh* 82 (1961), 225 has tried to use Dio's statement in 72. 14. 3 (296) that the plague of (probably) 189 was 'the greatest he had experienced' to show that the plague of 166 and the following years was not as great as has usually been thought. But when Verus' armies, bringing the plague, passed through Nicaea in 166—see *RE* 17 (1936), 233—Dio was about two or three years old and no doubt failed to notice.

[5] H. I. Marrou, *A History of Education in Antiquity* (trans. G. Lamb, London, 1956), 265 f.

[6] 71. 35. 1–2 (277).

purifying his style—τῶν Ἑλλήνων δέ τινες, ὧν τὰ βιβλία ἐπὶ τῷ
ἀττικίζειν ἀναγινώσκομεν.[1]

For the third stage of his education Dio might normally, as
a well-born Greek, have gone to hear one of the famous sophists
who taught in the great cities of Asia. Philostratus records that
pupils came to Scopelianus at Smyrna from all parts of Asia
Minor, Syria, and Egypt and to Heracleides from all Asia and
European Greece as well.[2] An Ephesian inscription lists the
pupils of Soter, with their native cities; one is from Nicaea.[3]
But when Dio comes to record the arrival of Commodus in
Rome in the autumn of 180 he states that from this point on he
speaks as an eyewitness of events—λέγω δὲ ταῦτά τε καὶ τὰ λοιπὰ
οὐκ ἐξ ἀλλοτρίας ἔτι παραδόσεως ἀλλ' ἐξ οἰκείας ἤδη τηρήσεως—
and carries on with a reference to Commodus' first speech in the
Senate.[4] He was not yet a senator himself (it is not until late in
his account of Commodus' reign that he begins to speak of the
Senate in the first person)[5] but he may well have been present,
for Augustus had laid down that the sons of senators, in order to
gain experience of public life, should, on assuming the *toga virilis*,
take the *latus clavus* and attend the Senate.[6]

It was thus at the age of sixteen or seventeen that Dio came to
Rome. He may have taken the sea-route to Thessalonica and
then travelled along the Via Egnatia, for it was perhaps on
this journey that he visited Apollonia in Illyria and tried the
prophetic powers of the river Aoos, of which he gives a rapt
description.[7]

To come to Rome did not, however, mean the loss of rhetorical
training in Greek. For, as Philostratus tells us, in the earlier part
of the reign of Commodus the famous sophist, Adrianos of Tyre,
occupied the chair in Rome; so popular were his declamations

---

[1] 55. 12. 4–5. See p. 41.
[2] Philos. *VS* 1. 21 (Teubner ed. 31), 2. 26 (113).
[3] J. Keil, 'Vertreter der zweiten Sophistik in Ephesos', *JOAI* 40 (1953), no. 7.
[4] 72. 4. 2 (284).
[5] The first instance is 72. 16. 3 (298) ἡμᾶς τε καὶ τὰς γυναῖκας ἡμῶν. See also 72.
18. 2 (299), 20. 1 (301), 21. 1–3 (302). All come in Dio's account of the year 192.
[6] Suet. *Div. Aug.* 38. 2. See J. C. P. Smits, *Die Vita Commodi und Cassius Dio*
(Leiden, 1914), 83–84. The age of assuming the *toga virilis* varied, but sixteen or
seventeen would be normal—*RE* 12A (1937), 'tirocinium fori' 1450–3.
[7] See 41. 45. The phrases 'ὅ τε μάλιστα διὰ πάντων ἐθαύμασα' and 'λιβανωτὸν δὴ
λαβών . . . ῥίπτεις' suggest that he is referring to a single personal experience.
See also pp. 180–1.

that senators and *equites* would leave their business and run to the Athenaeum to hear them.[1] But, if Dio did continue his education in Rome, it was soon interrupted, for the news of Commodus' murder of the Quintilii brothers, generally placed in 182/3, came to him while he was with his father in Cilicia—οὐδὲ ἔσχον αὐτὰ συμβαλεῖν, τῷ πατρὶ συνὼν ἄρχοντι τῆς Κιλικίας, πρὶν πυθέσθαι τούς τε ἀδελφοὺς ὑπὸ τοῦ Κομμόδου . . . τρόπον τινὰ πνιγέντας.[2] (The temporal reference seems clear enough and it is hard to see why this governorship has sometimes been placed in the late 170's.)[3] It was here, as Dio says, that Apronianus learnt the true story of Hadrian's accession—Trajan's death had been concealed for several days while the *coup* was effected.[4] Dio must have gone to Cilicia simply as his father's *comes*, for there were no legions there, and he could not have been doing his service as military tribune.

What posts Dio held before his praetorship is a matter of guesswork. One would expect the son of a senator to have had a post in the vigintivirate, to be a *tribunus militum laticlavius*, which is not found invariably, quaestor and tribune, or possibly aedile. The quaestorship should have come at twenty-five[5] (so in about 188–9), which accords well with the fact that it is after this that Dio begins to use ἡμεῖς in referring to the Senate, and that his information about the last three years of Commodus (in the form in which we have it) is very much fuller than for the earlier years.[6] Dio's military tribunate, if he held one, will have fallen in the mid-180's. His quaestorship was probably held at Rome or in a Greek province. No Greek senators seem to have served as quaestor in non-Greek provinces—Africa Proconsularis, Narbonensis, or Baetica. The only, partial, exception is the historian, Claudius Charax, who served in half-hellenized Sicily.[7] At one point Dio mentions in passing that he had visited Hierapolis in Phrygia and had tested the poisonous fumes of the cavern there;[8] it may be that Dio spent his quaestorship in Asia—at least we have no evidence to suggest on what other occasion he can have been there.

---

[1] Philos. *VS* 2. 10 (93).   [2] 72. 7. 2 (287). See also pp. 127, 180.
[3] So *PIR²* C 485.   [4] 69. 1. 3 (222).
[5] Mommsen, *Römisches Staatsrecht*, 1³, 573. Note 59. 9. 5. πρὶν ἄρξαι τινὰ ἀρχὴν δι' ἧς ἐς τὴν γερουσίαν ἐσερχόμεθα.
[6] See p. 131.
[7] See Chr. Habicht, 'Zwei neue Inschriften aus Pergamon', *Ist. Mitt.* 9/10 (1959/60), 109.   [8] 68. 27. 3 (215–16).

One may suppose that his tribunate fell in about 191, and it is certain that he was in the Senate during the latter years of Commodus; under Pertinax the venerable Claudius Pompeianus reappeared in the Senate, and Dio emphasizes that he had never seen him there in the previous reign.¹ We have only a single hint of his activities—he had reason to fear Didius Julianus since he had often accused him in the Courts.²

After the depressing scenes of Commodus' last years there came the all-too-short reign of Pertinax, in the first three months of 193. Dio was in favour now and he records that he received from the Emperor, among other unspecified honours, the appointment as praetor for the following year.³ Then followed the troubled months of Didius Julianus' régime and the arrival of Septimius Severus in Rome, backed by his army. Dio took the precaution of composing, and sending to the new Emperor, a pamphlet on the dreams and portents which had foretold to Severus his ascent to the throne.⁴ Thus, it seems, Dio won confirmation for his coming praetorship; common prudence dictated that Severus, after his successful *coup d'état*, should do nothing to upset the aspirations of safe and respectable senators.

Dio gives an enthusiastic eyewitness description of the deification of Pertinax in the summer of 193⁵ and must have been in Rome throughout his praetorship in 194. But from 193 until 197 his narrative follows the movements of Severus and the civil wars, in which he himself played no part. We therefore catch a glimpse of Dio's whereabouts only once, at the *ludi circenses* during the *Saturnalia* of December 196, when the crowd used the occasion to shout slogans hostile to Severus. Dio was present, and able to hear and record what happened, by virtue of being a friend of the consul.⁶

In 197 Severus returned from his bloody victory over the rival Emperor, Clodius Albinus, at Lugdunum. Dio was present when he addressed the Senate in threatening terms, praising the

¹ 73. 3. 2–3 (308). ² 73. 12. 2–3 (316).
³ 73. 12. 2 (316) ὑπό τε τοῦ Περτίνακος τά τε ἄλλα ἐτετιμήμην καὶ στρατηγὸς ἀπεδεδείγμην. It is perhaps possible that Pertinax was filling up a vacant place for 193. But it is far more likely that he was hopefully making his dispositions for the following year. Dio will then have been *candidatus Caesaris*. A parallel in the case of consulships is afforded by Tac. *Hist.* 1. 77, which shows that Nero must have made his dispositions of the suffect consulships for 69 before the beginning of June 68.
⁴ See p. 29.
⁵ 74. 4–5 (327–9). ⁶ 75. 4. 3 (341).

severity of Marius, Sulla, and Augustus.[1] At this point Dio once
again took care to keep himself in favour and presented Severus
with a history of the civil wars which had just ended. Inspired,
furthermore, by the success of his work he began preparation for
his Roman History, which he was not to complete until over
thirty years had passed.[2]

From 197 Dio recounts the Eastern wars and travels of Severus
up to his return in 202 and has no occasion to say anything of
himself. We should expect, however, that in this period he would
have held some praetorian governorship. A rescript of Severus to
'Dio' may well indeed refer to him (no other Dio is known who
could have been the recipient). It comes from the first book of
Paulus' *de officio proconsulis* and concerns the case of a man who
has promised aid to a city in some calamity.[3] It seems clear,
therefore, that the Dio in question is a provincial governor—
and probably in the Greek East, where the cities were vocal and
powerful.

From 202 or 203 until 208, when he went on his expedition to
Britain, Severus was in Rome and Dio's narrative thus includes
a number of incidents at which he was present himself. It was
during this period that he held his first consulship, probably as
suffect consul in 205 or 206. The date, much disputed, is certain
to within a few years. Once established, it removes all grounds
for the theory, based on the view that he was not consul until
about 223, that Dio was out of favour in Severus' reign.[4] He mentions in connexion with Severus' legislation on adultery that
while he was consul he saw a list of 3,000 cases pending on this
charge—τρισχιλίας γοῦν ὑπατεύων εὗρον ἐν τῷ πίνακι ἐγγεγραμμένας.[5] At this time he was also an *amicus* of Severus and was
a member of the imperial *consilium*.[6] He records, firstly, that he
took part in the trial of one Raecius Constans in 204— αὐτοῦ τοῦ
Σεουήρου νεανιευσαμένου πρὸς ἡμᾶς τοὺς συνδικάζοντας αὐτῷ.[7] Then

[1] 75. 8. 1–3 (344–5).   [2] See p. 29.   [3] *Dig.* 50. 12. 7 (Paulus).
[4] The date of Dio's first consulship is fully discussed in Appendix II.
[5] 76. 16. 4 (371).
[6] See J. Crook, *Consilium Principis* (Cambridge, 1955), 81. E. Gabba, 'Sulla
"Storia Romana" di Cassio Dione', *RSI* 67 (1955), 289 argues (p. 293, n. 5) that
these passages show Dio only as a member of the Senate. But the second passage
quoted here is conclusive.
[7] 75. 16. 2–4. Boissevain, vol. 3, p. 356 heads the page A.D. 200 but the date is
clear from internal evidence—16. 4 οὐδ᾿ ἀπηνιαύτισεν αὐτὸς οὗτος ὁ Πλαυτιανὸς
ἀλλ᾿ ἐσφάγη (A.D. 205).

at the end of his account of Severus he gives a description of the Emperor's working life in Rome—he would begin work before dawn, then have a stroll discussing official business and later, if there were not a festival, would sit in judgement, giving sufficient time to the defendants—καὶ ἡμῖν τοῖς συνδικάζουσιν αὐτῷ παρρησίαν πολλὴν ἐδίδου.[1] The reference is clearly to a meeting of the amici, for the procedure is described as part of the Emperor's routine early-morning business.[2] The composition of the consilium was not fixed, and there is no way of telling how often Dio took part or how close a friend of Severus he was; but that he was technically an amicus is certain and is confirmed by the fact that he appears in the same role under Caracalla. It was standard practice for the friends of one Emperor to remain as advisers to his successor.

Dio's reports of scenes in the Senate under Severus show him solely as a passive participant who does not intervene or speak. There is a selection of anecdotes about (apparently) several meetings after the fall of Plautianus, where he mostly uses the first person and is certainly reporting from personal observation.[3] A little later he shows a certain rueful sense of humour in describing the case of a proconsul of Asia accused in the Senate; the evidence implicated an unidentified bald senator and Dio has to admit that he was unable to refrain from putting up his hand to feel his own hair.[4] Dio and the rest of the Senate sat by while the bald Baebius Marcellinus was dragged out and executed; and later when his accuser, Pollenius Sebennus, lay and begged for his life in his turn, only to be saved at the last moment.[5]

For the last three years of his reign Severus was in Britain and Dio tells us nothing of himself. But the fragments of Dio's account of the brief joint reign of Caracalla and Geta and of Caracalla's doings in Rome up to his departure in 213 are full of vivid, anecdotal material, much of which probably comes from personal observations, though none actually attests it. It is likely that Dio was in Rome, and we can guess that he was there when a Thessalian sophist called Philiscus attached himself to the court

---

[1] 76. 17. 1–2 (371–2).   [2] Compare Pliny, Ep. 3. 5. 9.
[3] 76. 5–6 (360–1).
[4] 76. 8–9 (363–4) : 8. 4. οὐκ ἀποκρύψομαι τὸ τότε μοι συμβάν, εἰ καὶ γελοιότατόν ἐστιν· τοσαύτη γὰρ ἀμηχανίᾳ συνεσχέθην ὥστε καὶ τῆς κεφαλῆς τὰς τρίχας τῇ χειρὶ ζητῆσαι.
[5] 76. 9. 2–4 (364).

in about 213.[1] Philostratus, who tells the story of Philiscus' vicissitudes in Rome,[2] was himself a Court figure of the time— he was present on Caracalla's expedition of 213 to Gaul and Germany, when the sophist Heliodorus appeared before the Emperor[3]—and there are certain traces of a connexion between him and Dio which are worth examining. Dio makes two references to the philosophical circle which had formed round the Empress Julia. The first says that Julia Domna took to philosophy, and the company of sophists, when ousted by Plautianus from the main position of influence with Severus—the context dates this passage to some point during Severus' travels in the East in 199– 202, when Plautianus, who travelled with him, laid the basis of his power.[4] The second, which dates to the Court's stay in Nicomedia over the winter of 214/15, when Dio was present, relates how Julia, while doing most of Caracalla's work for him, still found time for philosophy.[5] Certainly the elder Philostratus (the author of the Lives and the Life of Apollonius) and, probably, Philostratus of Lemnos[6] travelled with the Court on Caracalla's Eastern expedition;[7] Philostratus' Ἡρωϊκός was written to celebrate Caracalla's visit to Ilium[8] in 214 and his Life of Apollonius was probably being composed in these years.[9] Philostratus of Lemnos won exemption from liturgies for a μελέτη before Caracalla at the age of twenty-four; he was born in 190 or 191,[10] so the performance took place in 214 or 215—perhaps during the winter of 214/15 at Nicomedia. It was about then too that Dio wrote, and probably declaimed, the dialogue of Agrippa and Maecenas which occupies most of Book 52.[11]

All this merely shows that Dio and Philostratus belonged in the same world, and in itself reveals little. But there are indications of a closer connexion. Dio tells a story about the sophist Favorinus and Hadrian, which Philostratus was later to incorporate in the Lives.[12] Far more significant than this are Dio's two

---

[1] See pp. 50–51.   [2] VS 2. 30.   [3] VS 2. 32 (Teubner ed. 124).
[4] 75. 15. 6–7 (354–5).   [5] 77. 18. 2–3 (397).
[6] See F. Solmsen, 'Philostratos' (8–12), RE 20 (1941), 124–77, on the various Philostrati.   [7] See Philos. VA 8. 31 and VS praef.
[8] Solmsen, op. cit. 154, argues that it was written before 219 and probably between 217 and 219.
[9] VA 1. 3. 4 f. See Solmsen, op. cit. 139.
[10] Solmsen, op. cit. 174–5.   [11] See p. 104.
[12] Dio 69. 3. 6 (225). Philos. VS 1. 8 (Teubner ed. 9). Philostratus does not use the anecdote about Dionysius of Miletus—69. 3. 5 (225).

references to Apollonius of Tyana. The first tells the story of how
Apollonius in Ephesus cried out encouragement to the slave
Stephanus at precisely the moment when he was murdering
Domitian in Rome;[1] the story differs in some details from the
version given by Philostratus,[2] but agrees in the main and ends
with a fervent affirmation of its truth—τοῦτο μὲν οὕτως ἐγένετο,
κἂν μυριάκις τις ἀπιστήσῃ. This will have been written in about
217; its tone contrasts strongly with his attitude when (some time
about 220) he described Caracalla's interest in Apollonius:

τοῖς δὲ μάγοις καὶ γόησιν οὕτως ἔχαιρεν ὡς καὶ Ἀπολλώνιον τὸν
Καππαδόκην τὸν ἐπὶ τοῦ Δομιτιανοῦ ἀνθήσαντα ἐπαινεῖν καὶ τιμᾶν,
ὅστις καὶ γόης καὶ μάγος ἀκριβὴς ἐγένετο, καὶ ἡρῷον αὐτῷ
κατασκευάσαι.[3]

It is reasonable to deduce from this contrast that while Julia
Domna (of whom Dio speaks with sympathy)[4] was alive and her
circle in existence, Dio was influenced by their interests and enthu-
siasms. Some years later his attitude was rather different.

It is not until Dio describes the Court's stay at Nicomedia in
214/15 that we learn anything further of his own movements. It
seems probable that it was only there that he joined the Court,
for in describing the conduct of the eunuch, Sempronius Rufus,
whom Caracalla left in charge of Rome in 214, he uses the first
person (εὐνοῦχος ἡμῶν . . . κατεκράτησε),[5] which implies that he
was there himself.

It is not difficult to see why Dio had to join the Emperor at
Nicomedia. The journeys of the imperial train were a burden on
the provincials comparable to the passing of an army; only the
intervention of a local magnate could save the situation, and
numerous inscriptions attest the generosity of rich men in the
East who produced supplies for armies or Emperors. A number
of such inscriptions come from Bithynia in just this period.[6] It
might be expected that Dio, as a landowner in nearby Nicaea,

---

[1] 67. 18. 1–2 (185). [2] VA 8. 25–26.

[3] 77. 18. 4 (397). See Philos. VA 8. 31. The Heroon was dedicated at Tyana as
the expedition passed there on its way through Asia Minor, cf. Magie, Roman
Rule, ch. 28, n. 43. γόης and μάγος were abusive terms in Dio's vocabulary—see
52. 36. 3.

[4] See 75. 15. 6–7 (354–5), 77. 2. 3–6 (374), 78. 24. 1–2 (430–1). Though compare 77. 10. 2 (383).

[5] 77. 17. 2 (396). [6] See Rostovtzeff, SEHRE², ch. 9, n. 46.

would come in for this obligation, and in fact he records that this was so himself:

ὁ δὲ (Caracalla) ἔλεγε μὲν μηδενὸς ἔξω τῶν ἀναγκαίων προσδεῖσθαι, καὶ ἐπὶ τούτῳ καὶ ἐσεμνύνετο ὡς ὅτι εὐτελεστάτῃ τῇ διαίτῃ χρῆσθαι δυνάμενος, ἦν δὲ οὐδὲν οὐκ ἐπίγειον, οὐ θαλάττιον, οὐκ ἀέριον, ὃ μὴ οὐ καὶ ἰδίᾳ καὶ δημοσίᾳ αὐτῷ παρείχομεν.[1]

If Dio did not join the court until it arrived at Nicomedia, he appears also to have left it before the winter was over. For he later says that after Caracalla's death he remembered the Emperor at dinner in Nicomedia quoting some lines of Euripides on the mutability of human fortune; this was at the *Saturnalia* (in December) and the last occasion on which he spoke to Dio— τελευταίαν ταύτην φωνὴν πρὸς ἐμὲ ἔρρηξε.[2] The inference that Dio took his leave of the court in mid-winter (presumably he simply retired to Nicaea) is confirmed by the fact that he was not present at the gladiatorial games which were held there on the Emperor's birthday (4 April).[3]

Life at Nicomedia was acutely unpleasant for Caracalla's senatorial friends. The Emperor would send for them soon after dawn to consult about a case or some public business and then keep them waiting outside the door, sometimes till evening—and not only that: before the horrified eyes of the *amici* he would send round cups of wine to the soldiers who guarded him within. Only then would he begin taking cases.[4] Moreover he would rarely dine with the *amici* (the occasion of the *Saturnalia* must have been an exception) and preferred the company of his freedmen.[5] What Dio recounts is confirmed by the headings of two documents from the reign of Caracalla: one, from the Codex of Justinian, an administrative hearing which probably belongs to the Eastern expedition; the other an inscription of a case at Antioch, in 216.[6] In both of them the *Praefecti praetorio* take precedence over the *amici* and the *principales officiorum*, who are classed together.

It was to Nicomedia also that an anonymous Ephesian made one of his numerous journeys to present before the Emperor the

---

[1] 77. 18. 3 (397).
[2] 78. 8. 4–5 (411).
[3] 77. 19. 3–4 (399)—ἔνθα λέγεται.
[4] 77. 17. 3–4 (396).
[5] 77. 18. 4 (397).
[6] *Cod. Just.* 9. 51. 1. W. Kunkel, 'Der Prozess der Gohariener vor Caracalla', *Festschrift H. Lewald* (Basel, 1953), 81. See Crook, op. cit. 82 f.

claims of Ephesus to have precedence in Asia and to be the seat of the proconsul's juridical *conventus*.[1] It is noteworthy that it was, as will be argued, under these circumstances that Dio wrote the speech of Maecenas, which is devoted to the reassertion of senatorial dignity and, among other things, takes a severely repressive line about the privileges of cities within the Empire.[2]

There is no certain evidence as to Dio's movements in the next two years, though it is likely that in the spring of 215 he returned to Rome. He quotes a letter to the Senate which Caracalla wrote from Antioch in 215,[3] and mentions an exploit of his about which he reported in 216;[4] the most probable inference is that Dio was in the Senate when the communications arrived.[5]

He was certainly in Rome during the reign of Macrinus, for he says that he was present in the Senate when the first letter from Macrinus announcing that he had taken power (on 11 April 217) was read out. It was in this letter that Macrinus, without awaiting the vote of the Senate, awarded himself the titles of *Caesar, Imperator, Severus, Pius, Felix* and *Augustus*.[6] Dio was there also when the Senate assembled (συνήλθομεν) to hear Macrinus' letter concerning honours for his son Diadumenianus,[7] and records various incidents in Rome throughout the reign.[8]

---

[1] See the inscription from Ephesus published by J. Keil, 'Ein ephesischer Anwalt des dritten Jahrhunderts durchreist das Imperium Romanum', *SBAW* 1956, 3. Also Piganiol, *REG* 70 (1957), 108, Robert, *BE* 1958, no. 422, and Duval, *REA* 60 (1958), 381. The importunities to which Emperors were subjected are vividly illustrated also by an inscription (*IGR* 3. 1422) from Prusias ad Hypium in honour of one M. Aurelius Asclepiodotianus Asclepiades who petitioned Caracalla, successfully, on his way through the town in the spring of 215 for the right to wear the *latus clavus*—αἰτήσαντα αὐτὸν τὴν πορφύραν καὶ λαβόντα. He is also described proudly as 'σεβαστόγνωστος'. See the parallels given by L. Robert, *Études Anatoliennes* (Paris, 1937), 228.

[2] See pp. 106 f.   [3] 77. 20 (399).

[4] 78. 1. 4–5 (403) ὡς αὐτὸς ἐπέστειλεν.

[5] If, as seems clear, Dio did not accompany Caracalla any further on his Eastern expedition, there must be an error in Boissevain's reading at 78. 3. 5 (405) where Dio is describing Caracalla's clothing in the last stages of his life; ὥσπερ καὶ ἐγὼ εἶδον is in any case ill supported by the manuscripts (see Boissevain's apparatus ad loc.). Similarly when Dio later says that Caracalla used to kill interpreters between himself and the Scyths and Celts 'so that nothing should leak out to us' and that 'we' later learnt of his dealings with them from the barbarians themselves—78. 6. 2–3 (409)—'we' must be the Senate, not the Emperor's *comites* on the expedition.

[6] 78. 37. 5 (446), 78. 16. 2–17. 4 (419–21).

[7] 78. 37. 5 (446).

[8] e.g. 78. 20. 1 (424), the birthday of Diadumenianus—14 September 217; 25. 2 (431), the *Volcanalia*—25 August 217.

At what must have been very near the end of his reign Macrinus appointed Dio as *curator* of Pergamum and Smyrna.[1] Dio was still in Rome when the Emperor first wrote concerning the rebellion of Elagabal,[2] but must have left soon after this, for the rebellion, which began on 16 May 218, was successful by 8 June. By the winter of 218/19 he was at Pergamum, for he says that he was able there to confirm the details of an attempted mutiny in the fleet while Elagabal was wintering at Nicomedia.[3] He was still there when there took place the strange incident of a pseudo-Alexander who appeared in Moesia near the Danube, and with a company of 400 men proceeded down to Byzantium, aided and fed by the people and untouched by the authorities, crossed to Chalcedon and disappeared.[4] The incident took place before Dio heard anything about Bassianus in Rome—the reference must be to the adoption of Bassianus by his cousin, Elagabal, his re-naming as 'Alexander' and his elevation to the title of *Caesar*, which took place on 26 June 221.[5] Dio's mission to Pergamum and Smyrna was perhaps concerned with the incessant rivalry over titles—Pergamum was deprived by Macrinus of titles granted by Caracalla, as Dio tells us himself, and had responded with insults.[6] The repeated journeys of the Ephesian dignitary are no doubt part of the same story.[7]

At the beginning of his brief account of Severus Alexander's reign Dio explains that, while he has so far recorded events as fully as possible, from now on he can only give a summary;[8] the reason was his absence from Rome, for on leaving Asia he went to Bithynia (that is, presumably, to his home in Nicaea), was ill there for a time and then went to Africa—as proconsul of the senatorial province, perhaps in 223. From there he returned to Italy and was appointed almost immediately to the unarmed province of Dalmatia as *legatus Augusti*, probably in 224–6, and then to Pannonia Superior, a military province with two legions, probably in 226–8.[9] If Dio was still in Pannonia in 228, then he

---

[1] 79. 7. 4 (461).
[2] 78. 36. 1 (444). Dio's presence is shown by 38. 2 (447).   [3] 79. 7. 4 (461).
[4] 79. 18. 1–3 (471). The context shows that Ἀσίας in line 13 should read Μυσίας. See App. V.
[5] *Feriale Duranum*, col. 2. 16–17. See *YCS* 7 (1940), 141–3 and Welles, Fink, Gilliam, *The Excavations at Dura-Europos. Final Report* V. 1. *The Parchments and Papyri* (New Haven, 1959), 209.   [6] 78. 20. 4 (425).
[7] So Keil, op. cit. 8 f.   [8] 80. 1. 2–2. 1 (474).
[9] These dates are suggested by Jagenteufel, op. cit. 94.

was consul-designate there, for in 229 he was given the honour of being consul for the second time, as *ordinarius* with the Emperor.[1] A reputation for disciplinary severity had preceded him from Pannonia, and such was the hostility of the praetorian cohorts that the Emperor allowed him to spend the two months of his consulship outside Rome. He also relieved Dio of the expenditures of his office (a further sign that Dio was not in the wealthiest group of senators) and after its termination invited him to spend a few days at Rome and in Campania— perhaps at Baiae where there were magnificent imperial villas.[2] With that, Dio, now aged about sixty-six and suffering from an ailment of the legs,[3] returned home to Nicaea to spend there the rest of his life.[4] Here he brings his History to a close, and if he lived to see the armies of Severus Alexander pass through Bithynia on the way to the East in 231[5] he does not record it.

Such was Dio's career, so far as it can be traced. The gaps in our information about it (principally the early posts and praetorian appointments) hardly allow its evaluation in technical terms. It is sufficiently clear at least that he did not enjoy the rapid ascent to the consulship which was granted to *viri militares* who were going to have important commands. The view, however, that such careers represent the maximum political success and power is perhaps a misconception. Public honour and status was one thing, power quite another; and power could be exercised only at the Emperor's side and depended not on status but on access and influence.

Dio himself played no traceable role in the politics of his time. A couple of pamphlets ensured his safety in the early years of Severus, and thereafter his position was respectable but inconspicuous: he neither records any actions on his own part nor is mentioned by Herodian or the *Historia Augusta*. On the other

---

[1] Documentary evidence listed in *PIR*[2] C 492; also a papyrus, *Dura Final Report*, V. I, no. 69, and an inscription published in *SCIV* 8 (1957), 317–21 = *AE* 1960. 348.

[2] See Josephus, *AJ* 18. 249.

[3] It is perhaps relevant that according to Galen (Kühn 18A, 42) ποδάγρα was common in his time as a result of gross over-indulgence in food and drink; on Dio's testimony the affliction was shared by the Empress Faustina, 71. 29. 1 (268), by Pertinax, 73. 1. 5 (307), and by Septimius Severus, 76. 16. 1 (370).

[4] 80. 4. 2–5. 3 (476).

[5] Gren, op. cit. 126 and D. R. Wilson, 'Two Milestones from Pontus', *Anatolian Studies* 10 (1960), 133, especially p. 135.

hand, there is not the slightest indication that he at any time fell into disgrace. While he makes certain criticisms of Severus' conduct in the early years,[1] it would be rash to assume that he expressed them publicly while Severus was alive; if he had, he would hardly have remained, as he did, the *amicus* of Severus and his son. Dio, it is clear, was a safe man, known perhaps to be engaged primarily on his History. This may explain why he had no consular appointment until sent to Pergamum and Smyrna by Macrinus, twelve years or more after his consulship. The main bulk of his History, to the death of Severus, will have been finished while he was there.

So far his career was respectable but not distinguished. Only with the reign of Severus Alexander did he begin to govern important provinces. By 222 he had reached, and perhaps exceeded, the normal interval which lay between the suffect consulship and the proconsulate of Africa or Asia. However, the honour now came, not disgracefully late, and perhaps, if the *Historia Augusta* is to be believed, by the decision of the Senate.[2] It was after this that his career became exceptional, for since the Julio–Claudian era no known legate of Dalmatia had come from the proconsulate of Africa.[3] The province, without legions since A.D. 86, was low in the hierarchy of consular offices and in the second century was normally governed within one to three years of the suffect consulship.[4] The legate of Dalmatia in the early third century commanded a standing force of, probably, two milliary and two quingenary cohorts, 3,000 men in all,[5] and his *officium* had to be manned from the legions of Pannonia and Moesia.[6]

It may well be that this command was given to Dio specifically to prepare him for that which followed, the governorship of Pannonia Superior. It was normal for the governors of Dalmatia to move on to major military commands, especially Germania Inferior and Pannonia Superior itself.[7] This province stood very high in the hierarchy, second only to Syria among the imperial

---

[1] See pp. 140–3. [2] *vita Sev. Alex.* 24. 1.
[3] Jagenteufel, op. cit. 125. [4] Ibid. 124.
[5] G. M. Bersanetti, 'Gli auxilia di stanza nella Dalmazia nei secoli I–III', *Bull. Mus. Imp. Rom.* 12 (1941), 47. I am very grateful to Professor E. Birley of Durham University for this reference and for his full and helpful reply to my query about the garrison of Dalmatia. See now also G. Alföldy in *A. Arch. Hung.* 14 (1962), 259 f.
[6] A. Betz, *Untersuchungen zur Militärgeschichte der römischen Provinz Dalmatien* (Baden bei Wien, 1939), 61–62.
[7] Jagenteufel, op. cit. 127.

provinces, and was normally governed between three and ten years after a man's suffect consulship.[1] Again, Dio is an exception in that Greeks are not often found governing the military provinces of central Europe—of the other known governors of Pannonia Superior only T. Pomponius Protomachus is thought to have been a Greek.[2]

Dio's sudden rise to important posts under Severus Alexander can only be seen as a by-product of the resurgence of the Senate in the face of the dynasty's weakness, discredited as it was by Elagabal, and with only the thirteen-year-old Alexander to put in his place. No one could have been more acceptable to the senatorial oligarchy[3] than the elderly Dio, whose δαιμόνιον had already, while he was in Bithynia in about 222, announced to him his retirement,[4] and whose views emphasized stability, the repression of the lower orders, and senatorial dignity.[5] It was thus perhaps that this rather unmilitary figure found himself commanding two legions and a key province in the defence of the Empire.[6] Once there, his efforts had to be directed against his own undisciplined troops;[7] and, when he records his experience of the fierce and blood-thirsty character of the Pannonians (θυμικώτατοι γὰρ καὶ φονικώτατοι, οἷα μηδὲν ἄξιον τοῦ καλῶς ζῆν ἔχοντες, εἰσί),[8] the knowledge was not, on the evidence, gained in battle. A second consulship was a fit reward for his pains, an honour granted to few Greeks among his contemporaries.[9]

---

[1] W. Reidinger, *Die Statthalter des ungeteilten Pannoniens und Oberpannoniens von Augustus bis Diokletian*, Antiquitas: Abh. z. alt. Gesch. 2 (Bonn, 1956), 120–2.

[2] Ibid. 127.

[3] On the leading figures in the senatorial reaction see H. G. Pflaum, *Le Marbre de Thorigny*, Bibl. Éc. Hautes-Ét. 292 (Paris, 1948), A. Stein, 'Le Marbre de Thorigny', *Eunomia* 1 (1957), 1, and P. W. Townsend, 'The Revolution of A.D. 238: the Leaders and their Aims', *YCS* 14 (1955), 49, on pp. 83 f.

[4] 80. 5. 2 (476).   [5] See pp. 108 f.

[6] On Pannonia see P. Oliva, *Pannonia and the Onset of Crisis in the Roman Empire* (Prague, 1962), and J. Fitz in *A. Arch. Hung.* 14 (1962).

[7] 80. 1. 2 (476).

[8] 49. 36. See Appendix III.

[9] C. Aufidius Marcellus (*Albo* no. 70), who perhaps came from Pisidia, was *cos. II ord.* in 226. Others were *ordinarii*—Clodius Pompeianus (*Albo* no. 1531 = 1256), L. Ti. Claudius Aurelius Quintianus (*Albo* no. 1001)—both connexions of the famous Ti. Claudius Pompeianus *cos. II ord.* 173; L.? Annius Maximus, 207 (*Albo* no. 31 = ? 773), perhaps from Lydia; Cn. Claudius Severus, 235 (*Albo* no. 1002), probably son of Ti. Claudius Severus Proculus *cos. ord.* 200 (*Albo* no. 171), probably from Phrygia; Pontius Proculus Pontianus, 238 (*Albo* no. 1137), had property at Philippi. None of these are apparently *cos. II*, and in all cases their Greek origin is not entirely certain.

The succession of provincial posts which Dio held towards the end of his life formed an epilogue to his career and came after the main bulk of his History was written. The work itself was the product of a long period in the middle of his life, when he was mostly in Rome and could watch, in safety, civil wars, proscriptions, alleged conspiracies, the murder of two Emperors, and then the ascent to the throne of an equestrian—all the phenomena of an age of instability in which the pre-eminence of his own order was for the first time seriously assailed.

II

THE COMPOSITION OF THE HISTORY

SCHOLARS have perhaps done themselves less than justice in assuming, as so often, that the most important thing to discover about a classical historian is the books from which he has copied. The material which confronts a historian does not of itself dictate the character of his work, any more than does the character of the historical works which he uses. A real historian, says Josephus, is one who does not just take over the structure and form of his predecessor's work but who creates an original composition of his own.[1] It was indeed the attempt at originality of form, as opposed to that of content, which was characteristic of ancient historians; the essential thing was not the discovery of new facts but the retelling of known facts in a certain style. Not only the literary taste of his own age but also other more elementary considerations, the time available for composition and the intended length and scope of the work, shaped what a historian wrote at any given point.

Dio's History is, to say the least, not a literary work of the first rank. It is hardly surprising that he has been used mainly as a source of individual facts and examined simply for his 'credibility'. Works which analyse his methods of composition have not been frequent.[2] Nevertheless, to understand the work and the man, it is necessary to make clear how he set about writing his History, what literary canons he followed, and what his style and technique of narration were. To do this effectively sections from various parts of the History have to be examined in detail. The first thing to establish is the time of composition, which will give the work its setting within Dio's career.

The Time of Composition

Dio records how and why he began to write his enormous work, and how he went through with it, in a passage which he inserts

---

[1] Jos. *BJ* 1. 15 φιλόπονος δὲ οὐχ ὁ μεταποιῶν οἰκονομίαν καὶ τάξιν ἀλλοτρίαν, ἀλλ' ὁ μετὰ τοῦ καινὰ λέγειν καὶ τὸ σῶμα τῆς ἱστορίας κατασκευάζων ἴδιον.

[2] Principally A. von Gutschmid, *Kleine Schriften*, 5 (Leipzig, 1894), 547–54, and G. Vrind, 'De Cassii Dionis Historiis', *Mnemosyne* 54 (1926), 321, on pp. 321–7.

after the death of Commodus.[1] He begins by mentioning the two
works with which his literary career opened: a pamphlet of
dreams and portents by which Severus was warned that he would
ascend the throne, and the history of the wars in the first part of
Severus' reign. Of the first of these Dio says that he published it
(ἐδημοσίευσα) and also sent a copy to Severus, who answered with
a warm and favourable acknowledgement the same evening. The
setting, it seems clear, is Severus' first stay in Rome as Emperor,
in June 193 after his march from Pannonia;[2] only then, in 196,
and in 197 was he in Rome—or near enough to reply to Dio on
the same day. Moreover, the dangerous and unpleasant period
when the new Emperor established himself in the capital at the
head of his army was just the moment for a senator to make some
form of propitiation. What Dio's second work was emerges from
two sentences which are separate but related to each other:

πόλεμοι δὲ μετὰ τοῦτο καὶ στάσεις μέγισται συνέβησαν, συνέθηκα
δ' ἐγὼ τούτων τὴν συγγραφὴν ἐξ αἰτίας τοιᾶσδε . . . καὶ οὕτω δὴ
ταῦτα περὶ ὧν νῦν καθίσταμαι ἔγραψα.

This too, Dio claims, won approval, both generally and with
Severus himself. That the work must have described the wars
after the death of Commodus is clear enough;[3] what is not so
clear is how far it went. The context again suggests that Severus
was in Rome at the moment when the work was completed. The
date must therefore be 196, 197—or not until the summer of 202
when he finally returned from the East. It seems unlikely that
Severus, who in that year celebrated his *decennalia* and the marriage of his son to Plautianus' daughter, would have welcomed
a reminder of the civil wars which had ended five years earlier.
If a date as late as this is excluded, 196 and 197 remain. The
expression στάσεις μέγισται which Dio uses ought to have included the last act of the civil wars, Severus' great victory over
Clodius Albinus in 197. It is tempting to assume that it was on
Severus' arrival in Rome later that year that Dio presented his
historical work (which could include at least one πόλεμος, the
expedition into Mesopotamia in 195) and that it was from that
moment that he began his major work, the whole history of
Rome from its foundation.

[1] 72. 23 (304–5).
[2] For evidence on chronology in the reign of Severus, see Chapter IV.
[3] See J. C. P. Smits, *Die Vita Commodi und Cassius Dio* (Leiden, 1914), 68 n. 81.

Preparation, then, began in the summer of 197. In a single
sentence at the end of this same paragraph Dio gives the vital
information about how long the work took and in what manner it
was done—συνέλεξα δὲ πάντα τὰ ἀπ' ἀρχῆς τοῖς 'Ρωμαίοις μέχρι τῆς
Σεουήρου μεταλλαγῆς πραχθέντα ἐν ἔτεσι δέκα, καὶ συνέγραψα ἐν
ἄλλοις δώδεκα.[1] The ten years of note-taking will thus have been
from 197 to 207 and the twelve years of composition from 207
to 219.[2]

That the work as we have it was not altered or revised by Dio
later cannot be assumed without question. The only available
check is to examine the references to dateable events within Dio's
lifetime which occur in the main body of the text. Since these, or
some of them, are of interest in themselves it is worth treating them
fairly fully: the passages are listed and discussed in Appendix III.

What emerges confirms the supposition that Dio's History was
not revised, but comes to us as he wrote it in the years 207 to 219.
Apart from a single passage referring to his own career, and one
clause interpolated at the end of a sentence, nothing is referred
to which took place later than the early years of Caracalla.
Even the most striking events that took place later in Dio's lifetime—the reigns of Macrinus and Elagabal, or the rise of Persia—
have left no trace; the case of Persia is especially clear, for Dio
refers to the Parthian Empire as being still in existence and a
danger to Rome. In the last part of his life Dio brought his
History up to his own second consulship in 229, treating the
reigns of Caracalla, Macrinus, and Elagabal in full and that of
Severus Alexander very briefly, but did not go back to the main
bulk of his narrative. This allows no inference about the 'publication' of his work—it cannot be assumed without evidence that
any ancient literary work which has come down to us was
'published' at all, in the sense of a simultaneous distribution of
a number of identical copies.[3] Parts of the History, such as
Philiscus' *consolatio* of Cicero[4] and the debate between Agrippa
and Maecenas,[5] were probably read out, or intended to be read

---

[1] 23. 5 (305).
[2] For this to be accepted, it must be taken that the sentence is not pedantically
correct, since the period of note-taking ends before the death of Severus. τὰ . . .
πραχθέντα is the object of both verbs and is placed where it is for stylistic reasons.
[3] See Th. Birt, *Kritik und Hermeneutik: nebst Abriß des antiken Buchwesens* (Munich,
1913), 307 f., especially pp. 325–6.
[4] See pp. 49–51.   [5] See pp. 102 f.

out, immediately after they had been written. But, so far as we
can tell, it was a long time before the work as a whole was much
known or used.[1]

Furthermore, Dio's references to events within his lifetime do
nothing to upset the natural inference that it is possible to establish the approximate date at which each book was written by
spacing them appropriately between the years 207 and 219. No
doubt, as in all literary or scholastic work, there were interrup-
tions and difficulties and periods of better or worse progress.[2]
But, if the formula which presents itself as the natural one is
applied, it is found to work; at only two points does Dio refer to
things which took place after the relevant part of the History will
have been written, while there are two passages, those referring
to the attachment of the legion I *Adiutrix* to Pannonia Inferior and
to the introduction of Egyptians into the Senate, which were
written within a year or two of the event. Finally, the formula
gives a satisfactory setting and relevance for both Philiscus'
consolatio and the debate of Agrippa and Maecenas.

If this scheme is accepted important results follow. Scholars
have for instance reproached Dio with lack of detail and grip of
technicalities in his narration of military operations; Schwartz
waxes strong on the point—'Und dabei ist Dio kein dem Staats-
leben fernestehender Deklamator gewesen, sondern ein hoher
Reichsbeamter von anerkannter Tüchtigkeit, der gefärhliche
Truppenkommandos geführt und wichtige Grenzprovinzen ver-
waltet hat . . . .'[3] The reference is clearly to Dio's governorship of
Pannonia, which began some seven years after the main body of
the History was completed. To disregard chronology and regard
Dio's posts as a sort of timeless characteristic of the man is a wild
error, though Schwartz is not the only one to commit it.[4] Dio
may have been a military tribune or governed a province as
a praetorian, but there is no certain evidence that he had so
much as seen a Roman army, except that which came with
Severus to Rome in 193, until he stayed with Caracalla's court in
the last part of 214.

It must be taken that passages in Dio were written when he

[1] See p. 72.
[2] See 76. 2. 1 (358) on Dio's villa at Capua—τοῦτο γὰρ τὸ χωρίον ἐξειλόμην . .
ἵνα σχολὴν ἀπὸ τῶν ἀστικῶν πραγμάτων ἄγων ταῦτα γράψαιμι.
[3] Schwartz 1690.
[4] See, for example, H. Haupt in *Philologus* 44 (1885), 558.

came to their place in his work unless there is evidence to the contrary. In considering the political background to his writing it is therefore necessary to dismiss Severus Alexander and the 'senatorial reaction' from the scene. Dio's History, and his thinking as it is reflected there, is the product of the age of Severus and Caracalla.

The First Stage: the Collection of Material

The enormous task which Dio imposed on himself set severe limits on the quality of his performance in detail. The method he adopted added others. The fact that he first went through the whole of Roman history taking notes and then, *ten to twelve years later*, went through his material again, arranging it and writing it out in finished style, must account for much of the vagueness in his narrative and for his failure to achieve any effective analysis of events. There is more to admire in the fact that the task was accomplished at all than to complain of in the fact that precise topographical details are missing in his battle-scenes. A hunger for accurate accounts of battles afflicts many scholars; but, even if such accounts are a central virtue in a historian, no man (and certainly not a senator, whose movements were controlled by the Emperor) could visit all, or many, of the battlefields in Roman history; and, had he done so, there is little probability that any of the existing accounts would have given him much to go on.

Ten years were spent in the taking of notes from previous historians. The purpose of this stage was to assemble (συλλέγειν) a mass of material in a raw state ready for reworking in a literary style.[1] It can reasonably be assumed that these notes were taken down on *membranae* or *chartae* and assembled in order;[2] the basic work of condensing a long text would most probably be done by the author himself—only in the final stage might he dictate his corrected version to a slave for a fair copy to be taken.[3]

The vital point was the selection of the material, but it is precisely here that Dio gives least help. The fragment which Boissevain prints first in his edition lays down a principle—⟨ . . . . ⟩ πάντα ὡς εἰπεῖν τὰ περὶ αὐτῶν τισι γεγραμμένα, συνέγραψα δὲ οὐ

---

[1] For a collection of illustrative passages, with discussion, see G. Avenarius, *Lukians Schrift zur Geschichtsschreibung* (Meisenheim-Glan, 1956), 85–104.

[2] See Birt, op. cit. 289–92.

[3] See N. I. Herescu, 'Le mode de composition des écrivains ("dictare")', *REL* 34 (1956), 132.

πάντα ἀλλ' ὅσα ἐξέκρινα.[1] A later fragment adds a further point—
σπουδὴν ἔχω συγγράψαι πάνθ' ὅσα τοῖς Ῥωμαίοις καὶ εἰρηνοῦσι καὶ
πολεμοῦσι ἀξίως μνήμης ἐπράχθη . . .[2] The first passage yields, or
can be made to yield, an important clue to Dio's method of
composition. συγγράφειν is his word for the second stage, that of
reworking the material in literary style. The verb in the first part
of the sentence is missing; the restoration ἀνέγνων has been suggested,[3] but it is permissible to assume that the word was not that
but συνέλεξα, which appears in the primary passage describing his
method. Even if this was not actually the word used, the contrast
between the two stages should be the same in each case. If this is
so, the implication is that the selection of material (ἐξέκρινα) took
place in the second stage—a conclusion supported by the second
fragment—he *wrote down* only what was 'worthy of mention'.
In other words it was in the years 207 to 219 and not 197 to 207
that the decisive shape was given to the work. The procedure
which is best attested for ancient historical works was that of
forming the material first into a ὑπόμνημα (*commentarius*), that is
making the basic selection and arrangement of it, and then in the
final stage simply rewriting it in correct literary style as a finished
work.[4] There is no indication that Dio followed this procedure;
his words, if taken literally, seem to mean that selection and
composition took place simultaneously in the second stage. It
would also be at this point that he inserted not only his references
to events after 207 but his personal comments and explanations[5]
and also his numerous and lengthy speeches.[6] If this was so, it is
hardly surprising that it took him two years longer to compose
his work than to read nearly all the existing works on Roman
history.

Inevitably, however, much must remain obscure in the working procedures of any ancient historian. A chance in a million
might one day produce a parchment or papyrus with the notes
for a known text; until then what can be said about this vital
stage in the production of a history must be largely guesswork.

[1] I. 2.
[2] I. I (Boissevain, p. 12). On these two fragments see A. G. Roos, 'Über einige
Fragmente des Cassius Dio', *Klio* 16 (1919), 75, on pp. 76 f.
[3] See Vrind, op. cit. 322–3.
[4] See Avenarius, op. cit. 85 f.
[5] See especially Chapter V and Appendixes III and IV.
[6] See pp. 78 f.

The Use of Sources

Quellenforschung makes up the vast majority of the literature on Dio,[1] but has hardly led to satisfactory results. It is difficult to see what, if anything, is proved by the retailing of the same fact by two ancient historians. It certainly does not prove that the later read the earlier one; nor does the fact that a later historian gives a different version of an event prove that he had *not* read his predecessor. Dio claims to have read nearly all works on Roman history and later refers to 'the many books which I have read'.[2] Passing references to Livy,[3] Sallust,[4] and Arrian[5] (none of them quoted as sources of information) show that, as one would expect, these writers were familiar figures to him. He could hardly have made such sweeping claims to wide reading if Livy at least were not included; again there are a couple of not quite certain references to Plutarch as a source.[6] But the only writers who are unmistakably quoted by name as the source of particular facts are Augustus in his autobiography (and here the quoted figure is wrong)[7] and Hadrian on the deaths of Vespasian and Antinous.[8]

Hopeless uncertainties prevail in the field of source-criticism. Even where a historian quotes a writer by name it is not certain that he had read him, for the name could have come from an intermediate source. No two historians covering the same period could fail to record *some* of the same facts, but what a historian

---

[1] There is no modern bibliography of work directly concerned with Dio. For the older literature see the 'Jahresberichte' by H. Haupt in *Philologus* 39–41 (1880–2), 43–44 (1884–5), Boissevain, vol. i, ci–iii, and Schwartz, 1685. The fullest recent survey is in *Fifty Years of Classical Scholarship*, ed. M. Platnauer (Oxford, 1954), 175–6 and notes.

[2] 53. 19. 6.   [3] 67. 12. 4.

[4] 40. 63. 4 τὸν τὴν ἱστορίαν γράψαντα. 43. 9. 2–3 on Sallust's governorship in Africa, his prosecution for *res repetundae* and the added shame ὅτι τοιαῦτα συγγράμματα συγγράψας καὶ πολλὰ καὶ πικρὰ περὶ τῶν ἐκκαρπουμένων τινὰς εἰπὼν οὐκ ἐμιμήσατο τῷ ἔργῳ τοὺς λόγους. The reference is to Sallust's denunciation of rapacity in his historical works, not to pamphlets allegedly by him. See R. Syme, 'Pseudo-Sallust', *MH* 15 (1958) 46, on pp. 49–50. Both passages show total ignorance of the chronology of Sallust's writings, for the first comes under 50 and the second under 46 B.C.

[5] 69. 15. 1. See p. 70. Note also references to Q. Dellius: 49. 39. 2, &c.; Asinius Pollio 57. 2. 5 (not explicit); Cremutius Cordus: 57. 24. 2, 4 (see p. 85); Cluvius Rufus: 63. 14. 3–4, and Josephus: 66. 1. 4.

[6] Fr. 40. 5. See Boissevain, ad loc. (1. 116). Fr. 107. 1, referring to Plutarch's comparison of Pompey and Agesilaus.

[7] 44. 35. 3. See p. 85.

[8] 66. 17. 1 (perhaps referring to a *remark* by Hadrian) and 69. 11. 2 (see p. 61).

actually wrote will have been dictated largely by the character of
his own work. No attempt will be made to discuss Dio's sources as
such, though the question inevitably arises at various points.
What can be done more usefully is to discuss some points about
Dio's explicit attitude to his sources and instances of his use of
them.

Like other ancient historians, he rarely names a source (we
cannot even *assume* that his own notes included the names of the
writers he had excerpted) but oblique, anonymous references are
fairly common.[1] They tend to appear either where a story is
attested, but prima facie improbable, or where he was confronted with a conflict of authorities. Even in the latter case
Dio lays down no principles (political experience or personal
acquaintance with events) for preferring one authority to another,
but simply says, for instance, that 'the more trustworthy' gave one
version—ταῦτα γὰρ οὕτω τοῖς τε πλείοσι καὶ ⟨τοῖς⟩ ἀξιοπιστοτέροις
γέγραπται[2]—or just gives one of the versions as the true one—
ταῦτα μὲν τἀληθέστατα· ἤδη δέ τινες καὶ ἐκεῖνο εἶπον.[3] It was sometimes possible to refer to special authorities—οἱ τὰ σαφέστατα
Σαβίνων εἰδότες[4]—but normally, where the narrative sources dis-
agreed, or agreed in recording something utterly improbable,
the only thing was to disclaim all power of interpretation[5] or
to resort to the test of common sense. This he does for instance in
giving the reason why Octavian's fleet failed to pursue that of
Pompey after the battle of Lilybaeum in 36 B.C.; as he thought
and as was probable (ὡς μὲν ἐμοὶ δοκεῖ καὶ τὸ εἰκὸς συμβάλλεται) it
was because they could not catch them and feared shipwreck;
others supposed that Agrippa felt he had done enough, since he
was fighting for Octavian, not for himself.[6]

As a supplement to what appeared in the narrative sources
an historian could use what he had seen himself or what he had
heard from others.[7] Dio knew the value of recording his personal
experience as a means of adding weight to his account—he can
testify to the character of the Pannonians not from hearsay or
reading alone but from his own dealings with them.[8] He gives

[1] The full list would serve no purpose. For examples of the manner in which
he refers to his authorities see: Fr. 43. 26; 40. 27. 3; 41. 14. 4; 47. 3. 3; 57. 14. 3;
57. 22. 3; 62. 11. 4.

[2] 56. 31. 1. [3] 44. 19. 5. [4] Fr. 6. 5.

[5] e.g. Fr. 35. 7–8; compare 38. 13. 5. [6] 49. 4. 1.

[7] See Avenarius, op. cit. 71 f. [8] 49. 36. 4. See Appendix III.

accounts of things he had seen in Campania, where his villa was, and in various provinces,[1] but always, it must be said, of things which were curiosities rather than germane to his narrative. He does not use personal knowledge of the terrain to clarify his account of any military operations in his History.

Information from eyewitnesses of events or from participants was only possible, of course, with the history of the recent past. The furthest into the past that his personal inquiries took him was to 117, the death of Trajan. His father, as governor of Cilicia, heard the true version and passed it on; Dio was able to use the information when writing about the death of Trajan a century after the event.[2] For the reign of Marcus Aurelius, during which he was born but which ended before he came to Rome, there was much more to be learnt from hearsay. He heard from men who had been there how the Emperor, on his Danubian campaigns, had once used the ancient Fetial rite for declaring war;[3] and he was told, and believed, the story that Marcus had been killed by his doctors on the instructions of Commodus.[4] In another passage he seems to refer to contemporary discussions of Marcus' rule, and refutes those who thought him parsimonious.[5]

Apart from these references to eyewitness reports there are a considerable number of passages where he introduces information with the word ἤκουσα, the earliest from his account of the building of Pompey's theatre in 55 B.C.[6] This paragraph is a medley of different elements: the story of how the elephants which took part in the first show there appeared to trumpet for mercy, some information on elephants' foresight, and a version according to which the theatre was built by one Demetrius, not Pompey himself. It is not surprising that stories should circulate about the foundation of a major public building which, as Dio says, was still in use. In considering the sources used by ancient historians we perhaps underestimate the part played by the vague area of knowledge about figures and events in the past, and anecdotes and legends, which would be common to any given society.[7]

---

[1] See pp. 11, 180–1.
[2] 69. 1. 3. See p. 62.
[3] 71. 33. 3 (273).
[4] 71. 33. 4² (275).
[5] 71. 32. 3 (273).
[6] 39. 38. Note 38. 4 λέγεται γὰρ ... ἤδη γάρ τινες καὶ ἐκεῖνο εἶπον. See also 42. 2. 5; 50. 12. 5; 54. 35. 3; 57. 3. 3.
[7] See Plut. *Dem.* 2. 1 καὶ ὅσα τοὺς γράφοντας διαφυγόντα σωτηρίᾳ μνήμης ἐπιφανεστέραν εἴληφε πίστιν, ὑπολαμβάνων ἀκοῇ καὶ διαπυνθανόμενος . . . .

Equally, items about events in the more distant past which Dio says he has 'heard' might derive from the historical or antiquarian reading of his friends.

Finally, documentary evidence was a possible source, but although a number of inscriptions are *mentioned*, as curiosities or to give colour to the narrative, they were not used as basic evidence.[1] There is no trace of his using the *acta Senatus* or any other 'archives'. Two documents are mentioned, one merely referred to, the other actually used as evidence. Relating how Cicero was too terrified to utter more than a few words of his *Pro Milone* he says 'the speech which now circulates as the *Pro Milone* he wrote later at leisure when he had got up his courage'.[2] There is nothing to show that he used it, however; the speeches of Cicero were in current circulation, but were regarded as literary models, not as the material of history.[3] The other document was a letter of Hadrian to Antoninus, perhaps even an autograph letter (ἔστι γε αὐτοῦ καὶ ἐπιστολὴ αὐτὸ τοῦτο ἐνδεικνυμένη) ; it is not impossible that we have a transcript of it on a second-century papyrus.[4]

Only in one place does Dio discuss seriously the nature of his sources. This is the much-quoted chapter 19 of Book 53 where he analyses the difference between the material for Republican and for Imperial history. Two main factors governed the change—in the Republic everything was publicly known, being brought before the Senate and People; while in the Empire all important political business was done in private by the Emperor and his advisers, and what was made public was disbelieved, even if it happened to be true. Secondly, the sheer size of the Empire meant that many things which happened were known to none except the participants. The truth in Republican history could be checked from the accounts of various historians and even from public records (παρὰ . . . τοῖς τε ὑπομνήμασι τοῖς δημοσίοις τρόπον τινὰ εὑρίσκετο)—he is referring, it should be noted, to the way in which the sources from which he worked were built up, not to possible consultation of archives by himself.

All that could be done therefore was to record what was made

[1] See D. R. Stuart, 'The Attitude of Dio Cassius towards Epigraphic Sources', *Univ. Michigan Stud.* 1 (1904), 101.

[2] 40. 54. 2.

[3] See, for example, Fronto, ed. van den Hout, 108, 109, 139, &c.

[4] 69. 17. 3. See p. 70.

public, whether it were true or not. Beyond that Dio could only use his own judgement, on the basis of any further information he had from all that he had read, heard or seen.[1] This comes near to being a complete list of the critical weapons available to a historian in Dio's time.

The question of exactly which authorities an ancient historian used in each section of his narrative, while important for those whose sole concern is with the truth or falsehood of the facts he records, is not essential for the study of the historian himself. What was distinctively his was not any new array of facts but the composition of a new literary narrative on the basis of accepted facts.

The Second Stage: Composition

It was in the second stage of the composition of Dio's History, in the years from 207 to 219, that the economy and form of the work will have been established. The Suda indicates that the work was divided into eight decads;[2] and, within the limits set by the state of the text, it is possible to see how this was done. The most important division was that which marked the beginning of the Empire, the re-establishment of monarchy, which Dio dates from the battle of Actium; this is placed at the beginning of Book 51.[3] So 50 books covered the 723 years of the Kings and the Republic, and 30 the remaining period of some 250 years. Precisely up to what date the 80 books went is not at all clear. To achieve an exact total of 80 books, and a division into round numbers, the terminal point ought, one would have thought, to have been fixed in advance. The main passage in which Dio describes the composition of his work implies that the original terminal point was the death of Severus. Photius, on the other hand, writing about Dio's History in his *Bibliotheca*, seems to imply that the 80 books went up to the death of Elagabal,[4] the

---

[1] 53. 19. 6: προσέσται μέντοι τι αὐτοῖς καὶ τῆς ἐμῆς δοξασίας . . . ἐν οἷς ἄλλο τι μᾶλλον ἢ τὸ θρυλούμενον ἠδυνήθην ἐκ πολλῶν ὧν ἀνέγνων ἢ καὶ ἤκουσα ἢ καὶ εἶδον τεκμήρασθαι.

[2] Suidas s.v. Δίων, ὁ Κάσσιος (ed. Adler vol. 2, pp. 116–17) ἔγραψε Ῥωμαϊκὴν ἱστορίαν ἐν βιβλίοις π´· διαιροῦνται δὲ κατὰ δεκάδας.

[3] See p. 74.

[4] Photius, *Bib.* 71 ἀνεγνώσθη βιβλίον . . . ἐν λόγοις π´ ἄρχεται μὲν . . . διέρχεται δὲ καθεξῆς ἀποπαυόμενος εἰς τὴν τοῦ Ἀντωνίνου, ὃν Ἐλαγάβαλον ἀπεκάλουν, σφαγήν . . . οὐ μόνον δὲ ἀλλὰ καὶ εἰς τὴν ἀρχὴν κάτεισιν Ἀλεξάνδρου.

point at which in his own narrative Dio disclaims further direct acquaintance with events. This version is confirmed by the fifth- or sixth-century Vatican Codex which contains the text of Dio, with some gaps, from the last part of Caracalla's reign to the middle of Elagabal's.[1] It gives the numbering of the books it covers as 79 and 80.[2] The few pages that Dio then wrote on the reign of Severus Alexander should therefore, as Photius implies, be considered as an appendix to the main work and numbered separately.[3] At any given stage Dio must have had a rough idea of how many books he intended to write, but in the nature of the case the aim was constantly being revised. He says that the main bulk of the narrative took him to the death of Severus; but, when Severus died, on 4 February 211, Dio will already have completed some 24 books. Then, between the deaths of Severus and of Geta, he had a dream which instructed him to record the reign of Caracalla,[4] and by 219 he was intending to go on as long as fate allowed. It is not surprising therefore that in the end he went slightly over the round total of 80 books.

Apart from his main division of 50 books for the regal period and Republic and 30 for the Empire, it is clear that Dio made an attempt to end each decad at a major turning-point. Boissevain's arrangement of the early fragments makes Book 11 open at the beginning of the First Punic War and Book 21 at the beginning of the Third, which is probable, though it cannot be formally proved.[5] The beginning of the fourth decad is irretrievably lost, but Book 41 opens at New Year 49 B.C., the start of the civil war of Caesar and Pompey. So far the divisions appear to have been neat and successful. For the books on the Empire no satisfactory pattern can be discovered. It is possible that the seventh decad began with the accession of Nero[6] and the eighth with that of Marcus Aurelius, but there can be no certainty.

Within this framework Dio's History is in principle annalistic.

[1] 78. 2. 2 (404)–79. 8. 3 (461). See Boissevain, vol. 3, pp. iii–ix.
[2] See Boissevain, vol. 3, p. viii.
[3] It is not practicable to follow the implications of this rigidly, and in references to Dio's text the numbering used in the index to Boissevain—vol. 4, ed. Smilda (1926)—has been followed.
[4] 78. 10. 1–2 (412–13). See pp. 120, 180.
[5] The opening of the third decad is fairly certain. Bekker, Anecd., p. 124, 9 (Fr. 71. 2), has Δίωνος κα′ βιβλίῳ "ὅ τε Φαμέας ἀπογνοὺς τὰ τῶν Καρχηδονίων πράγματα". See Zon. 9. 27. 6.
[6] See Boissevain, ad loc. (vol. 3, 19) and vol. 2, pp. xxi f.

In the books which are extant in full the consuls of each year are given—and at the point where suffect consuls make their appearance he explains that, while the *suffecti* may or may not be mentioned (depending on whether they play a part in the narrative), the *ordinarii* will continue to be recorded as a matter of principle, for the sake of clarity.[1] The principle, however, was by no means rigidly adhered to, and to say that Dio wrote 'not *historiae* but *annales*'[2] is an oversimplification. Not only must the regal period have been divided by reigns: in the imperial period also each reign begins and ends with a collection of material taken out of its chronological setting and designed to illustrate the character and manner of government of the Emperor concerned.[3] The design is conscious and shows a fair degree of regularity from reign to reign, and the introduction is often marked off explicitly from the chronological section, as for instance with Claudius— τοιοῦτος οὖν δή τις, ὥς γε συνελόντι εἰπεῖν, ὧν . . . λέξω δὲ καὶ καθ' ἕκαστον ὧν ἐποίησε.[4] Even in the supposedly chronological sections, however, he does not keep strictly to the annalistic structure,[5] and the practice of giving the names of the consuls year by year seems, from our fragmentary text, to have been maintained until he reached about the end of the first century, and then abandoned.[6] There is no trace of it in his account of his own time. Even in the books which cover the end of the Republic much of the period of the civil wars is handled in long resumptive sections which are conspicuously weak in chronology and ill related to each other.[7]

Style

The essential thing in composing an historical work was to produce an even flow of narrative, interspersed with speeches, and with comments by the author, in correct and suitably elevated diction. It is clear that Dio made great efforts to achieve

[1] 43. 46. 6.

[2] Schwartz, 1687. The distinction made here relates solely to the arrangement of material, not to the nature and purpose of historical writing (as in Sempronius Asellio, Peter, *HRR* fr. 1 and 2).

[3] See C. Questa, 'Tecnica biographica e tecnica annalistica nei libri LIII–LXIII di Cassio Dione', *Studi Urbinati* 31, N.S., B. 1–2 (1957), 37.

[4] 60. 3. 1 (665).

[5] See below on the reign of Hadrian.

[6] The last instance is 67. 14. 5, the consuls of 96.

[7] See below, pp. 55 f.

a correct style and he reveals in passing that he read Atticist writers in order to imitate them:

χρυσοῦν γὰρ δὴ καὶ ἐγὼ τὸ νόμισμα τὸ τὰς πέντε καὶ εἴκοσι δραχμὰς δυνάμενον κατὰ τὸ ἐπιχώριον ὀνομάζω· καὶ τῶν Ἑλλήνων δέ τινες, ὧν τὰ βιβλία ἐπὶ τῷ ἀττικίζειν ἀναγινώσκομεν, οὕτως αὐτὸ ἐκάλεσαν.[1]

The reference is not to Thucydides and the Attic orators[2]—*they* had no need to find a word to translate *aureus*—but to writers who followed the Atticist convention which reigned supreme in his own day,[3] and long afterwards. τῶν Ἑλλήνων δέ τινες means men of Greek culture; if he wished to refer to the Greeks of the classical era he used a different expression, οἱ ἀρχαῖοι Ἕλληνες.[4]

A fragment from the very beginning of the History refers to his efforts to write in pure style (as far as the subject-matter allowed) and offers a defence against the suspicion that this might be incompatible with truth:

μὴ μέντοι μηδ' ὅτι κεκαλλιεπημένοις, ἐς ὅσον γε καὶ τὰ πράγματα ἐπέτρεψε, λόγοις κέχρημαι, ἐς τὴν ἀλήθειαν αὐτῶν διὰ τοῦτό τις ὑποπτεύσῃ ... ἐγὼ γὰρ ἀμφότερα, ὡς οἷόν τε ἦν, ὁμοίως ἀκριβῶσαι ἐσπούδασα.[5]

It was impossible, however, as Dio admits, to write a history of Rome in entirely pure Attic. Not only had certain Latinisms crept into Dio's style,[6] but there was also the constant problem of Latin constitutional terms and various others which were no less difficult. Dio uses three methods for handling this problem: transcription (Γαλλίας τῆς τογάτης), translation (ἑταιρικά for *collegia*), and equivalents (θρίαμβος for triumph).[7] There are times

---

[1] 55. 12. 4–5. The discussion of this passage by T. F. Buttrey, 'Dio, Zonaras and the Value of the Roman Aureus', *JRS* 51 (1961), 40, adds nothing of importance. His historical conclusions are vitiated by his belief that the passage was written in the reign of Severus Alexander and by his ignorance of Pekáry's article in *Historia* 8 (1959), 443.

[2] So Schwartz, 1709.

[3] See W. Schmid, *Der Atticismus* (Stuttgart, 1887–97).

[4] 75. 13. 5 (351). See p. 178.

[5] 1. 2 (p. 1).

[6] See K. Niemeyer, 'Zu Cassius Dion', *Jahrbücher für classische Philologie* 22 (1876), 583–4.

[7] See G. Vrind, *De Cassii Dionis vocabulis quae ad ius publicum pertinent* (Leiden, 1923), 22 f. The problem was not, of course, Dio's alone and many of the terms he uses for Roman institutions were common currency.

when he is unable to find any effective way of dealing with a Latin term except by a long explanation, as for instance with *auctoritas* (*senatus*)—τοιοῦτον γάρ τι ἡ δύναμις τοῦ ὀνόματος τούτου δηλοῖ· ἑλληνίσαι γὰρ αὐτὸ καθάπαξ ἀδύνατόν ἐστι.[1] Troublesome as it was to Dio, this was not something which much affected the character of his work as a whole. More important was his imitation of Thucydides—and, more important than that, the influence of rhetoric. As Photius remarked, the influence of Thucydides is most obvious in his speeches,[2] and it affects not only his language but sometimes the whole cast of his thought.[3] The same is true of some passages outside the speeches. It has been shown that his account of the fighting against Sextus Pompeius in 36 B.C. is largely modelled on Thucydides, in particular on the sea-battle in the Great Harbour at Syracuse.[4] The same is perhaps true of his paragraph on the causes of the First Punic War—the alleged reasons (αἰτίαι) were Carthaginian aid to Tarentum and the Roman alliance with Hiero, but the real cause was the power and continuing expansion of Rome.[5] Again, his description of the character and generalship of Hannibal perhaps owes something to Thucydides' summing-up of the abilities of Themistocles.[6]

A much more pervasive influence was that of rhetoric, the canons of which supplied what there was of historiographical theory in the ancient world.[7] The majority of Dio's work is written in periodic style as appropriate to narrative. His rhetorical training shows itself most clearly in moments of heightened tension or drama, for instance in his description of the two sides at the battle of Pharsalus, which is a mass of antitheses ending with an asyndeton—συνέβαλον ἀλλήλοις τοὺς ὁμοφύλους, τοὺς

---

[1] 55. 3. 4–5. Compare 42. 26. 4: 'Fortuna Respiciens' was τρόπον τινὰ οὐκ εὐαφήγητον Ἕλλησιν. For 'auctoritas' in other contexts Dio was able to use ἀξίωμα. Fr. 91 ὅτι ὁ Σερουίλιος ὑπὸ τοῦ πρὸς τὸν συνάρχοντα φθόνου (τὰ μὲν ⟨γὰρ⟩ ἄλλα ἐξ ἴσου οἱ ἐπετέτραπτο, τῷ δὲ δὴ ἀξιώματι οἷα ὑπατεύοντος αὐτοῦ ἠλαττοῦτο). . . .

[2] Photius, *Biblioth.* 71. See E. Litsch, *De Cassio Dione imitatore Thucydidis* (Diss. Freiburg, 1893) and E. Kyhnitzsch, *De contionibus, quas Cassius Dio historiae suae intexuit, cum Thucydideis comparatis* (Diss. Leipzig, 1894).

[3] See e.g. p. 137.

[4] 49. 1 f. See J. Melber, 'Dio Cassius über die letzten Kämpfe gegen Sextus Pompeius 36. v. Chr.', *Abh. W. Christ dargebracht* (Munich, 1891), 211.

[5] Fr. 43. 1–3.

[6] Fr. 54. 1–3. Compare Thuc. 1. 138. 3.

[7] See P. Scheller, *De hellenistica historiae conscribendae arte* (Diss. Leipzig, 1911) and Avenarius, op. cit.

συσκήνους, τοὺς συσσίτους, τοὺς ὁμοσπόνδους.[1] A little later there is
a reference to Corinth and Carthage—πόλεις ἀρχαίας, λαμπράς,
ἐπισήμους, ἀπολωλυίας.[2] Antithesis was a favourite trick, used
above all in his summings-up of the careers of famous men,[3]
where he presents his own political views, and in his speeches. On
occasion he allowed himself some more enterprising rhetorical
conceits, as for instance about Nero's appearances on the stage:

τίς γὰρ ἂν προγραφὴ ταύτης χαλεπωτέρα γένοιτο ἐν ᾗ ⟨οὐ⟩
Σύλλας μὲν ἄλλους Νέρων δὲ ἑαυτὸν προέγραψεν; τίς δὲ νίκη
ἀτοπωτέρα, ἐν ᾗ τὸν κότινον ἢ τὴν δάφνην ἢ τὸ σέλινον ἢ τὴν πίτυν
λαβών, ἀπώλεσε τὸν πολιτικόν; . . . ἐδεῖτο ὡς δραπέτης, ἐπο-
δηγεῖτο ὡς τυφλός, ἐκύει ἔτικτεν ἐμαίνετο ἠλᾶτο. . . .[4]

Then there were occasions of a different type, horrors and calami-
ties where vivid detail could be used to arouse the emotions of the
reader or audience. This was the genre which, with all due
reservation, may still be given the label 'tragic history'.[5] Dio
gives, for instance, a vivid description of the earthquake at
Antioch in 115, with a mass of details of buildings falling, trees
uprooted, and men buried alive—and a woman who survived by
feeding herself and her baby on her own milk.[6] But above all
there is his account of the proscriptions carried out by Sulla,[7]
which comes near to being a piece of great writing and shows
a man who lived through a similar, if much less terrible, period in
the civil wars under Severus. But, dramatic as is the detail which
he uses—men rushing to look at the *album* as if it contained good
news, then killed even for frowning, or for smiling, when they had
done so, and much more besides—it is conspicuous that the
passage contains not a name nor a figure nor any indication of
the course of events. The design is to create a certain emotional
climate, not to reproduce particular facts.

This avoidance of detail is a characteristic of his work throughout, not merely in the rhetorical passages. It is the result of a
conscious literary principle which Dio follows, that the narrative
should not be overburdened with details which were trivial,

[1] 41. 57. 1-3.　　　　　　　　　　[2] 43. 50. 4.
[3] See p. 47.　　　　　　　　　　[4] 63. 9. 3-4 (74-75).
[5] See F. W. Walbank, 'Tragic History: A Reconsideration', *BICS* 2 (1955), 4,
and 'History and Tragedy', *Historia* 9 (1960), 216; C. O. Brink, 'Tragic History
and Aristotle's School', *PCPhS* 186 (1960), 14.
[6] 68. 24. 1-25. 4.　　　　　　　　[7] Fr. 109. 6-21.

tedious, or unworthy of the dignity of history. It is unfortunate that by following this principle he often deliberately leaves out just those facts which we should now wish him to have included. The most striking example is perhaps that of Caesar's legislative programme in 59—τούτους μὲν οὖν (the *leges Juliae*), ὅτι πάμπολλοί τέ εἰσι καὶ οὐδ᾽ ὁτιοῦν τῇδε τῇ συγγραφῇ συμβάλλονται, παραλείψω[1]— but there are many other places where he indicates that unseemly detail is being omitted or cut short for reasons of style.[2] Similarly, he feels it necessary to explain on occasion why an apparently unworthy item has been included—it revealed an example of virtue[3] or showed in a nutshell the character of an historical figure.[4]

The same stylistic considerations applied to the indication of exact dates, which he scrupulously avoids for most of his History. He knew, for instance that Augustus entered on his first consulship in the month of August,[5] but does not say so at the relevant point in his narrative.[6] Only with the lives and reigns of Emperors does he make a regular practice of giving an accurate record in years, months and days, even devoting a short excursus to explaining how he numbered the overlapping reigns of the year of the four Emperors.[7] The battle of Actium, to Dio the major turning-point in Roman history, was an exception to his normal rule, and here he gives the exact date, and explains why:

τοῦτο δὲ οὐκ ἄλλως εἶπον (οὐδὲ γὰρ εἴωθα αὐτὸ ποιεῖν) ἀλλ᾽ ὅτι τότε πρῶτον ὁ Καῖσαρ τὸ κράτος πᾶν μόνος ἔσχεν, ὥστε καὶ τὴν ἀπαρίθμησιν τῶν τῆς μοναρχίας αὐτοῦ ἐτῶν ἀπ᾽ ἐκείνης τῆς ἡμέρας ἀκριβοῦσθαι.[8]

Only when he comes to the reign of Macrinus does he drop the literary convention and give various dates in days and months.[9]

These were some of the conventions which Dio adopted, and followed with some consistency throughout his work. There were

---

[1] 38. 7. 6–8. 1.
[2] e.g. 44. 14. 3: ἐγὼ δὲ τὰ μὲν τῶν ἄλλων ὀνόματα οὐδὲν δέομαι καταλέγειν: 47. 10.1 ἐγὼ οὖν τὸ μὲν πάντα αὐτὰ ἀκριβῶς καθ᾽ ἕκαστον ἐπεξελθεῖν παραλείψω (πάμπολύ τε γὰρ ἔργον ἂν εἴη, καὶ οὐδὲν μέγα τῇ συγγραφῇ παρέξεται): 48. 13. 1 καὶ αὐτῶν ἐγὼ τὰ μὲν πολλά, καὶ ἐν οἷς οὔτε τι μέγα οὔτ᾽ ἀξιόλογον ἐπράχθη, παρήσω, τὰ δὲ δὴ λόγου μάλιστα ἄξια συντόμως διηγήσομαι.
[3] 64. 6. 5 (105). Compare 65. 14. 1 (148).
[4] 65. 9. 4 (143).
[5] 55. 6. 7.
[6] 46. 45.
[7] See W. F. Snyder, 'On Chronology in the Imperial Books of Cassius Dio's Roman History', *Klio* 33 (1940–1), 39.
[8] 51. 1. 1–2.
[9] See 78. 20. 1 (424), 31. 4 (440), 39. 1 (447).

others which he announces but which seem to have had little
effect on his practice. He states fairly near the beginning of his
work that he 'is not accustomed to inserting excursuses in his
text'[1]—but in fact throughout it there are numerous, and often
valuable, digressions on antiquities, customs, constitutional practice, geographical points and the like.[2] Again, at the conclusion
of some reflections on the Senate's responsibility for the civil strife
of the late Republic, he makes a general pronouncement on
historical method:

καὶ γὰρ καὶ παίδευσις ἐν τούτῳ τὰ μάλιστα εἶναί μοι δοκεῖ, ὅταν
τις τὰ ἔργα τοῖς λογισμοῖς ὑπολέγων τήν τε ἐκείνων φύσιν ἐκ
τούτων ἐλέγχῃ καὶ τούτους ἐκ τῆς ἐκείνων ὁμολογίας τεκμηριοῖ.[3]

Schwartz took this to be the principle which justified the omission
of awkward detail from the narrative.[4] But this does not seem to
be the meaning of the sentence, which must be translated in more
general terms—'I consider it to be the chief characteristic of
a trained mind to be able to apply rational principles to historical
facts, thereby demonstrating the true nature of the facts and also,
by co-ordinating the facts, showing the truth of the principles.'
This is not a reference to a stylistic convention but a formulation
of the view, expressed for instance by Sempronius Asellio,[5] that
history is by definition the meaningful interpretation of past events
and not merely a record of them. The application of this principle,
however, is not discernible in Dio's writing of history, from which
large-scale interpretations are clearly absent.[6] It is tempting to
conclude that it is merely a passing thought, which has no relevance to the actual structure of his History.

Such is the general character of Dio's work, dictated largely by
the sheer bulk of material to be handled and the methods Dio
adopted from the start in tackling it. A full analysis of how it
worked out in all the various parts of Roman history would not
be practicable. But a selection of three types of material, the
career of a political figure, the course of civil wars and the reign

[1] Fr. 32: οὐκ εἰωθὼς ἐκβολαῖς τοῦ λόγου χρῆσθαι. Compare Thuc. 1. 97. 2: τὴν
ἐκβολὴν τοῦ λόγου ἐποιησάμην, and see Cic. ad Att. 7. 1. 6.
[2] See especially Chapter V and Appendixes III and IV.
[3] 46. 35. 1.   [4] op. cit. 1689.
[5] Peter, HRR, Fr. 1 and 2 (Aulus Gellius, NA 5. 18). For a discussion of the text
see R. Till, 'Sempronius Asellio', Würzburger Jahrbücher 4 (1949–50), 330–4.
[6] See Chapter III.

of an Emperor, may help to illustrate in greater detail what sort
of history Dio wrote.

Cicero

To write a connected narrative of late Republican political
history is a task that might daunt anyone. For Dio, who came to
it only as part of the whole sweep of Roman history, the chances
of dealing with it in a way that was profound or original were
small indeed. None the less it had to be done, and the results are
best seen in his portrait, if such it can be called, of Cicero.[1] That
he fails to deal adequately with Cicero, and indeed appears to
show a marked prejudice against him, has long been a subject of
comment.[2] But, as will appear, there is a vein of hostility to
Cicero which persists in writers of the Imperial period,[3] to which
Dio owes many, perhaps all, of his expressed views on him. It is
not clear that we should look for personal motives in Dio's
hostility, and there is certainly nothing in the view that he disliked Cicero for his opposition to monarchy.[4] That misrepresents
his own attitude to monarchy,[5] and also attributes to Dio more
feeling about Republican politics than he had time to acquire.

The framework of Dio's history did not enable him to present
Cicero in his context in a meaningful way. Cicero could hardly be
understood, for instance, without some indication of his social
position and upbringing. But there was no space for giving
introductions to the careers of important figures; their names
simply make their appearance in the text at the first historical
event in which they take part. In the history of the Republic only
one figure, Octavian, is introduced with a brief description of his
background and education[6]—and this may owe its existence to
Augustus' autobiography, or to the Greek version of it by Nico-

[1] Much of the material in this section (as in the section on Dio's speeches in
Chapter III) was used in an article, 'Some Speeches in Cassius Dio', *MH* 18 (1961),
11. It has been re-used here with various changes in emphasis and conclusions, and
the article will not be quoted except for peripheral points.
[2] See, for example, Conyers Middleton, quoted in *MH* 18, p. 15, n. 48, and G. I.
Vossius, *De Historicis Graecis* (ed. Westermann, Leipzig, 1838), 283.
[3] See Th. Zielinski, *Cicero im Wandel der Jahrhunderte*[3] (Leipzig–Berlin, 1912),
280–8, and E. Gabba, 'Note sulla polemica anticiceroniana di Asinio Pollione',
RSI 69 (1957), 317.
[4] So K. Wachsmuth, *Einleitung in das Studium der alten Geschichte* (Leipzig, 1895),
600.
[5] See Chapter III.   45. 1. 1–2.

laus of Damascus.[1] On the other hand, Dio is fond of composing a brief summing-up, normally built up from rhetorical antitheses, when he records the death of any famous character;[2] a highly developed example of this type of writing is his comment on the death of Capitolinus:

τά τε γὰρ πολέμια ἀκριβώσας εἰρηνεῖν οὐκ ἠπίστατο καὶ τὸ Καπιτώλιον ὃ ἐσεσώκει κατέλαβεν ἐπὶ τυραννίδι, εὐπατρίδης τε ὢν οἰκέτου ἔργον ἐγένετο, καὶ πολεμικὸς νομισθεὶς ἐν ἀνδραπόδου τρόπῳ συνελήφθη, κατά τε τῆς πέτρας αὐτῆς ἀφ' ἧς τοὺς Γαλάτας ἀπεώσατο ἐρρίφη.[3]

A similar example, at greater length, is his summing up of Pompey's career, which goes into considerable detail, contrasting his conquests as a youth with his defeat and death in middle age, his former command of a thousand ships with his murder in a small boat, and so on.[4] It cannot be pretended that Dio achieved great depth at these points, but none the less even a rhetorical paragraph of this type served to mark the passing of a great man, to recall the events of his life, and to emphasize a recurring, if conventional, theme in Dio, the instability of human fortune.[5]

Cicero is given no elogium. His death is mentioned twice—once in recording that his head was brought to the Triumvirs[6] and again in giving a version of his murder by Popilius Laenas.[7] Here there is a sardonic comment—ἀρετῆς μὲν δὴ καὶ εὐσεβείας τοσαῦτα τότε ἐπιφανῆ ἔργα ἐγένετο—but nothing more. It is necessary, therefore, to turn directly to the examination of how Dio deals with Cicero in the various scenes in which he appears. It is noteworthy that there are three speeches by Cicero, or rather scenes in which Cicero speaks at length: his dialogue with Philiscus, his speech on the Amnesty, and the debate with Calenus.[8] Given the use of speeches in ancient historians to illustrate character and situation, these episodes should be important and can be

[1] See H. Malcovati, *Imperatoris Caesaris Augusti Operum Fragmenta*[3] (Turin, 1948), xlii f.; Nicolaus, Jacoby, *FGrH* 90, Fr. 125–30.
[2] e.g. 51. 15. 1–4 (Antonius and Cleopatra), 58. 11. 1–2 and 12. 6 (Sejanus).
[3] Fr. 26. 2.   [4] 42. 5.
[5] See p. 76.   [6] 47. 8. 3.
[7] 47. 11. 1–2. Compare Plut. *Cic.* 48.
[8] Philiscus, 38. 18–29; amnesty, 44. 23–33; debate, 45. 18–47 (Cicero), 46. 1–28 (Calenus).

treated as a group after a discussion of the way in which Dio presents Cicero directly.

In the extant text Cicero is mentioned first in 66[1]—he supported the *lex Manilia* neither in the public interest nor to please Pompey but to advance himself and demonstrate to both sides that he could help them if he chose. Similar charges of ambition and disloyalty, not with regard to this particular episode, are a commonplace, and can be found in Pseudo-Sallust, Seneca, and Plutarch's Life.[2] Then comes the conspiracy of Catiline, which Dio has inevitably to recount in compressed and abbreviated form, missing all the real course of events and only able to treat a few of the main scenes in anything like adequate detail.[3] He sums it up by claiming that the fame of Cicero and of his speeches had made it seem much more important than it really was,[4] but none the less it is here alone that he awards Cicero some slight measure of praise—it was lucky for Rome that Cicero remained in the city (instead of going to Macedonia).[5] This is not much from an author whose own views on public order were so strict.[6]

The hostile tone continues in later references. On Cicero's speech *Pro C. Antonio* in March 59[7] Dio mentions his attack on Caesar (without making clear that it was indirect—Caesar's name was not mentioned)[8] and interprets it solely in terms of Cicero's desire to make himself the equal of a man who was his superior, by the exchange of abuse. Caesar was too noble to reply in the same terms.[9] Then, when he comes to Clodius' plans to bring down Cicero, Dio says that Cicero's support among senators and *equites* came from fear rather than goodwill, for he gained more hostility among those whom his eloquence harmed than favour from those it helped. Only enmity resulted from his attacks on the powerful, his unbridled tongue and his evident preference for a reputation for brilliance and eloquence rather than for that of being a good citizen. His arrogance and self-praise made him burdensome, envied and disliked even by his

---

[1] 36. 43. 2–44. 2. There is one previous mention in Xiphilinus, see Boissevain vol. I, p. 359.

[2] Ps.-Sallust *Invectiva in Ciceronem*, 4. 7; Sen. *Contr.* 7. 3. 9; Plut. *Cic.* 5. 2–3; 6. 4–5.

[3] For instance the senatorial meeting of 5 December. See 37. 35. 4–36. 3.

[4] 37. 42. 1.   [5] 37. 34. 1.

[6] See pp. 108 f.

[7] See M. Gelzer, *RE* 13A (1939), 'M. Tullius Cicero', 907–8.

[8] *de domo sua*, 41.   [9] 38. 10. 4–11. 2.

supporters.[1] Comments on the same lines can be found in Plutarch's Life.[2]

Further hostile comments come in the period after Cicero's return from exile. Caesar and Crassus showed him outward friendship. But Cicero knew that they were the authors of his exile and, while he could not show open hostility, composed what Dio calls βιβλίον . . . τι ἀπόρρητον which contained περὶ τῶν ἑαυτοῦ βουλευμάτων ἀπολογισμόν τινα. He filled it with dire charges against Caesar, Crassus, and others and gave it to his son with instructions not to publish it until after his death.[3] This is clearly a garbled reference to the work referred to as *Anecdota*, or better *de consiliis suis*. Dio has misplaced the time of its composition, for it was still being completed in 44, and also blundered in the reference to Cicero's son, who was now aged eight.[4] Dio seems to have got hold of the fact that the *de consiliis suis* made some charges against Crassus and Caesar[5] and arbitrarily thrust it in where there seemed to be an occasion for it. Two further references emphasize Cicero's cowardice—his inability to get out more than a few words of his *Pro Milone* for fear of the soldiers,[6] and his fear of going as legate of the Senate to Antonius in 43.[7]

Dio's explicit opinion of Cicero—that he was vain, self-seeking, cowardly and, in a word, contemptible—is consistent, but in no way original, and does not begin to take into account the realities of politics at the end of the Republic. Much the same picture emerges from the three episodes in which Dio employs direct speech.

The first in order is Cicero's dialogue with Philiscus, which takes place during his exile from Rome.[8] Philiscus meets Cicero and in a long conversation consoles and fortifies him. Cicero's despair and contemplation of suicide are known from his letters,[9]

[1] 38. 12. 4–7.
[2] Plut. *Cic.* 5. 6; 24; 27. 1. It is possible that a phrase in Dio 38. 12. 7: φορτικός τε καὶ ἐπαχθὴς ἦν is an echo of Plutarch 24. 3 καὶ τὸν λόγον (of his own achievements) . . . ἐπαχθῆ καὶ φορτικὸν ἐποίησε τοῖς ἀκροωμένοις. Dio uses the phrase in only one other place, 61. 3. 2, of Pallas.
[3] 39. 10. 2–3.
[4] See Büchner, *RE* 13A (1939), 'M. Tullius Cicero', 1267–9.
[5] See Plut. *Crassus*, 13. 4.
[6] 40. 54. 1–4. Compare Plut. *Cic.* 35.　　　　[7] 46. 32. 3–4.
[8] The statement in *MH* 18 (1961), 15 that the dialogue takes place in Athens was due to a misreading of 38. 18. 1 ἐντυχὼν δ' αὐτῷ Φιλίσκος τις ἀνὴρ ἔν τε ταῖς Ἀθήναις συγγεγονὼς οἱ καὶ τότε κατὰ τὴν τύχην συντυχών.
[9] e.g. *Ad Att.* 3. 3; 3. 8. 2–4; 3. 10; 12; 15.

and Plutarch makes his lack of fortitude a reproach—it was not to be expected of a man of his education.[1] But there is no trace in the other sources of a figure called Philiscus or of any specific scene in which Cicero received consolation. Philiscus must be an invention. It may be that the invention was taken over by Dio from some predecessor, but a much more interesting possibility is to hand, for a Philiscus is known who was a contemporary of Dio's, a rhetor who held the chair of rhetoric at Athens.[2] Not only was he a contemporary, but he travelled to Rome in the reign of Caracalla to pursue a lawsuit and attached himself closely to the circle of Julia Domna (through whom he now obtained the chair at Athens). After a time he was made to defend his case before Caracalla and by displeasing the Emperor lost the immunity from taxation which normally went with the chair. Caracalla was in Rome as sole ruler from the murder of Geta in late February 212 to the spring of 213 and again over the winter of 213–14. So the story of Philiscus' appearance before him, told by Philostratus, must date to one of these two periods. Dio will have been writing Book 38 in about 212 or 213. It is possible to suggest, tentatively, that the name was taken from the rhetor, Philiscus, and even that the dialogue was written, perhaps as a compliment and display of its author's literary taste, while Philiscus was in Rome. There is some evidence to suggest that Dio had connexions with the Empress's circle.[3]

Dio's Philiscus speaks the conventional language of popular philosophic tracts, influenced by the later cynicism.[4] Various *consolationes* and tracts περὶ φυγῆς are known, but none of them can be distinguished as Dio's source; on the other hand, a number of parallels and resemblances can be listed, showing that Dio was familiar with the common stock of ideas on the subject.[5] In

[1] Plut. *Cic.* 32. 5. See Ed. Meyer, *Caesars Monarchie und das Principat des Pompeius*[3] (Stuttgart–Berlin, 1922), 120, n. 1, comparing Appian *BC* 2. 55–57 on Cicero's cowardice in the face of Clodius.

[2] Philos. *VS* 2. 30. See *RE* 19. 2 (1938), 'Philiskos' (10), 2387–8, and a dedication from Delphi published in *BCH* 73 (1949), 473–5 = *AE* 1951. 58.

[3] See p. 19.　　　　[4] So *RE* 19. 2 (1938), 'Philiskos' (8), 2384.

[5] The following parallels are worth noting. Teles and Musonius are quoted by page and line in Stobaeus 3, ed. Hense, Favorinus' περὶ φυγῆς from Norsa and Vitelli, *Il papiro Vaticano greco XI*. Studi e Testi 53 (Vatican, 1931). Dio 23. 2 : Teles, pp. 738–9 (on the soul and the body) ; 23. 3 : Cic., *Disp. Tusc.* 5. 107, Musonius 755. 15 f., Plut. *Mor.* 599 c (only convention makes exile a disgrace) ; 24. 1–3 : *Disp. Tusc.* 5. 106, Sen. *ad Helv.* 6, Plut. *Mor.* 601 b, Favorinus 8. 35 f. (residence abroad

brief, Philiscus reproves Cicero for the unphilosophical weakness he displays in spite of his education, points out that he has physical health and needs nothing more, and that his soul is unaffected; that his exile was destined by fate, that many people live abroad anyway—including famous men in the past who left their native land to avoid dishonour, and others who later prospered again. Cicero has had honour enough and can afford to retire to an estate by the coast, to farm and write history, like Thucydides and Xenophon—this should be a personal touch, if Dio was thinking of his own Campanian villa, and his use of it.[1] He ends with an unashamed *vaticinium post eventum*—death might await Cicero on his return, for those who seek power will betray even their dearest friends.

The dialogue has no function within the History, unless to underline the weakness of Cicero's character, and no justification from historical evidence. But if the suggestion made is correct, Dio's ἐντυχὼν δ' αὐτῷ Φιλίσκος τις ἀνὴρ ἔν τε ταῖς Ἀθήναις συγγεγονώς οἱ[2] is a personal allusion. If there were earlier rhetorical pieces using this theme and setting, we do not know of them. As the evidence stands, we have a rare, probably unique, case of initiative in composition by Dio and perhaps the circumstances to explain how it came about.

The case of Cicero's speech supporting the Amnesty, at the meeting of the Senate on 17 March 44,[3] is very different, for it is amply attested, first by Cicero himself in the first paragraph of his first Philippic—'ieci fundamenta pacis Atheniensiumque renovavi vetus exemplum, Graecum etiam verbum usurpavi, quo tum in sedandis discordiis usa erat civitas illa.'[4] There can be no doubt that the speech was made by Cicero, but there is no evidence that it was published and none of the sources seems to know anything of its contents in detail. There can be little doubt that the speech in Dio is a free composition by himself, though it has been suggested that the excerpts made by the freedman, Tiro, played their part

---

is common); 26. 1 f.: Teles 742. 5 f., Musonius 753. 4 f., Favorinus 21–22 (cases where exile has been the honourable course); 26. 3: Plut. *Mor.* 605 e, Teles 739. 9 f., Musonius 753. 9 f. (famous men gaining by exile); 28. 2: Musonius 749. 20 f. (profit from leisure of exile). Compare also Philo, *In Flaccum*, 183–4.

[1] 76. 2. 1 (358).   [2] 38. 18. 1.   [3] 44. 23–33.

[4] Repeated in substance by Vell. Pat. 2. 58. 4 and Plut. *Cic.* 42. 3. Other references (see *MH* 18, p. 17, n. 62) either omit mention of Cicero or do not enlarge on the part he played.

in the tradition.[1] As it stands, the speech is in Dio's style and
language,[2] and the presence of occasional Ciceronian mannerisms
—for instance τῆς ἀρίστης καὶ ἀρχαιοτάτης πόλεως[3]—is no dis-
proof, for such things were easy to imitate. Nor is there any
reason to suppose that Livy included here a speech by Cicero,
so he cannot be taken as the source.[4] It must be assumed that Dio
set out to write the speech with no clearer evidence than was given
at the beginning of the First Philippic, or by sources deriving from
it. The task was not especially difficult, and Dio does not make
much of it. A reference to the Amnesty of 403 B.C. in Athens,[5]
some obvious examples from Republican history[6] and some
general indications of the current position[7] were all that was required, and all that he provided. That Dio wrote the speech at
all, thus emphasizing Cicero's importance and conciliatory role,
must be a result of his fondness for the theme of civil concord and
the exercise of mercy.[8]

Finally, there is the debate between Cicero and (Q. Fufius)
Calenus which occupies the last half of Book 45 and the first of 46,
evidently an attempt to sum up in the two balanced speeches the
complex political situation at the beginning of 43 B.C. The same
thing is attempted by Appian who, however, gives the second
speech to L. Calpurnius Piso.[9] Like Appian, Dio sets the debate
in the context of the senatorial meeting which covered the first
three days of January 43.[10] It is not clear on which of the days Dio
intended to place the speeches (if indeed he was thinking in such
detailed terms), but a reference to the temple of Concordia in
Calenus' speech suggests that it was the second or third.[11] But
it is in fact fruitless to attempt to give an actual point at which
either Dio's or Appian's debate took place. Both are fictional, and

[1] See H. Haupt, *Philologus* 43 (1884), 689–90.
[2] Kyhnitzsch, op. cit. 26 f., finds five cases where he has imitated the language of Thucydides: 25. 4: Thuc. 2. 43. 1; 27. 2: 4. 62. 3–4; 30. 5: 3. 66. 2; 32. 1: 3. 44. 4; 32. 4: 3. 46. 4—and others which are less certain.
[3] 44. 26. 1. See Haupt, op. cit. 692–3.
[4] As suggested by E. G. Sihler, *Cicero of Arpinum*[2] (New York, 1933), 396.
[5] 26. 2 f.   [6] 25; 28; 30. 4–5.
[7] 31–33.
[8] See pp. 78 f.
[9] *B.C.* 3. 213–20, 222–48. Both Piso and Calenus are mentioned by Cicero in the Philippics as prominent opponents of his. See e.g. *Phil.* 12. 3 f.
[10] See 45. 17. 1.
[11] 46. 28. 3. See P. Stein, *Die Senatssitzungen der ciceronischen Zeit* (Diss. Münster, 1930), 80–82, 206–9 and *RE* 13A, 1060.

designed as a substitute for the complex political history of the time.[1]

The question is simply—what sort of fiction? The speech of Calenus is more rich in obvious clues, since it includes many of the elements common to anti-Ciceronian literature; a recent study concludes that it derives from the polemics of Asinius Pollio.[2] The fundamentally non-historical character of it is shown by a reference to Cicero's letters to his friends—ἐφ' οἷς οὕτω σαυτῷ ἀδικοῦντι σύνοισθα ὥστε μηδὲ δημοσιεύειν αὐτὰ τολμᾶν.[3] This charge, sufficiently absurd in itself, is carried further a few chapters later, where Calenus speaks of Cicero's correspondence with Caerellia, a blameless elderly lady interested in philosophy,[4] makes an otherwise unrecorded allegation of immorality with her, and casts aspersions on the character of his letters— πρὸς ἣν καὶ αὐτὴν τοιαύτας ἐπιστολὰς γράφεις οἵας ἂν γράψειεν ἀνὴρ σκωπτόλης ἀθυρόγλωσσος πρὸς γυναῖκα ἑβδομηκοντοῦτιν πληκτιζόμενος.[5] This item cannot have taken its place in the repertory of Cicero-abuse at least until the publication of his letters, which took place after his death, perhaps many years after.

A common assumption is that Dio derived at least the main elements of the speech from a Greek rhetor, probably of the early Empire.[6] One item which seems to support this is the row of puns on Cicero's name to which Calenus gives vent—ὦ Κικέρων ἢ Κικέρκουλε ἢ Κικεράκιε ἢ Κικέριθε ἢ Γραίκουλε.[7] The last expression reflects the prejudice against Cicero's Greek education, to which Plutarch also refers.[8] The others are punning allusions to the slur that Cicero's father was a fuller.[9] Dio is not given to punning, and it is legitimate to doubt whether he himself made up this elaborate play on words.

There were numerous possible sources of anti-Ciceronian material. Antonius' criticisms of Cicero in his speech of 19 September 44 can be reconstructed in part from Philippic II, and

---

[1] Appian commits serious chronological errors. For instance 3. 253 mentions the death of Trebonius and the declaration of Dolabella as *hostis* (late February 43 B.C.). On these points see Gabba, 'Note sulla polemica . . .', 328–31.
[2] Gabba, op. cit.   [3] 46. 8. 1.
[4] See *RE* 3 (1897–9), 'Caerellia' (10), 1284. The correspondence was known to Quintilian (*Inst.* 6. 3. 112) and Ausonius (*Cent. Nupt.*, p. 218, Peiper).
[5] 18. 4.
[6] So Haupt and Zielinski, op. cit.
[7] 18. 1.   [8] Plut. *Cic.* 5. 2.
[9] See also 46. 5. 2 and 7. 3 f. and Plut. *Cic.* 1. 2. See Zielinski, op. cit. 284.

a number of them reappear in Calenus' speech;[1] similarly, Calenus' attack on Cicero's divorce and remarriage[2] is said by Plutarch to have been made by Antonius in his anti-Philippics.[3] Again, Asinius Pollio's *Pro Lamia* made various sordid charges so clearly false that even he did not include them in his Histories.[4] As a secondary source there is the, surely spurious, Sallustian *Invectiva in Ciceronem*,[5] where again there are parallels to passages in the speech of Calenus.[6] In other words, Dio was well acquainted with the sort of material which would go into a speech against Cicero, as his own comments on him show. There is no reason to suppose a single source for the whole speech.[7]

Cicero's speech cannot from internal evidence be attached to any identifiable moment in the political history of the winter 44/43. As has long been recognized, it uses material from all the first eight Philippics, especially the Second, Third and Fifth.[8] It is clear that the Philippics have been sifted to provide a selection of the charges which were brought against Antonius over this period and that these were put together to make a speech which has no real historical context. It is, however, worthy of note that in it Dio makes use of a number of details which derive from the Philippics but are not to be found in his own narrative.[9] It is hardly possible to escape the inference that Dio read the Philippics for the express purpose of composing this speech (the supposition of a proto-Dio, his 'source', who read Cicero for him, will not help). If so, this illustrates a curious, but important, feature of ancient historiography—while it was possible to use Cicero's speeches for putting together a speech 'by Cicero', it was

---

[1] Gabba, op. cit. 321–2.   [2] 18. 3.
[3] Plut. *Cic.* 41. 6.   [4] Sen. *Suas.* 6. 15.
[5] See especially G. Jachmann, 'Die Invektive gegen Cicero', *Misc. Acad. Berol.* 2. 1 (1950), 235.
[6] Gabba, op. cit. 320–1.
[7] Some further, inconclusive speculations on the source in *MH* 18, pp. 18 f.
[8] See Haupt, op. cit. 687–92.
[9] e.g. 45. 26. 4: *Phil.* 2. 19 (Antonius' visits to Gabinius in Egypt and Caesar in Gaul); 27. 5: *Phil.* 2. 2 and 32, 5. 3 (Antonius' claim to the augurate); 28. 1: *Phil.* 2. 25 (Antonius vomiting from the tribunal); 28. 2: *Phil.* 2. 24 (Antonius' progress through Italy); 28. 3: *Phil.* 2. 27 (purchase of Pompeius' property); 30. 1: *Phil.* 3. 5 (naked procession as consul). Note also 27. 4 οὗτος ὁ τὸ σπέρμα τῶν κακῶν τῶν μετὰ ταῦτα ἐκφύντων ἐμβαλών: *Phil.* 2. 22 huius luctuosissimi belli semen tu fuisti; and 28. 4: *Phil.* 2. 27 (comparison to Charybdis). The list could be greatly extended. See the parallels in the edition of Dio by F. G. Sturzius, vol. 5 (Leipzig, 1824), 457–71.

THE COMPOSITION OF THE HISTORY

not possible to use them to provide evidence for the main narrative; that was supplied by the narrative sources alone. None the less, the use of contemporary material does bring these speeches perceptibly closer to their context than is the case with the majority of Dio's speeches.[1] The richness of the material must account for the length of the debate (thirty-six pages in Boissevain), for Dio himself has no discernible axe to grind here. Once again, however, he manages to end the exchange with an attack on Cicero—he was always outspoken in his attacks on others but was not prepared to suffer outspokenness in return from his opponents.[2]

Dio's handling of Cicero is a failure, perhaps the most complete failure in his History. The character of it can be explained largely—though not entirely—in literary terms. It was governed by two factors: firstly Dio's extensive knowledge of anti-Ciceronian literature, which meant that there was always a derogatory comment to hand; and secondly by the nature of Dio's narrative, which of necessity moved from one major scene to the next. Cicero suffered defeat and public humiliation, and this was all that could emerge in Dio. There was no time to explain the forces at work, even if Dio understood them.

Brutus and Cassius from the Ides of March to Philippi

The handling of complex political events in a single city presented certain difficult problems to a narrative historian. Quite different problems had to be dealt with in organizing his account of a period when important events were taking place simultaneously in different parts of the world. Thucydides had solved the problem by arranging his narrative on a strict chronological basis, which largely preserved the relations of events to each other but meant the total loss of continuity in dealing with operations in any particular area. Dio, like most later historians, chose rather to arrange the narrative in large resumptive sections, thus breaking through the annalistic framework of his History. The pattern can be seen in simple form in his account of Caesar's Gallic Wars, which he treats in considerable detail, even developing a brief speech of Caesar's into a full-length oration of his own.[3] Initially, the annalistic pattern is retained, with a long section

---

[1] See pp. 78 f.   [2] 46. 29. 1.
[3] 38. 36–46. Compare *BG* 1. 40. See pp. 81–83.

which forms the last part of Dio's account of 58 B.C. and the first of 57 B.C.[1] The story is taken up again under 55 B.C. with a passage covering the events of 56 and 55.[2] Then the operations of 54 are given under the right year.[3] Finally, the pattern breaks down and under 51 he goes back with a weak indication of chronology (ἐν δὲ τῷ αὐτῷ ἐκείνῳ χρόνῳ) to give the events of 53 onwards, or rather a résumé of them—ὧν ἐγὼ τὰ ἀξιολογώτατα διηγήσομαι μόνα—and takes the story down to 50 B.C.[4]

In his narrative of events from the murder of Caesar to Philippi Dio throws aside the annalistic convention completely. He concentrates on the story of political events in Italy, including the very long orations of Cicero and Calenus, and leaves his account of the movements of Brutus and Cassius until he has brought the narrative down to the formation of the Triumvirate and the proscriptions of the winter 43/42 B.C. This scheme is, as far as can be seen, his own. Neither Appian[5] nor Livy (if the Periochae are any guide)[6] used it. Plutarch's Life could have provided Dio with a continuous account of Brutus' movements and it is possible, though perhaps unlikely, that he used it. The various ways in which the people appealed to Brutus to imitate his namesake, the Liberator, and the scene in which Porcia proved herself worthy to share in the conspiracy are recounted in similar terms by both writers.[7] Dio's narrative of Brutus' operations from 44 to 42 is not, however, strikingly similar to that of Plutarch (which is of course much longer). Some passages are fairly similar[8] but there are also items in Dio which Plutarch omits[9] and others where the details are rather different.[10] The answer is not clear; but the relation between Dio and Plutarch's Roman biographies is one area of source-criticism which might repay attention.

Given this scheme, it is striking how little attempt Dio made to indicate in his narrative the connexions between events in different areas. The speeches of Cicero and Calenus each have a single reference to the fact that Brutus had been given the command of Crete,[11] but in the narrative itself, there is only a single,

---

[1] 38. 31–39. 5. [2] 39. 40–53. [3] 40. 1–11.
[4] 40. 31–44. 1. [5] BC 3–4. 373. [6] 117–124.
[7] 44. 12: Plut. 9. 5–7; 44. 13. 1–14. 1: Plut. 13. 2–11.
[8] e.g. 47. 20. 4 and Plut. 24. 1.
[9] e.g. 47. 22. 2—the Senate's vote of maius imperium.
[10] Compare 47. 34. 4–6, on the siege of Patara, with Plut. 32.
[11] 45. 32. 4; 46. 23. 3.

oblique reference to the whereabouts of Brutus and Cassius up to
the point where the account of their own movements begins—the
senatus consultum of March 43 B.C. giving them Macedonia and
Syria for the war against Dolabella.[1] In turn, while Dolabella's
appointment to Syria had been mentioned before this,[2] his actual
position at the time is not made clear until much later.[3]

Similarly, the movements of Brutus and Cassius themselves
are brought in when Dio narrates the departure to the war of
Antonius and Octavianus in the early summer of 42.[4] The
reader is not, however, told where they were going, and Dio does
not revert to them until he comes to the preliminaries of Philippi
itself, when he recounts how Antonius delayed at Brundisium and
Octavianus watched Sextus Pompeius in Sicily.[5] To bring the
movements of Brutus and Cassius up to date, Dio has now to go
right back to the events which followed the Ides of March and to
their stay in Italy in the summer of 44.[6] There they stayed until
Octavianus began to win power in the city, an event which Dio
had related two books earlier.[7] When they learned, while in
Athens, that Octavianus' power had increased still further, they
abandoned all thought of the governorships of Crete (mentioned
only in the speeches of Cicero and Calenus) and Bithynia (not
mentioned previously) and planned to gain Syria and Macedonia
instead. Cassius now went off to Syria, where, as Dio says, he was
popular from his conduct on the expedition of Crassus,[8] and the
following chapters are devoted to Brutus.[9] The narrative is
straightforward and, within the limits of its style, accurate—
though there is a curious statement that Brutus was preparing to
sail to Italy in the early summer of 43.[10] There are no formal
indications of chronology; the whole section is treated as an
excursus; and the consuls, Dio's normal method of dating, are not
given here as they are in the main narrative. A number of dates
are indicated implicitly, by the connexions with contemporary
events already narrated. But it is hard to believe that Dio's

---

[1] 46. 40. 3.   [2] 45. 15. 2.   [3] 47. 28. 5 f.
[4] 47. 20. 1.   [5] 47. 36. 2 f.
[6] 47. 20. 1–3. There is an implicit indication of chronology in the mention of the
ludi Apollinares (6–13 July).
[7] 45. 8–9.
[8] Mentioned in 40. 28. 1–2.   [9] 47. 21. 2–25. 3.
[10] 22. 3. See the remarks by M. Gelzer, *RE* 10. 1 (1917), 'M. Iunius Brutus',
1004.

readers, or hearers, could have known (if they cared) what year
the narrative had reached unless they already had a considerable
acquaintance with the period. For instance, Dio says that Brutus
invaded Macedonia when C. Antonius had just arrived in the
province[1] (having in fact received it at the senatorial meeting of
28 November 44);[2] to recollect that, Dio's readers would have
had to rely on passing references in Book 45 and in Cicero's
speech.[3] A further fixed point is provided by the Senate's confirmation of Brutus as proconsul in Macedonia, Achaea, and
Illyricum, towards the end of March 43.[4] This Dio had not mentioned in his narrative of events in Rome; what he had given was
the joint grant, late in April 43, of *maius imperium* to Brutus and
Cassius for the war against Dolabella[5]—which he gives in his
section on Cassius,[6] but not in that on Brutus. Then, as another
fixed point, there is a reference to Octavianus' march on Rome in
43 and the *lex Pedia* providing for the prosecution of Caesar's
murderers.[7] This, however, merely serves to expose a mistake on
Dio's part, for he says that after receiving the news Brutus remained in Macedonia and only later moved east into Thrace;[8]
but it is known that he was already on the march in May.[9] Dio
goes on to say that Brutus now crossed into Asia, returned to
Europe, and then crossed again in the autumn.[10] Some have
doubted whether the first crossing is a reality, but Dio's account
is at least self-consistent.[11]

Dio thus brings Brutus' movements up to the autumn of 43,
and now goes back to recount Cassius' operations over the same
period (ἐν δὲ τοῖς αὐτοῖς ἐκείνοις χρόνοις).[12] Here the narrative is
rather more complicated. Over the winter of 44/43 Cassius arrived in Asia, acquired from Trebonius some cavalry sent on by
Dolabella, brought over the Tarsians, and arrived in Syria.[13] The
situation here needed some explanation (ἡ δὲ δὴ κατάστασις ἡ ἐν
τῇ Συρίᾳ τότε τοιάδε ἦν) and Dio was forced to go back and cover

[1] 21. 4.
[2] See T. R. S. Broughton, *The Magistrates of the Roman Republic*, 2 (New York,
1952), 319.   [3] 45. 9. 3 and 22. 3.
[4] 22. 2. For the date see Gelzer, op. cit. 1002, Broughton, op. cit. 346.
[5] 46. 40. 3. For the date see Gelzer, loc. cit., Broughton 343 and 346.
[6] 47. 28. 5.   [7] 22. 4. Narrated in 46. 42 f.
[8] 22. 4–24. 2.   [9] Gelzer, op. cit. 1005 f.
[10] See 24. 2; 25. 1; 25. 2.
[11] For the doubts see Magie, *Roman Rule*, ch. 17, n. 52. For Dio's consistency see
the preceding note.   [12] 26. 1.   [13] 26. 1–2.

the military history of the province from 46 B.C. onwards[1]—thus
having in effect an excursus within an excursus.

Cassius managed to acquire all the troops operating in the
province and it was then, in April 43, that his governorship of
Syria and *maius imperium* against Dolabella were granted by the
Senate.[2] Here again Dio has to make an excursus, which he
begins by repeating the one fact about Dolabella that he had
related before, his departure for the province while still consul, in
44.[3] The first chapter on Dolabella seems to be muddled, for
Dio says that, after making his way slowly through Macedonia
and Thrace, he stayed in Asia and there heard of τὸ δόγμα (which
must mean the grant of *imperium* to Brutus and Cassius); he goes
on to describe the murder of Trebonius and the Senate's declaration of Dolabella as *hostis*.[4] Dio has reversed the true order of
events, for Trebonius was murdered in January, the Senate's
declaration was in late February or early March,[5] and the grant
of *imperium* in April. The right chronology is in fact implicit in the
following lines,[6] where Dio says that Dolabella was made a *hostis*
before Octavianus had defeated Antonius (at Mutina in April)
and before the Senate knew that Cassius was master of Syria.
Dolabella's remaining actions, his advance into Syria, his defence
of Laodicea against Cassius and his death are retailed fairly
briefly by Dio[7] and need no comment. Dio then collects in a
chapter[8] the operations of Tillius Cimber against Tarsus, which
began before Dolabella's death and continued until after the
formation of the Triumvirate in November.

The news of the measures which the Triumvirs had taken
against them[9] caused Brutus and Cassius to meet again in Asia.[10]
Dio briefly sets out their plans and then turns to the mopping-up
operations which they conducted before advancing into Macedonia, listing them—against Ariobarzanes of Cappadocia, Rhodes,
and Lycia[11]—before taking them in succession. Cassius' campaign
against Rhodes is treated very briefly, in contrast to the long
account, complete with speeches, which Appian gives it.[12] Dio

---

[1] 26. 3–27. 5.   [2] 28. 5. See above.
[3] 45. 15. 2; 47. 29. 1. On his movements see Magie, ch. 17, n. 48.
[4] 29. 1–4.   [5] See Magie, loc. cit.   [6] 29. 4–6.
[7] 30. 1–7.   [8] 31.
[9] Dio had recorded these in 46. 56. 1.
[10] 32. 1. This gives a further fixed point in Dio's narrative.
[11] 33. 1.   [12] *BC* 4. 66–74.

however includes a colourful detail, the Rhodians boastfully sailing up to the mainland and displaying fetters for their prospective prisoners,[1] which no other source has, and another, that Cassius stripped the Rhodians of everything except the chariot of the Sun, an item which he shares only with Valerius Maximus.[2] Brutus' campaign against the Lycians, with the sieges of Xanthus and Patara, gets more vivid treatment and here Dio may well, in spite of some differences in detail, be condensing the account in Plutarch's *Brutus*.[3] The relation persists in the following section, where Dio's brief note of the differences between Brutus and Cassius which were composed at Sardis could be a condensation of Plutarch's long account of the same business.[4] With that Dio comes to the crossing into Macedonia and a detailed treatment of how they made contact with the hostile forces under C. Norbanus and Decidius Saxa (who are now mentioned for the first time) and of the topography of the area. All that remained to set the scene of the battle was to go back and relate how Antonius and Octavianus, with many delays, made their way over from Italy to the scene of operations.[5]

Dio's treatment of these years is a prime example of how narrative history was written. A great number of things vanish, nearly all links between events in Rome and in the East, all facts and figures as to the size of the forces involved, and even most details about the character of Brutus and Cassius and the relations between them. Dio did no more, and tried to do no more, than write down 'what happened' in each area in succession, in correct style and easily digestible form.

The Reign of Hadrian

The history of the Empire, from the point of view of the historian, was a very different thing from that of the Republic. Not only did the withdrawal of major decisions from public debate mean a decline in the weight and reliability of the information available; such information as there was inevitably centred on the persons of the Emperors themselves, and the details of their

[1] 33. 3.
[2] Dio 47. 33. 4: Val. Max. 1. 5. 8.
[3] Dio 34: Plut. 30. 4–32. 4 (compare Appian, *BC* 4. 316–43). For the differences in detail see, for example, Dio 34. 5—Brutus parading leading prisoners before the walls of Patara and Plut. 32. 1–2—mentioning female prisoners only.
[4] Dio 47. 35. 1. Plut. *Brut.* 34–35.   [5] 36. 2–37. 3.

conduct might be more fully recorded than many an important war. Dio made no attempt to avoid what the nature of his material implied and used a clearly-marked biographical technique by which much of the information on each reign was collected in illustrative sections at the beginning and end.[1] The model, may, for all we know, have been adopted from some predecessor,[2] but Dio made it his own and used it for all the reigns he recorded, up to and including those of his own time.[3] In the case of Hadrian's reign the introduction takes seven of a total of twenty pages in Boissevain and the resumption of the narrative is clearly indicated—ταῦτα περί γε τοῦ τρόπου, ὡς ἐν κεφαλαίῳ εἰπεῖν, προείρηκα· λέξω δὲ καὶ καθ' ἕκαστον, ὅσα ἀναγκαῖόν ἐστι μνημονεύεσθαι.[4] The closing section is comparatively brief: a note of the chronology of his reign, of the location of his mausoleum, and of popular reactions and memories of him.[5]

Whether there were any formal histories of the reign, or biographies, which Dio consulted, remains a mystery. He mentions the autobiography of Hadrian once, on the death of Antinous, only to refute it;[6] the references to the autobiography in the *Historia Augusta* are not sufficient to give much idea of its scope or contents.[7] References to a work on the reign by Philon of Byblos and to an *encomium* of Hadrian by Aspasius of Byblos[8] take us no further. Nor are there the slightest grounds for supposing any relationship between Dio's work and the imperial biographies of his contemporary, Marius Maximus.[9] Dio mentions him several times, as *Praefectus Urbi* under Macrinus,[10] but there is no indication that he knew of his literary activity. Then there was yet

---

[1] See p. 40 and Questa, op. cit.
[2] Questa, op. cit. 52, suggests Plutarch's imperial biographies.
[3] See F. Millar, 'The Date of the *Constitutio Antoniniana*', *JEA* 48 (1962), 124.
[4] 69. 8. 1[1] (228).   [5] 69. 23 (241–2).
[6] 69. 11. 2 (231) εἴτ' οὖν ἐς τὸν Νεῖλον ἐκπεσών, ὡς Ἀδριανὸς γράφει, εἴτε καὶ ἱερουργηθείς, ὡς ἡ ἀλήθεια ἔχει. Dio's expression does not suggest that he was refuting Hadrian from another *written* source.
[7] See Peter, *HRR* 2. 117–18 and CLXXVI–CLXXVIII. For the connexion of this work with that of Phlegon of Tralles see Jacoby, *FGrH* 257, T. 5, F. 35, and commentary.
[8] *FGrH* 790, T. 1, and 792.
[9] L. Marius Maximus Perpetuus Aurelianus. See *Albo* no. 1100 and addenda (p. 620), Peter, *HRR* 2. 121–9, CLXXX–VIII, and G. Barbieri, 'Mario Massimo', *RFIC* 32 (1954), 36 f. and 262 f. Subsequent documentary evidence on his career in *AE* 1955. 188, *Dura Final Report*, V. 1. *The Parchments and Papyri*, no. 56, 60 B, C. See also J. F. Gilliam, 'The Governors of Syria Coele from Severus to Diocletian', *AJPh* 79 (1958), 225, on p. 230.
[10] 78. 14. 3 (418); 78. 36. 1 (444); 79. 2. 1 (453).

a third senator of the Severan age, Asinius Quadratus, whose work, covering all Roman history, will also have dealt with Hadrian.[1] He is not mentioned as a person, or quoted as a source,[2] by Dio—and here again there is nothing to show any connexion. Nor is it necessary to chase once again the ghost of the 'annalistic historian' whom a former generation detected in the *Historia Augusta*.

It is permissible to wonder whether a major 'source' in the form of a history or biography was in fact required. The only part of the text as it stands where a coherent source seems to underlie Dio's account is on the Jewish revolt of 132–5.[3] It is possible that Dio's information here was derived, directly or indirectly, from Hadrian's reports to the Senate, for he mentions the wording of one of the letters explicitly,[4] and the only points of detail which his account contains are the number of places taken and men slain and the name of the commander, Julius Severus.

We tend perhaps to disregard the fund of common knowledge which would be available to a historian in recording events which took place not more than a century before he wrote—Book 69 will have been written in 217 or 218. There was, for instance, the information which Cassius Apronianus was able to gather in Cilicia and transmit to his son, about the death of Trajan at Selinus and the accession of Hadrian. But there is also an incident from Dio's account of his own time which is significant; Quintillus, an elderly and respected senator, was forced to suicide after the execution of Plautianus, and before his death proclaimed: 'I offer up the same prayer which Servianus made against Hadrian's[5]—that he should wish for death and not find it.[6] The saying would have been pointless if the story had not been well known. To this one might add various details about Hadrian to be found in writers who were not concerned formally with history, the *sententiae et epistulae* of Hadrian in a grammarian,[7] or

---

[1] C. Asinius Protimus Quadratus; see *Albo* no. 59 and Jacoby, *FGrH* 97. According to the Suda s.v. Κοδράτος he wrote a history of Rome in Ionic dialect from the foundation to Severus Alexander.

[2] Christ–Schmid, *Geschichte der griechischen Literatur*[6], 2. 2 (Munich, 1924), 801 and n. 6, claims that the quotation in Xiphilinus—Dio 70. 3. 3 (244)—originates from Dio. But Xiphilinus is quoting a number of authors, on the death of Antoninus Pius, precisely because he had no text of Dio here.

[3] 69. 12–14 (232–4).   [4] 14. 3.   [5] 76. 7. 5 (362).

[6] 69. 17. 2 (236–7).

[7] *Corpus Gloss. Lat.* 3. 31 f.

Epiphanius' description of Hadrian's travels and the foundation of Aelia Capitolina,[1] and other references in Athenaeus, Aulus Gellius, and Philostratus' Lives of the Sophists.[2] The latter's Life of Apollonius of Tyana shows how far a Severan writer could assume a general basis of historical knowledge, not necessarily accurate or detailed, in the readers of a religious novel.[3] In the Lives of the Sophists Philostratus was later to re-use one story included by Dio.[4]

It has to be assumed, until evidence to the contrary is produced, that what Dio wrote about Hadrian was compiled by himself. It is clear enough that Hadrian's autobiography, the only source we know he used, could not have provided all or even a large part of his material, in which a hostile and critical spirit prevails. Dio's text is of course seriously defective, being constructed substantially from Xiphilinus, supplemented by a number of excerpts. But by studying what is there, without indulging in extensive surmises about what is lost, it is possible to gain a fair conception of what and how he wrote.

His father's inside information allowed Dio to start the reign with an unusually bold and polemical sentence—Ἀδριανὸς δὲ ὑπὸ μὲν Τραϊανοῦ οὐκ ἐσεποιήθη. In spite of his close association with Trajan Hadrian had never been specially honoured by him and the thing was only put through by Plotina and Attianus, the Prefect of the Guard.[5] It is probable that the circumstances of Hadrian's accession were from the first a subject of dispute[6] and that Dio was trying to clinch the argument with a piece of evidence which had not yet been produced.

Dio completes his account of the first days of the reign with a prophetic dream of Hadrian's and some details about his first letter to the Senate, in which he refused various honours and promised not to execute any senators.[7] Then he turns to a systematic introduction to the reign, which embraces in succession

---

[1] περὶ μέτρων 14.
[2] Athenaeus, Deip. 361 f., 574 f., 677 e. Aulus Gellius, NA 3. 16. 12, 13. 22. 1, 16. 13. 4–5. Philostratus, VS 1. 8 (Teubner ed. 9) 1. 22 (37), 1. 25 (42, 44), 2. 1 (57 f.).
[3] For an exhaustive discussion of this work's relation to historical fact, see F. Grosso, 'La "Vita di Apollonio di Tiana" come fonte storica', Acme 7 (1954), 333–530.
[4] See p. 19.
[5] 69. 1. 1–4 (222).
[6] See SHA, vita Had. 4. 8: 'Frequens sane opinio fuit. . . .'
[7] 69. 2. 1–3 (222–3). Compare vita Had. 6. 1–5.

Hadrian's executions of prominent men, his origin and personal character, his finances, military measures and travels, his treatment of the people, and various facets of his conduct and manner of government. The first thing to be dealt with was the executions at the beginning and end of his reign, which made him hated in spite of his generally benevolent rule and almost prevented his deification after death.[1] On the 'conspiracy of the four consulars' Dio gives only their names, Palma, Celsus, Nigrinus, and Lusius, and the fact, which he does not believe, that two of them attempted to assassinate Hadrian while on a hunting expedition (οἱ μὲν ὡς ἐν θήρᾳ δῆθεν ἐπιβουλευκότες αὐτῷ). The attempt to prove that what Dio disbelieved was in fact the case cannot ultimately be sustained.[2] The hostility aroused by the executions, Dio says, was such that Hadrian was forced to defend himself and swear that he had not given the order. The *Historia Augusta*, where the conspiracy is given as a fact, says that Hadrian's defence appeared in his Autobiography.[3] At the end of the reign came the deaths of Servianus and Fuscus, to which Dio returns when he comes to them in the narrative.[4]

The next section, which opens with a brief reference to Hadrian's father, the praetorian (P. Aelius) Hadrianus Afer, is entirely devoted to anecdotes illustrating the Emperor's character, chiefly his restless intellectual ambition and his jealousy of the major literary and intellectual figures of his time.[5] He tried, Dio claims, to humiliate Favorinus of Arelate and Dionysius of Miletus by favouring their (inferior) rivals. This view is ill supported, for Philostratus emphasizes the favour in which Hadrian held Dionysius,[6] and all that Dio can bring as evidence is a story of Dionysius sarcastically dismissing the claims of Avidius Heliodorus, the *ab epistulis*, to be a rhetor. As for Favorinus, Dio may be referring obliquely to the high favour which his rival, Polemo, enjoyed with Hadrian,[7] but in telling a story of his appearance in a lawsuit before Hadrian he omits (at least in the extant text) to record what Philostratus tell us, that through Hadrian's mercy Favorinus

---

[1] 69. 2. 5–6 (223). This is repeated in substance in the final summing-up 69. 23. 2 (241).

[2] See von Premerstein, *Das Attentat der Konsulare auf Hadrian im Jahre 118. n. Chr.* Klio: Beiheft 8 (1908), criticized by P. L. Strack, *Untersuchungen zur römischen Reichsprägung des zweiten Jahrhunderts* 2 (Stuttgart, 1933), 197–9.

[3] *vita Had.* 7. 1–2.   [4] 69. 17. 1 (236).   [5] 69. 3–4 (224–6).
[6] *VS* 1. 22 (Teubner ed. 37).   [7] *VS* 1. 25 (44).

escaped serious consequences.[1] It would be idle to claim that 'the facts' can be disentangled from these conflicting stories; but it is clear that Dio is using his material with hostile intent.

The story of Hadrian's relations with the architect Apollodorus, which is designed to serve the same end, offers considerable difficulties. Apollodorus plays a peculiarly large part in Dio's narrative, for he earlier devotes a long paragraph to an enthusiastic description of the bridge he built over the Danube in Trajan's reign,[2] not forgetting to note that Hadrian, through fear, had the upper part of it removed. In the extant text (that of Xiphilinus) the name of Apollodorus does not appear in connexion with the bridge, but it is clear that it stood there originally.[3] In his account of Hadrian and Apollodorus Dio goes back again to the reign of Trajan and recounts an incident when Apollodorus and Trajan were discussing plans for buildings (apparently the Forum Traianum, Odeum, and Gymnasium)—when Hadrian interrupted, the architect sharply dismissed him. The course of events which Dio then narrates is obscure in itself but can be dated with reasonable certainty. He begins by saying that Hadrian, once on the throne, first exiled and then killed Apollodorus. With that he brings in a notorious difficulty, the building of the temple of Venus and Roma; Hadrian sent the plan of the temple to Apollodorus, to show him that a great work could be built without his help, and Apollodorus wrote back pointing out numerous errors in construction. Hadrian was angry and distressed ὅτι καὶ ἐς ἀδιόρθωτον ἁμαρτίαν ἐπεπτώκει, and had Apollodorus executed.[4] It is clear that the story implies a moment at which the temple, if not complete, was at least well under way. It was inaugurated on 21 April 121 (the *Parilia*, which the festival of *Roma* was designed to supersede)[5] but not dedicated until 136/7.[6] This chronological scheme removes the difficulties which were once felt[7] and allows

---

[1] 3. 6. Philos. *VS* 1. 8. [2] 68. 13 (199–200).
[3] See Tzetzes, *Chil.* 2. 65 f. and 4. 504–5. Procopius, *de aed.* 4. 6.
[4] 69. 4. 1–5 (225–6). [5] Athenaeus, *Deip.* 361 f.
[6] So G. A. S. Snijder, 'Kaiser Hadrian und der Tempel der Venus und Roma', *JDAI* 55 (1940), 1. Platner–Ashby, *Topographical Dictionary of Ancient Rome* (Oxford, 1929), 553, has A.D. 135. F. Préchac, 'La Date du déplacement du colosse de Rome sous Hadrien', *MEFR* 37 (1918–19), 285, brings some evidence, not entirely convincing, to show that the colossus was not moved, to make way for the temple, until 128.
[7] See J. Plew, *Quellenuntersuchungen zur Geschichte des Kaisers Hadrian* (Straßburg, 1890), 89 f.

the extant letter of Apollodorus to Hadrian, on the building of military engines,[1] to refer, as it should, to the Jewish War. The date of Apollodorus' death is therefore fixed to within a few years. The whole story is an admirable illustration of the way in which, by concentrating on the delineation of personality, Dio could record things of the greatest importance in the history of Rome[2] in an utterly trivial context. He follows it with an absurdity, the claim that Hadrian replaced Homer by Antimachus 'whose very name many had not known before'.[3]

The three remaining sections of the introduction cover Hadrian's dealings with the army, the provinces, and the Roman people; and some items from his manner of government, particularly his relations with senators. Although Dio begins these sections in a hostile spirit—ᾐτιῶντο μὲν δὴ ταῦτά τε αὐτοῦ καὶ τὸ πάνυ ἀκριβὲς τό τε περίεργον καὶ τὸ πολύπραγμον[4]—the tone is in fact entirely favourable. The benefactions in the provinces and the reforms of the army (to which he returns later) are given only in the most general terms. But various other aspects of his rule, his holding of *cognitiones* in public, his respect for the consuls, his visits to sick senators, and so forth, are given in considerable detail.[5]

Of the annalistic, or semi-annalistic, section, on Hadrian's activities between 117 and 132, very little remains;[6] and although Xiphilinus must be responsible for some of the omissions—for there is a reference to the Alexandrian *stasis* which appears only in a fragment of Petrus Patricius[7]—it is clear that Dio himself did not treat the period in detail. He gives a full description of the *character* of Hadrian's military reforms,[8] but it is only a few rhetorical phrases that reveal where Hadrian's travels had in fact taken him—ἐν ταῖς χιόσι ταῖς Κελτικαῖς (121/2)[9] καὶ ἐν τοῖς

---

[1] Plew, op. cit. 92–93. Revised text by R. Schneider, *Gött. Abh.*, hist.-phil. Kl., N.F. 10 (1908), 1.

[2] On the festival of *Roma* see Fink, Hoey, Snyder, 'The *Feriale Duranum*', *YCS* 7 (1940), 1, on pp. 103 f.

[3] 4. 6 (226). On the 'catachannae' which Hadrian wrote in imitation of Antimachus (*vita Had.* 16. 2), see Bardon, *Les Empereurs et les lettres latines* (Paris, 1940), 414–15.   [4] 5. 1 (226).   [5] Compare *vita Had.* 9. 7–8.

[6] 69. 8. 1a (229) – 11. 4 (232).   [7] 8. 1a.

[8] 9. 1–6 (229–30). The authorities are discussed by Plew, op. cit. 61 f.

[9] Hadrian passed the winter of 121/2 in Germany, Raetia, and Noricum. So W. Weber, *Untersuchungen zur Geschichte des Kaisers Hadrianus* (Leipzig, 1907), 108–9.

καύμασι τοῖς Αἰγυπτιακοῖς (123?)[1]—and then the story of how
the Batavian cavalry swam the Danube, thus impressing the
barbarians (124).[2] The references to places are more or less in
chronological order, for what that is worth. But the value of the
passage lies more in the revelation of Dio's own attitude to military matters. Hadrian's regulations, he says, lasted until his own
time.[3] By his revival of military training and discipline he was
able to preserve peace, for the barbarians, seeing this and not
being given any occasion for grievance—and in fact receiving
payments—made no warlike moves. The relevance of this opinion
in 217 or 218, when Caracalla's Eastern expedition had achieved
nothing except his own murder, is obvious. The passage reaffirms
the attitude Dio took to Severus' military operations.[4]

A brief appendix to the account of the Emperor's first journey
concentrates on his personal conduct, his abandonment of the full
Imperial train, and his love of hunting, and mentions the foundation of Hadrianoutherai in 123.[5] This takes Dio back to the
monument which Hadrian set up to his horse Borysthenes—in
Narbonensis in 121—and to the verses which he wrote himself
and had inscribed on the tomb.[6] From there he runs on by a
natural progression to the death of Plotina and to the temple Hadrian dedicated to her memory.[7] Dio (or at least Xiphilinus) does
not mention the place or time, Nemausus in (probably) 122.[8]

It is clear, even from the fragmentary text we have, that the
annalistic section is not as annalistic as it might be, for here too
the material tends to be grouped round leading characteristics of
the main figure and the chronological sequence, if never entirely
lost, is often vague in the extreme.

In the narrative of the next few years Xiphilinus has done more
than his usual damage to the text, for successive sentences make
a further reference to Hadrian's hunting,[9] to his visit to Greece—

[1] This is perhaps a slip, and refers to Hadrian's visit to *North Africa* in 123—
Weber, op. cit. 119 f. If not, then the reference is entirely out of context, for Hadrian
did not visit Egypt until 130. See E. Breccia, 'Il viaggio dell'imperatore Adriano in
Egitto e cio' che resta della città di Antinoo', *Atti IV Congr. naz. Stud. Rom.* (1938) 1,
119, on p. 120.
[2] Weber, op. cit. 153 f. See especially *CIL* 3. 3676.   [3] 9. 4.
[4] See pp. 82, 141-3.
[5] 10. 2 (230). For the date see Weber, op. cit. 131. For the site, Magie, *Roman Rule*, ch. 2, n. 20, also ch. 26, n. 20.
[6] Weber, op. cit. 105. Bardon, op. cit. 419 f.   [7] See 10. 3¹ (231).
[8] *vita Had.* 12. 2. Weber, op. cit. 112.   [9] 10. 3² (231).

ἀφικόμενος δὲ ἐς τὴν Ἑλλάδα ἐπώπτευσε τὰ μυστήρια—which must be that of 128/9,[1] and his journey through Judaea to Egypt in 129/30.[2] At this point the narrative becomes more complete, though still anecdotal, and Dio records Hadrian's sacrifice to Pompey and the rebuilding of his tomb.[3] Then came the death of Antinous and the foundation of Antinoopolis, and all the rest of the paragraph deals with rumours about his death,[4] and the honours then paid to him. This is followed by another incident, the death of Paulina, and Hadrian's failure to give appropriate honour to her at once—which is again used as an illustration of character.[5]

The revolt of the Jews under Bar Kochba which covered the years 132 to 135 is given at length in Xiphilinus' text of Dio,[6] no doubt because it was of greater religious interest than much else in his narrative. The text as we have it opens abruptly with Hadrian's decision to rebuild Jerusalem as Aelia Capitolina and establish there a temple of Jupiter. This is the sole reason that Dio mentions and he knows nothing of the cause adduced by the *Historia Augusta*, the banning of circumcision.[7] The decision was clearly taken on Hadrian's visit in 129/30,[8] for Dio indicates that, while Hadrian was in Egypt (130–1) and then again in Syria (131), the Jews, though indignant, remained quiet. When he was 'far away' (at Athens in 131/2)[9] they revolted. The passage reveals that Dio had better information about Hadrian's movements and their chronology than its style might suggest. Dio's account of the war itself amounts to a general description of its character but in no degree to an account of its course. The name of Bar Kochba (which was known to Eusebius)[10] is not mentioned;

---

[1] Weber, op. cit. 207, and P. Graindor, *Athènes sous Hadrien* (Cairo, 1934), 37–39.

[2] See W. F. Stinespring, 'Hadrian in Palestine 129/30 A.D.', *Journal of the American Oriental Society* 59 (1939), 360.

[3] 11. 1 (231). Compare *vita Had.* 14. 4.   [4] Compare *vita Had.* 14. 5–7.

[5] 11. 4. διὰ ταῦτά τε ἐσκώπτετο, καὶ ὅτι τῇ Παυλίνῃ τῇ ἀδελφῇ .... The date of Paulina's death is not known. *PIR*² D 186.

[6] 69. 12–14 (232–4).

[7] *vita Had.* 14. 2. See also *Dig.* 48. 8. 11 *praef.* For the rabbinical tradition of a period of persecution which can be placed before the outbreak of the war, see E. M. Smallwood, 'The Legislation of Hadrian and Antoninus Pius against Circumcision', *Latomus* 18 (1959), 334, and ibid. 20 (1961), 93.

[8] See Epiphanius περὶ μέτρων 14 and Stinespring, op. cit.

[9] Weber, op. cit. 268 f.; Graindor, op. cit. 49 f.

[10] Euseb. *HE* 4. 6. 2. The literary evidence is most fully discussed by E. Schürer, *Geschichte des jüdischen Volkes im Zeitalter Jesu Christi*, 1⁵ (Leipzig, 1920), 670 f.

nor are any place-names or any indications of chronology. Dio describes the preparations of the Jews, their fortifications and underground refuges,[1] and the outbreak of the revolt, followed by the participation of neighbouring Gentiles and disturbances throughout the *oikoumene*.[2] Hadrian then sent (Sextus) Julius Severus from Britain, and the rest is the account of his slow but steady progress, taking the strongpoints of the Jews in succession. Dio gives the figures, 50 major fortresses and 985 villages taken and 580,000 slain.[3] Typically, he ends with two illustrative details, the one trivial the other not: firstly he gives some portents which foretold the devastation of the land; and secondly refers to Hadrian's letter to the Senate which, because of the heavy Roman losses, omitted the usual formula 'If you and your sons are well, it is well; I and the army are well.'[4] This is the only indication he gives that Hadrian visited the scene of operations. When he did so is obscure[5] but it was probably before his return to Rome in 134,[6] so this item refers back to the early years of the war, perhaps to the loss of the legion XXII *Deiotariana*.[7] It is not necessary to suppose that Dio discovered the omission of the formula in the course of his researches in the *acta Senatus*.

After the Jewish War Xiphilinus provides brief and compressed notes of events and measures in the East, which are supplemented by three excerpts. The first item, the dispatch of Cn. Julius Severus to Bithynia, as *legatus Augusti pro praetore ad corrigendum statum provinciae*, reveals another type of tradition of which Dio was able to make use—καὶ ὁ μὲν διήγαγε καὶ διῴκησε καὶ τὰ ἴδια καὶ τὰ κοινὰ αὐτῶν, οὕτως ὥσθ' ἡμᾶς καὶ ἐς δεῦρο ἀεὶ αὐτοῦ μνημονεύειν.[8] Then comes a reference to an invasion by the Alani,

---

[1] This detail is amply confirmed by recent discoveries. See Benoît, Milik, de Vaux, *Discoveries in the Judaean Desert*, 2, *Les Grottes de Murabba'at* (Oxford, 1961) and *Israel Exploration Journal* 11 (1961), especially 16–24, 36–52, 77–81.

[2] No other source suggests this. It is just possible that the papyrus *IEJ* 11 (1961), 46, no. 11, mentioning one Thyriss bar Tinianus, offers some confirmation of the detail that Gentiles in the area took part in the war.

[3] 14. 1.

[4] 14. 2–3.

[5] See Schürer, op. cit. 690, and Weber, op. cit. 276.

[6] Strack, op. cit. 133 f., brought some evidence to show that Hadrian went to Judaea after his return to Rome in 134. This is not accepted by H. Mattingly, *Coins of the Roman Empire in the British Museum*, 3 (1936), cxlii f.

[7] See Ritterling, *RE* 12 (1925), 'Legio', 1794–5.

[8] 14. 4. On the appointment see Magie, *Roman Rule*, ch. 26, n. 54. On the puzzling clause which follows—τῇ δὲ δὴ βουλῇ καὶ τῷ κλήρῳ ἡ Παμφυλία ἀντὶ τῆς

bribed by Pharasmanes of Iberia, and its repulse by Flavius
Arrianus, the legate of Cappadocia. The reference to him is too
brief to afford much support for the Suda's statement that Dio
wrote his biography.[1]

Dio now reverts to the visit of Hadrian to Athens in 131/2[2]—
another indication of how far he had abandoned annalistic
methods. He gives Hadrian's measures there in unvarnished
detail (omitting, for instance, the oration given at the consecration of the Olympieion by the famous sophist, Polemo) ;[3] all the
details seem to be correct, except the statement that Hadrian
granted all Cephallenia to Athens. An inscription from Pale makes
clear that this city at least remained free and autonomous.[4]

Of the years after Hadrian's return to Rome in 134, everything
that Dio records, except for an incident at the moment of return,[5]
relates to the problem of the succession, along with some details
about prominent figures of the time. The purpose of this latter
material is probably to form a telling contrast to what he says of
Hadrian's first choice for the succession, L. Ceionius Commodus.
He balances a reference to the adoption of Commodus with the
murder of Servianus and Fuscus,[6] giving Hadrian's opinion that
Servianus was *capax imperii* and quoting Servianus' dying wish,
which was not fruitless, that Hadrian should long for death and
not find it. It is here that he mentions an extant letter of Hadrian
in which he expressed his desire for death, and of which we may
have a copy on a second-century papyrus.[7]

Then two other prominent contemporary figures, the Praetorian Prefects (Q. Marcius) Turbo and (Ser. Sulpicius) Similis,
are brought in solely to be praised (γεγόνασι δὲ καὶ ἄλλοι τότε
ἄριστοι ἄνδρες ὧν ἐπιφανέστατοι . . .).[8] Of Turbo he notes merely

---

Βιθυνίας ἐδόθη—see Magie, ch. 28, n. 7. The suggestion that the clause is misplaced in the *Excerpta Valesiana* (*Exc. de virt. et vit.* 296) will not do, as it contains
a reference to the first half of the sentence (and it is difficult to see how in making
excerpts this sort of mistake could occur). It is possible that the reference is to a tem-
porary measure, but far more probable that Dio is referring to the transfer under
Marcus Aurelius. He does not say that *Hadrian* made the transfer.

[1] 69. 15. 1 (235). See the Suda s.v. Δίων ὁ Κάσσιος and K. Hartmann, 'Über das
Verhaltnis des Cassius Dio zur Parthergeschichte des Flavius Arrianus', *Philologus*
74 (1917), 73, on pp. 89 f.

[2] 69. 16. 1–2 (236).   [3] Philos. *VS* 1. 25 (Teubner ed. 44).

[4] *IG* 3. 481. See Graindor, op. cit. 55.   [5] 69. 16. 3 (236).

[6] 17. 1–3.

[7] 17. 3. See P. J. Alexander, 'Letters and Speeches of the Emperor Hadrian',
HSCPh 49 (1938), 141, on pp. 170–2.   [8] 18. 1–19. 2.

an unidentified prefecture before that of the Praetorian cohorts,[1] and goes on to give two anecdotes illustrating the devotion with which he applied himself, at Hadrian's side, to public business. Similis is even more highly praised—entirely, it should be noted, for the modesty with which he conducted himself. Dio goes back to an incident in the reign of Trajan, when the Emperor admitted Similis, who was still a centurion, to his presence before the *Praefecti*; Similis reproved him for upsetting the due order of precedence. In the year 217 or 218, when Dio was writing, not all Praetorian Prefects were equally self-effacing. The reference to Similis is out of place chronologically, for he left office soon after Hadrian's accession, probably in 119, and died, as Dio says, seven years later.[2]

With the death of L. Ceionius Commodus and the adoption of Antoninus, Dio had the opportunity to introduce a brief speech by Hadrian.[3] That it is his own composition is beyond question,[4] and is confirmed, if necessary, by the appearance of familiar features of his language and style—τὸ δαιμόνιον, the neutral term for divine agency, and some much-used rhetorical devices.[5] The arguments for adoption bear some resemblance to those which Tacitus put into the mouth of Galba, adopting Piso Licinianus. Chance might give an Emperor an unworthy son but the exercise of free choice would mean that only the best could come to the throne.[6]

With that, all that remained was to give a sketch of Hadrian's complicated adoption scheme[7] and of his painful and protracted death,[8] and to bring the narrative to a close in the accustomed manner.[9]

What Dio records of Hadrian is largely a collection of anecdotes, from a variety of sources, centred round the Emperor and the leading men of his time. Some chronological structure is preserved, but it is vague and uncertain. Hadrian is seen from the point of view of the Roman aristocracy, and while his military reforms are praised there is no indication that his philhellenism,

[1] On his career see E. Frézouls, 'Inscription de Cyrrhus relative à Q. Marcius Turbo', *Syria* 30 (1953), 247, and Pflaum, *Carrières* no. 94, and compare R. Syme, 'The Wrong Marcius Turbo', *JRS* 52 (1962), 87.

[2] See *RE* 7A (1931), 871–2.   [3] 69. 20. 2–5 (239–40).

[4] See Bardon, op. cit. 402.

[5] See 20. 4 εὐγενῆ πρᾷον εὔεικτον φρόνιμον, μήθ' ὑπὸ νεότητος προπετὲς μηθ' ὑπὸ γήρως ἀμελὲς ποιῆσαί τι δυνάμενον.

[6] 20. 2–3: Tac. *Hist.* 1. 15–16. See Ch. Wirzubski, *Libertas* (Cambridge, 1950), 154 f.   [7] 21. 1–2.   [8] 22. Compare *vita Had.* 24. 8–25. 7.   [9] 23. See p. 61.

which led him, among many other things, to benefit Nicaea, seemed to Dio either important or praiseworthy.

Conclusion

A historian who set out with Dio's aims and methods ought perhaps to be judged by purely literary standards, or even narrower canons of style and language. To apply to Dio modern standards of historical criticism—that is, in effect, to compare what he wrote with what we should like him to have told us—is in itself a solecism. The exercise is worth while, however, if it is used precisely to show by contrast what Dio's methods of composition were and how the conventions he followed allowed him to handle the various types of narration required.

How far this massive work, which in its original state must have approached twice its present length, satisfied the literary taste of Dio's contemporaries we cannot tell. History was in vogue, as we know from Lucian, and above all histories which followed the rules of rhetoric and paid lip-service to Thucydides. The earliest literary judgement on Dio is that of Photius, who praises him for his pure and elevated diction.[1] But, while we cannot be sure that the History was in any way 'published' on completion, it is perhaps significant, not only that there are no papyrus fragments of it, a thing which proves nothing in itself, but that there is no certain mention of it in any writer before the sixth century. Byzantine writers used it largely as a storehouse of facts.[2]

Even if it is admitted that the task of making a satisfactory literary work out of an 80-book history of Rome was beyond Dio, as it might be beyond any man, neither the magnitude of the achievement nor Dio's personal contribution to the work should be underestimated. It is not possible to show, and there is no reason to believe, that for long stretches of the work Dio would follow a single source, contributing little of his own. On the contrary, the whole structure and composition of the History is his alone; and beyond that, he put into it much of his own knowledge and attitudes. If the work is not a masterpiece, its author still deserves attention and respect.

[1] *Biblioth.* 71.

[2] On Dio's *Nachleben* see Schwartz, 1720–21, and Christ–Schmid, op. cit. 799. The suggestion made in the latter work that there is a trace of Dio in Julian's *Caesares* rests on a passage of Xiphilinus where he had no text of Dio—70. 3. 3 (244). See p. 62, n. 2.

III

POLITICAL AND HISTORICAL VIEWS

THE question of a historian's political and historical views is not summed up in the mere definition of what he was for and what against, of what he approved and of what disapproved. It is necessary to consider first in what terms he viewed historical development: whether, like Polybius, he interpreted events in the light of a political theory or, like Thucydides, was able to see the economic basis which underlay historical change. Above all, with Dio, who lived in a period which most historians have taken to be crucial in the change from the early to the late Empire, it is worth considering whether this left any recognizable mark on his thinking, either in his political views or in his attitude to earlier periods.

The widest issue is easily settled: Dio has no explicit framework in terms of which he interprets the events he narrates, and there is nothing to show that he had any specific aim in view save that of composing the work itself and leaving his name with it to posterity. His views must therefore be looked for throughout his text, beginning with those passages in which he makes formal statements about Rome's successive constitutions. Then there are various passing comments on historical figures and situations, and generalizations about politics; it was precisely for such *ad hoc* judgements that, according to the basic tenets of ancient history-writing, his political experience should have fitted him. Even more valuable are the numerous and lengthy speeches which he inserts, not so much to show his formal political attitudes—the assumption that some of them are political pamphlets is sometimes made but can rarely be justified—as to make clear, first, which were the questions that troubled him and to which he would return, and, second, what was the philosophical, or semi-philosophical, background of his thinking. That is to say, the speeches illustrate primarily the scope and limits of his political thought, rather than his own views. The clear exception is the speech of Maecenas, the part of the History which reveals most about Dio and his time. To appreciate it properly, however, it is necessary to discuss its context, Dio's account of the reign of Augustus. This in its turn has much to reveal, for in describing it Dio is dealing with the period which definitively shaped the world in which he lived. That world too should be better understood when the examination is complete.

Political Judgements and Generalizations

Dio makes clear statements of his attitude to different types of constitution only in those books which cover the fall of the Republic and the establishment of the Principate. Three types of constitution are concerned—monarchy, democracy, and 'dynasties':

ταῦτα μὲν ἔν τε τῇ βασιλείᾳ καὶ ἐν τῇ δημοκρατίᾳ ταῖς τε δυνα-
στείαις . . . καὶ ἔπραξαν οἱ Ῥωμαῖοι καὶ ἔπαθον· ἐκ δὲ τούτου
μοναρχεῖσθαι αὖθις ἀκριβῶς ἤρξαντο.[1]

The period of the dynasties is not accurately defined; he uses the term to denote a state of affairs, characterized by violence and illegality,[2] in which one or more faction-leaders held power unconstitutionally. 'Monarchy' in Dio means the established rule of a single man, or even by an extension of the term two or three men ruling together.[3] It applies equally to the regal period and the Empire, which he regards as effectively equivalent—the Emperors avoided only the *name* of King.[4] Summing up Augustus' achievement, however, he gives a rather different interpretation of the Principate—τὴν μοναρχίαν τῇ δημοκρατίᾳ μίξας.[5] Here δημοκρατία has no philosophical overtones but simply refers to a state of affairs in which order and due social distinctions were preserved and Republican institutions functioned[6]—he says that Marcus Antonius by summoning the Senate εἰκόνα τινὰ τῆς δημοκρατίας παρείχετο[7]—and in this sense Dio's statement is literally correct. In discussing democracy and its alternatives Dio's concern is not with the responsible participation of citizens

---

[1] 52. 1. 1.
[2] See Fr. 83. 4 πολλὰ μὲν καὶ βίαια, ὥσπερ ἐν δυναστείᾳ τινὶ ἀλλ' οὐ δημοκρατίᾳ, ἔπραξαν. Compare Appian, *BC* 1. 7.
[3] 53. 17. 1.   [4] 53. 17. 2.   [5] 56. 43. 4.
[6] See C. G. Starr, 'The Perfect Democracy of the Roman Empire', *American Historical Review* 58 (1952–3), 1, especially p. 15.
[7] 42. 27. 2.

in the management of their affairs, or any similar formulation, but with the formal outward functioning of the State. His preferences are dictated solely by considerations of public order. It was clear that the free functioning of the Republican constitution meant disorder and the imposition of a single ruler order; within these terms the conclusion that monarchy was preferable was inescapable.

Four passages set out the conclusion in detail. Introducing his account of the murder of Julius Caesar he mentions the claim of the assassins to the title of Liberators and refutes it by a disquisition on the merits of democracy and monarchy: democracy had a fair name but brought discord; historically, democracies had flourished only for short periods; Rome above all, with her Empire, wealth, and mixed population, could not have both democracy and concord. Monarchy had an ill name but was effective—it was easier to find one good man than many.[1] In his commentary on the battle of Philippi he seems at first to take a different view—this was the greatest battle of the civil wars for it was fought for democracy and freedom. But in fact, he goes on, the Romans gained by the defeat of the Liberators. Democracy, incapable of bringing order, would have meant slavery or mass destruction.[2] Then, after a brief statement that the Principate was better and safer,[3] he comes to his summing-up of Augustus's career and achievements, which gives a convenient opportunity for a closely-packed set of rhetorical antitheses:

τὴν μοναρχίαν τῇ δημοκρατίᾳ μίξας τό τε ἐλεύθερόν σφισιν ἐτήρησε καὶ τὸ κόσμιον τό τε ἀσφαλὲς προσπαρεσκεύασεν, ὥστ' ἔξω μὲν τοῦ δημοκρατικοῦ θράσους ἔξω δὲ καὶ τῶν τυραννικῶν ὕβρεων ὄντας ἔν τε ἐλευθερίᾳ σώφρονι καὶ ἐν μοναρχίᾳ ἀδεεῖ ζῆν, βασιλευομένους τε ἄνευ δουλείας καὶ δημοκρατουμένους ἄνευ διχοστασίας.[4]

The conclusion was the only one to which a man could come. The rule of one man was a necessity,[5] and freedom had henceforth to mean the preservation of personal dignity and no more;[6] if a ruler allowed that, if he behaved as a *Basileus*, or even a *civis*,

---

[1] 44. 2. 1–4. [2] 47. 39.
[3] 53. 19. 1. [4] 56. 43. 4.
[5] Compare Tac. *Hist.* 1. 1, 'postquam bellatum apud Actium atque omnem potentiam ad unum conferri pacis interfuit . . . .'
[6] See Ch. Wirzubski, *Libertas* (Cambridge, 1950), especially 167 f.

not a *Tyrannos*, that was the most that could be expected. Acceptance of this position did not mean, however, that Dio in writing history had to abandon political comment or pass over without mention the gap that lay between political reality and constitutional façade.

Apart from such formal statements of his political position there are numerous comments on politics and human nature scattered throughout the text, most of them pessimistic. Human nature is the key and he looks no further for the explanation of events. Defects of character explain the career of political figures in the later Republic. Tiberius Gracchus was perverted by φιλο-τιμία,[1] while his brother was worse—ταραχώδης τε φύσει ἦν.[2] Marius was the same—στασιώδης καὶ ταραχώδης, καὶ παντὸς μὲν τοῦ συρφετώδους ... φίλος.[3] The same went for social phenomena —piracy would always be rife *while human nature remained the same.*[4] The judgement contrasts with the passage from his contemporary history where he notes that it was Severus' exclusion of Italians from the Praetorian guard which caused the youth of Italy to turn to banditry.[5]

Most of his judgements are no more than commonplace. Especially in the early books he is fond of emphasizing the instability of human fortune—success leading to over-confidence and over-confidence to disaster.[6] Almost as common are comments on the behaviour of the mob in politics, the people's dislike of being ruled by those familiar to them,[7] their fickleness,[8] their search for novel remedies in crises,[9] their habit of casting blame on those who have already fallen from power,[10] and so on. Other things he says are more interesting and show a man who had seen something of politics—that two or three men who hold power together are not likely to agree,[11] that those who have brought a man into power cannot necessarily take it away again when they wish to,[12] or that civil wars are always fatal to the

---

[1] Fr. 83. 1–3.   [2] Fr. 85. 1.   [3] Fr. 89. 2.

[4] 36. 20. 1. οὐ γὰρ ἔστιν ὅτε ταῦτ' οὐκ ἐγένετο, οὐδ' ἂν παύσαιτό ποτε ἕως δ' ἂν ἡ αὐτὴ φύσις ἀνθρώπων ᾖ (compare Thuc. 3. 82. 2 ... ἕως ἂν ἡ αὐτὴ φύσις ἀνθρώπων ᾖ). The passage is illuminating for Dio's period and reinforces the contemporary evidence for piracy—see H. von Domaszewski, 'Die Piraterie im Mittelmeere unter Severus Alexander', *RhM* 58 (1903), 382.

[5] 74. 2. 5–6 (326).

[6] See, for example, Fr. 39. 3; 50. 2; 57. 79; 36. 1. 2; 39. 6. 1; 47. 11. 5.

[7] Fr. 5. 12.   [8] Fr. 19; 53. 24. 1.   [9] Fr. 24. 1.

[10] 58. 12. 4.   [11] 48. 1. 2.   [12] 61. 7. 3.

noble.[1] The first two of these can hardly fail to be direct references to his own experience. The same is perhaps true of another passing generalization—rulers know everything except what happens in their own households.[2]

The list of his passing comments on men and situations need not be continued. It is clear enough that just as there was no overall interpretation of history, there was no detailed analysis of historical events. Narrative ruled supreme and Dio's comments are mere adornments to it. The same is in part true of the immense number of prodigies and portents which fill his pages.[3] They could serve a literary and dramatic aim in forming a prelude to a great event or, alternatively, light relief and contrasting detail.[4] But it is clear also that, for all the inconclusiveness of the one passage where he discusses the genuineness of portents, he really believed in them;[5] this is shown most clearly in a passage where he gives alternative explanations of the flooding of the Tiber banks but rejects natural causes in favour of divine intervention—εἴτε καὶ μᾶλλον, ὡς ὑποπτεύετο, ἐκ παρασκευῆς δαιμονίου τινός.[6] None the less it would be going much too far to say that divine intervention functions as an alternative type of historical explanation in his History, and only on a single occasion does he represent a god taking an active part in human affairs; Hatra was protected by its local deity, Helios, against the assaults of both Trajan and Septimius Severus.[7] In sum, his use of prodigies and portents is harmless and trivial, not affecting his treatment of events, and hardly deserving the scorn which some have poured on it.[8]

Except in his set pieces on the fall of the Republic, where he presents a firm and coherent, if unoriginal view, Dio contributes little of interest in his comments on events—only in his treatment of the early years of Augustus' reign does his own interpretation give structure and force to the narrative. Before that, something can be gained from a study of his speeches.

---

[1] 52. 42. 5; compare 47. 5. 1–2. [2] 55. 10. 13.
[3] See the index in Boissevain, vol. 4 (ed. Smilda), s.v. 'prodigium'.
[4] See the remarks of P. G. Walsh, *Livy: His Historical Aims and Methods* (Cambridge, 1961), 62 n. 3, and 175 f.
[5] See p. 179. [6] 39. 61. 1.
[7] 68. 31. 2. On dedications to *Deus Sol Invictus* at Hatra see A. Maricq, 'Les dernières années d'Hatra: l'alliance avec Rome', *Syria* 34 (1957), 289–90.
[8] See *CAH* 10, 876.

The Speeches

The majority of Dio's speeches come in the first two-thirds of his History, on the Republic and the reign of Augustus.[1] The few which come later, all except one addressed by generals to troops, are much shorter, more related to the context in which they are set, and are not used for the extended development of political ideas. It may be that the fragmentary nature of the text in the later books has exaggerated this sharp distinction; but the distinction persists and the reasons for it remain obscure. Possibly the structure of the sources Dio used for the Principate was more anecdotal and gave less opportunity for rhetorical set-pieces; or it may be that he was writing more hurriedly in the later years (the books from Tiberius to Septimius Severus will have been written in about 215 or 216 to 219) and was unable to give the text its full adornment.

It is therefore the earlier speeches which give a picture of the range and direction of Dio's political thought. The most important preoccupation which emerges is with two closely related themes: firstly the need for the exercise of mercy by the powerful, and secondly the contrast between the vicious and the benevolent rule of a single man—in other words they are devoted to the conventional subject of how a *Basileus* should behave.[2] The fullest development of this theme is the long dialogue between Augustus and Livia on the conspiracy of Cn. Cornelius Cinna Magnus.[3] As has often been noted, this must derive from Seneca's *de clementia*; it has been suggested that because Dio misdated the conspiracy to A.D. 4, he must have been using some intermediate source.[4] This is possible, but the argument allows too little for the limitations on accuracy which his methods of work imposed. It seems equally likely that Dio read the *de clementia* itself, for he mentions, and appears to be acquainted with, two other works by Seneca, the *ad Polybium* and the *Apocolocyntosis*,[5] a type of

---

[1] They are listed by Schwartz, 1718–19. He omitted two, Antonius' funeral oration for Caesar—44. 36–49—and a speech by Hadrian—69. 20. 2–5.

[2] See the sketch of Hellenistic views on kingship in T. A. Sinclair, *A History of Greek Political Thought* (London, 1951), 287 f.   [3] 55. 14–22. 1.

[4] So M. Adler, 'Die Verschwörung des Cn. Cornelius Cinna bei Seneca und Cassius Dio', *Zeitschr. für die Öst. Gymn.* 60 (1909), 193, on p. 198, and H. R. W. Smith, 'Problems Historical and Numismatic in the Reign of Augustus', *Univ. Calif. Pub. Class. Arch.* 2. 4 (1951), 133, especially pp. 183 f.

[5] 60. 35. 3–4 (18); 61. 10. 2 (31). See F. Giancotti, 'La consolazione di Seneca a Polibio in Cassio Dione, LXI, 10. 2.' *RFIC* 34 (1956), 30.

reference not common in ancient historical works. Dio's dialogue
owes to Seneca not only its setting and characters[1] but a good deal
of its argument.[2] It was certainly normal practice for historians
in antiquity to rely on historical sources in building up a narrative; we should not assume too readily that they did not sometimes include facts from literary sources of other types.

Two of the early fragments of speeches cover the same theme.
The first is that of Fabius Rullus the elder in 325 B.C., of which
a version in *oratio obliqua* is given by Livy.[3] The speech in Dio, as
it stands, is no more than a series of generalities about human
nature—savage punishments do not deter, men are better per-
suaded than driven, and so forth. It forms an illuminating contrast
with the speech in Livy, whose argument is entirely built up with
material from its historical context. Livy's speech belongs in its
setting, Dio's could have been put in at any point in his History
at which the relevant moral situation occurred. It illustrates what
is a general, though not quite universal, tendency in Dio, to use
his speeches not to focus a particular political situation or a particular character,[4] but to set forth the moral sentiments appropriate
to the situation.

Very shortly afterwards there follows another speech on the
same theme[5] which seems to be that of the Samnite, Herennius
Pontius, recommending the release of the Roman army trapped
at the Caudine Forks.[6] The same unexceptionable sentiments are
expressed—those who have done wrong should be pitied, advised
and schooled, mercy can make friends out of enemies, and the
like; only a reference to the Romans in the third person and a
mention of the speaker's age and experience make it possible to
recognize the context. Finally there is Cicero's speech on the
Amnesty after the murder of Julius Caesar, the only moment in
Dio in which he is allowed an honourable role.[7]

The related theme of *Basileus* and *Tyrannos* is given more
detailed treatment, beginning with a debate at the establishment of the Republic,[8] perhaps suggested by that in Dionysius of

---

[1] See *de clem.* 1. 9.   [2] See Adler, op. cit. 200 f.
[3] Fr. 36. 1–5: Livy 8. 33. 12–22.
[4] See the accurate formulation of the functions of speeches in ancient historians
by M. F. Dibelius, *Studies in the Acts of the Apostles* (London, 1956), ch. 9.
[5] Fr. 36. 11–14.
[6] See Boissevain, vol. 1. pp. 98–99. Schwartz, 1718.
[7] See pp. 51–52.   [8] Fr. 12.

Halicarnassus.[1] From Zonaras[2] it appears that the debate takes place on the arrival of ambassadors from Tarquin to request his restoration, and the majority of the fragments seem to come from their speech—observations on mob psychology and the dangers of μεταβολαί in constitutions.[3] Then there are some sentiments about the qualities required in a king:

> ὅτι τὸ τῆς βασιλείας πρᾶγμα οὐκ ἀρετῆς μόνον ἀλλὰ καὶ ἐπιστήμης καὶ συνηθείας, εἴπερ τι ἄλλο, πολλῆς δεῖται, καὶ οὐχ οἷόν τέ ἐστιν ἄνευ ἐκείνων ἀψάμενόν τινα σωφρονῆσαι.[4]

It is unfortunate that more of this debate is not preserved, for there are traces in the last two fragments of the Republican case also.[5] This would have been a valuable exposition of the range of Dio's political thinking.

The tyrant-theme comes into its own with the invasion of Pyrrhus in 280 B.C., the first fully historical event in Roman history, but none the less suitable as an occasion for rhetorical discourse and improving sentiments. First there comes a fragment which cannot be placed satisfactorily but which, starting from the principle that equality is necessary to friendship and co-operation, develops the point of the inevitable friendlessness and suspiciousness of a tyrant.[6] The subject gets its full dramatic treatment in the dialogue between Fabricius and Pyrrhus.[7] Pyrrhus offers Fabricius a post as general and adviser; Fabricius reproves him, pointing out at some length the evils of his greed and ambition, and the fact that it is as dangerous to himself as to others.

Apart from the debate of Agrippa and Maecenas the fullest treatment of the sole ruler's position and duties comes in the speech of Julius Caesar to the Senate in 46 B.C.[8] Some have taken this as evidence that Caesar made a speech, even indeed for what he said.[9] But it is clearly a fiction, a propaganda speech, as Béranger has put it, packed with imperial slogans.[10] Perhaps that is going too far; for the demands which the propertied and noble

---

[1] Ant. Rom. 4. 72–75.   [2] 7. 12. 1.
[3] Fr. 12. 3a. Compare Dion. Hal. Ant. Rom. 4. 73. 1.   [4] Fr. 12. 9.
[5] Fr. 12. 7 and 10.   [6] Fr. 40. 14–16.
[7] Fr. 40. 33–49. See RE 6 (1909), 'Fabricius' (9), 1934 f.
[8] 43. 15. 2–18. 5.
[9] See P. Stein, Die Senatssitzungen der ciceronischen Zeit (Diss. Münster, 1930), 69; Klotz, RE 10 (1917), 'Julius' (131), 244.
[10] J. Béranger, Recherches sur l'aspect idéologique du Principat, Schweiz. Beitr. zur Altertumswiss. 6 (Basel, 1953), 197.

classes made of their monarchs remained fairly constant—and the political thought of the Hellenistic and Roman age was largely reduced to pious exhortation to rulers to preserve the lives, dignity, and property of the upper classes. Thus, in this speech Caesar is made to say (in brief) that, in contrast to Marius, Cinna, and Sulla, he will be milder after gaining power than before, that he will be not a despot or tyrant but a champion and leader, that there will be no executions, he will act as a father, the soldiers will be kept to protect the Senate not to oppress it, his money will be spent on public needs and he will not attack the rich or introduce any new taxes.

No other source mentions this speech and it must be concluded that not only the content but the occasion was fabricated by Dio.[1] The only works to which it might have some relation are the *Epistulae ad Caesarem senem* (surely not by Sallust).[2] The first of these (in the manuscript order) also touches on the need for exercising mercy;[3] Dio might have read it,[4] though there is nothing to prove that he did. All that emerges is that the relationship between Caesar and the Senate could be used as a vehicle for laying down those precepts which Emperors were supposed to follow. Dio's sentiments in the speech were applicable to any age, but perhaps particularly to that of Severus and Caracalla. They can be regarded as a stage between the rhetorical moralizings of the early fragments and the detailed proposals (whose relevance to his own age is barely disguised) in the dialogue of Agrippa and Maecenas.

Outside the sphere of internal politics a senator's attention fell naturally on military affairs, and Dio adorned his History with a large number of addresses to troops.[5] One at least of these (Julius Caesar's speech to the army at Vesontio)[6] has been thought to reflect Dio's experiences with the legions of Pannonia, and therefore to be a late insertion[7]—a view for which there is no

---

[1] Plutarch, *Caesar*, 55. 1, mentions only a speech to the Plebs.

[2] See Latte, *JRS* 27 (1937), 300–1, and Fraenkel, *JRS* 41 (1951), 192–4. But the point cannot be argued here—and is perhaps not worth arguing.

[3] 4. 1; 13.

[4] R. Syme, 'Pseudo-Sallust', *MH* 15 (1958), 46, suggests (p. 54) that the second *Suasoria* might be a product of the Antonine age.

[5] Fr. 40. 14–16 (not certainly an address to troops. See Boissevain, vol. 1, p. 122. It is referred to above, on the tyrant theme). 57. 5; 57. 6a–b(?); 57. 47 (49)? 107. 2–3; 38. 36–46; 41. 27–35; 50. 16–22, 24–30; 62. 3–6, 9–11; 63. 22. 3–6; 64. 13. (111); 71. 24–26 (265–67).

[6] 38. 36–46. [7] H. R. W. Smith, op. cit. 188–91.

82 POLITICAL AND HISTORICAL VIEWS

evidence and which the frequent recurrence of the theme elsewhere effectively disproves. In fact there is nothing of note in
Dio's use of this theme, which, for all its frequency, is never
employed without justification from his sources.[1]

There is more of interest in his treatment of the question of war
and peace. This theme is first developed in the debate between
Fabius and Lentulus in the Senate in 218 B.C.[2] Lentulus' arguments echo those of the Athenians in the Melian debate—ὅτι
πέφυκε πᾶν τὸ ἀνθρώπειον δεσπόζειν τε ἐπιθυμεῖν τῶν ὑπεικόντων καὶ
τῇ παρὰ τῆς τύχης ῥοπῇ κατὰ τῶν ἐθελοδουλούντων χρῆσθαι—and
urge the advantages to be gained by war. Fabius gives the conventional arguments for caution, using the commonplace of men
destroyed by rash use of good fortune. Neither side, as represented
in the extant fragments, makes any specific reference to the current situation; the debate is once again solely a development of
commonplace moral attitudes to the issue at stake.

The type of argument used by Lentulus is taken up and expanded in the speech of Caesar at Vesontio—an amplification of
the speech in the *Bellum Gallicum*[3]—and joined with stoic concepts
of the mission of Empire and Rome's duty of trusteeship towards
the provinces. All this has been fully discussed by Gabba and
recapitulation would serve no purpose.[4] Gabba, however, failed
to note the connexion with the debate set in 218 B.C. (where Dio
presents both sides of the case) and regards this as a straightforward exposition of Dio's views on the military policy of the
Empire. Dio's explicit comments on the campaigns of his own
time, however, present an entirely different picture—he regarded
Severus' Eastern expeditions as a waste of men and money and
a source of future trouble, and looked on the British campaign
without apparent enthusiasm.[5] What we have here is evidence
not for Dio's views but for his acquaintance with a certain
range of political thought, that is Greek philosophical justifications of empire.[6] Caesar's speech in Dio is an extrapolation in

[1] See the parallels listed by Schwartz, 1718–19.
[2] Fr. 55. 1–8. Polybius 3. 20 denies that any such debate took place. See F. W.
Walbank, *Commentary on Polybius*, 1 (Oxford, 1957) ad loc., who regards it as
genuine.
[3] 1. 40.
[4] E. Gabba, *RSI* 77 (1955), 301–11.   [5] See pp. 141–3, 149.
[6] See W. Capelle, 'Griechische Ethik und römischer Imperialismus', *Klio* 25,
N.F. 7 (1932), 86.

commonplace philosophical terms (with some examples from Republican history thrown in) of a speech in which a general urged his soldiers to fight.

Dio's speeches carry further the tendency towards generality and lack of apposite detail which characterizes his History as a whole. Not all of them are built up so completely from general considerations as those just discussed, and one, Cicero's 'anti-Philippic', actually adds details not given in the text.[1] But in general their interest must lie not in what they can contribute to historical knowledge, but in the insight they can give into the mind of a senator writing under the Severi, the political questions which were uppermost in his mind and the sort of reasoning he could apply to them. In the former respect they are undoubtedly an accurate reflection of Dio's time, when the principal causes of tension lay in relations between the Emperor and the governing class and between the army and society. In the second respect they are disappointing, for Dio's reasoning is banal and unoriginal. Only in one place, the debate of Agrippa and Maecenas, does he seriously come to grips with the problems of his time. Its context, Dio's account of Augustus, is of equal significance and must be taken first.

The Reign of Augustus

It is curious that Dio's account of this reign, the most complete and satisfactory one we have, has never been studied for its own sake.[2] There are certain passages which are important for the constitutional positions taken up by Augustus, and these have been discussed and examined over and over again. But the whole account, that is Books 51–56, deserves consideration in its own right; for, as will be seen, it is here that the structure of the narrative owes more to Dio himself than at any other point in his History. In the course of doing this he gives a good deal of explicit comment of his own and also outlines the constitution of the Principate as it was in his own time.

Before discussing Dio's own contribution it will be necessary to consider the various types of material in these books and, briefly, his sources. It is possible to see this problem in very simple terms—

[1] See p. 54.
[2] Though one may note the pages devoted to Dio by A. E. Egger, *Examen critique des historiens anciens de la vie et du règne d'Auguste* (Paris, 1844), 280–311.

where does he stop using Livy and begin using Aufidius Bassus?[1] This approach is no great help, for it is not even certain that Aufidius wrote about this period; the only evidence is that of the elder Seneca who says that, among other historians, he dealt with the death of Cicero[2]—it is convenient but not necessary to assume that this was in an early book of his Histories, and that consequently these continued over Augustus' reign. It would be equally possible to assume that just as Pliny began *a fine Aufidi Bassi* so Aufidius began *a fine Titi Livi*—9 B.C.[3] The attractive suggestion has been made that the reason why Dio says so little about Germanicus' campaigns in Germany from A.D. 14 to 16 is that he was using Aufidius' Histories—and he, having given a full account in his German Wars, did not repeat it here.[4] But, if this is accepted, it does not help for the first half of Augustus' reign. So there can be little force in the suggestion that Dio 53. 17–19 marks the end of Livy and the beginning of Aufidius.

A rival version makes Dio's use of Livy continue for another book—the break comes probably in Book 54: there was however 'a strong secondary anti-Augustan source (perhaps Timagenes?)'.[5] The *testimonia* on Timagenes indicate that, while he was a historian with an anti-Roman bias who also said rude things of Augustus, the books he wrote about Augustus were burned by him.[6] Moreover none of the extant fragments of Timagenes' work, as distinct from reports of things he said, refers to Augustus. This suggestion will not help—and it is doing Dio less than justice to assume that an equivocal judgement in his work will simply be the result of using sources with opposing views.

Source-criticism normally ends in mere speculation. It is probable that Nicolaus of Damascus continued his Histories down to 4 B.C.,[7] but there is no guarantee that Dio used them; though Dio's account of the Indian embassy of 20 B.C.[8] probably goes

---

[1] So M. A. Levi, 'Dopo Azio: appunti sulle fonti Augustee: Dione Cassio', *Athenaeum*, N.S. 15 (1937), 3; *Il tempo di Augusto* (Florence, 1951), 415–34.

[2] *Suas.* 6. 18. 23 (Peter, *HRR*, frr. 1 and 2).

[3] A view which gets some support from Cassiodorus, *in fin. chron.* p. 659, Mom. (*HRR* fr. 3).

[4] F. A. Marx, 'Die Quellen der Germanenkriege bei Tacitus und Dio', *Klio* 26 (1933), 323; 'Aufidius Bassus', ibid. 29 (1936), 94; 'Die Überlieferung der Germanenkriege besonders der augusteischen Zeit', ibid. 202.

[5] *CAH* 10, 875–6.   [6] Jacoby, *FGrH* 88.

[7] Ibid. 2. C 229. R. Syme, 'Livy and Augustus', *HSCPh* 64 (1959), 27 on p. 65.

[8] 54. 9. 8–10.

back ultimately to Nicolaus' eyewitness report.[1] Dio does quote
the autobiography of Augustus—but the quoted figure (on the
amount of Caesar's legacy) is wrong.[2] If there is any profit in
coming to the decision that Dio used one author whose works are
lost rather than another whose works are lost, then the most
reasonable choice would be Cremutius Cordus. Dio treats the
lectio senatus of 18 B.C. in some detail,[3] and Suetonius quotes
Cremutius on the searching of senators on this occasion.[4] Moreover, in his account of Tiberius, Dio mentions with approval
Cremutius' history of Augustus—he had praised Brutus and
Cassius, taken the side of the Senate and People and, while not
slandering Caesar and Augustus, had not lauded them either.[5]

The search for a proto-Dio is futile. Dio's sources were various
and complex, including at one point Seneca. His reference to
sources on the death of Augustus should, if pressed, indicate at
least five separate accounts—the majority of writers, and the
more reliable, said that his death was concealed until Tiberius
arrived; others said that Tiberius was at the death-bed.[6] There are
a certain number of other, colourless, references to sources, and
some, typical of his method, indicating that he is leaving out some
details for stylistic reasons or to avoid boring the reader—for instance ταῦτά τε οὕτως, ὅσα γε καὶ ἐς ἱστορίαν ἀναγκαῖά ἐστι, διενομο-
θετήθη.[7] Similarly, he makes clear on occasion that the evidence
of his sources is obscure or inadequate; in this category there
are two passages of particular interest, one on the difficulties of
Imperial history in general and another on the added difficulties
of discovering the truth about real or alleged conspiracies.[8]

In effect, while Dio makes fairly frequent references to his
sources in the Augustan books he neither names them nor reveals
anything of their character—and we cannot even tell whether his
primary sources were in Latin or Greek. It may not be an accident, however, that a number of passages indicate a close relation
with Suetonius. For instance, where he describes a portent of

[1] Strabo 719–20.
[2] 44. 35. 3. See Malcovati, *Imperatoris Caesaris Augusti Operum Fragmenta*³ (Turin,
1948), 86.
[3] 54. 13–14.   [4] Suet. *Div. Aug.* 35. 2.
[5] 57. 24. 2–3. Not derived from Tac. *Ann.* 4. 34–35.
[6] 56. 31. 1. See C. Questa, 'La morte di Augusto secondo Cassio Dione', *Parola
del Passato* 14 (1959), 41.
[7] 56. 27. 4. Compare pp. 43–44.   [8] 53. 19 and 54. 15. 2–4. See pp. 37–38.

Augustus' death (a thunderbolt struck the letter 'C' from the word 'Caesar' leaving 'aesar', the Etruscan for 'god') he gives a direct translation of Suetonius' account of the same incident (with the necessary addition of a phrase meaning 'in Latin'—παρὰ τοῖς Λατίνοις—a curious expression).[1] Again, his explanation of the word 'Augustus' is close to Suetonius; Suetonius gives some etymology—'loca quoque religiosa et in quibus auguratu quid consecratur augusta dicuntur, ab auctu vel ab avium gestu gustuve'—and quotes Ennius. Dio is limited to a more colourless version—πάντα γὰρ τὰ ἐντιμότατα καὶ τὰ ἱερώτατα αὔγουστα προσαγορεύεται.[2] Similarly, he repeats Suetonius' explanation of why Augustus had the month *Sextilis* and not *September* named after him.[3] Apart from agreement in major matters of fact (which proves nothing) there are numerous other significant correlations between Suetonius and Dio—references to minor matters, explanations, and anecdotes.[4] There can be no proof that Dio used Suetonius directly, though it is an attractive possibility; one objection is that in his account of Augustus' death he tacks on to the story which Suetonius has, of how the Emperor had his friends come in and applaud him as he died,[5] the saying of Augustus which Suetonius records in another connexion[6]— 'I found Rome brick and leave it marble'—and makes it his last words.[7]

Whether Suetonius was used or not, there is a certain amount of anecdotal material which Dio uses to illustrate the characters of the main figures in the narrative. Just as the death of Augustus is followed by illustrative anecdotes[8] so also are the deaths of Vedius Pollio[9] and Maecenas;[10] then there is the aphorism of Pylades the dancer—'it is fortunate for you, Caesar, that the people waste their time on us';[11] the anecdote of Augustus' intervention in a lawsuit involving Appuleius and Maecenas,[12] and of an appeal to Augustus by a veteran who had served under him (possibly an

---

[1] 56. 29. 4: Suet. *Div. Aug.* 97. 3.
[2] 53. 16. 7–8: Suet. *Div. Aug.* 7. 4.   [3] 55. 6. 7: Suet. *Div. Aug.* 31. 2.
[4] 51. 3. 6–7 and Suet. 50 (compare Pliny, *NH* 37. 8–10); 51. 14. 3–4 and Suet. 17. 8; 53. 22. 3 and Suet. 52. 1; 54. 4. 3 and Suet. 91. 3; 54. 11. 7 and Suet. 42. 1; 55. 3. 1 and Suet. 35. 4; 55. 10. 7 and Suet. 43. 2 (see *Res Gestae*, 23); 55. 10. 16 and Suet. 65. 5; Boissevain vol. 2, p. 557, n. 4 (attributed to Dio by Boissevain vol. 3, p. xvii) and Suet. 88. 2.
[5] Suet. *Div. Aug.* 99. 1.   [6] 28. 5.
[7] 56. 30. 3–4.   [8] 56. 43.   [9] 54. 23. 1–6.
[10] 55. 4. 2–3.   [11] 54. 17. 5.   [12] 54. 30. 4.

expansion of a story in Suetonius).[1] It is hard to tell whether material of this type was in position in the sources Dio read or was arranged by him for his own purposes. There is, as will be seen, little trace of a strong annalistic source in these books; but on the other hand it has been shown that on Tiberius he retells in the introduction items which occur as late as the year 37 in Tacitus.[2] Certainty is impossible, but the impression remains of material gathered from a number of separate sources, not necessarily annalistic histories.

One of these sources was perhaps Ti. Claudius Balbillus, the Claudian *littérateur* and Prefect of Egypt; it has been suggested that some material in Suetonius goes back to him[3] and, if the suggestion can be followed, more can be found in Dio. Thrasyllus the astrologer is prominent in this material and it is significant that a story in Suetonius—of how Tiberius in Rhodes was deterred from hurling Thrasyllus into the sea by the latter's announcement that a ship on the horizon was bringing good news (Tiberius' recall to Rome)[4]—is repeated by Dio, less firmly in context (καὶ λόγον γε ἔχει ὅτι μελλήσας ποτὲ ἐν τῇ ῾Ρόδῳ) and with changes in detail.[5] The same chapter of Suetonius tells of the portents of Tiberius' accession which occurred as he passed Philippi—and this too is repeated elsewhere, with slight changes, by Dio.[6]

The most serious chronological problems are presented by Dio's accounts of various conspiracies against Augustus. So marked is this tendency that it is tempting to follow the suggestion of a separate source which dealt with the opposition to Augustus without much regard for chronology;[7] some reflection of it might be found in a passage of Suetonius giving a list of conspiracies.[8] Dio leaves his general introduction to the conspiracies to Book 54, but the chronological difficulties begin much earlier. Under 26 B.C. he discusses the career of Egnatius Rufus: Egnatius τότε . . .

---

[1] 55. 4. 2: *Div. Aug.* 56. 7.

[2] See C. Questa, 'Tecnica biographica e tecnica annalistica nei libri LIII–LXIII di Cassio Dione', *Studi Urbinati* 36. 1–2 (1957), 37, on p. 43.

[3] See G. B. Townend, 'The Sources of the Greek in Suetonius', *Hermes* 88 (1960), 98, especially 115–17.

[4] Suet. *Tib.* 14. 6.

[5] 55. 11. 2.   [6] 54. 9. 6.

[7] So H. A. Andersen, *Cassius Dio und die Begründung des Principates*, Neue deutsche Forschungen; Abteilung alte Geschichte (Berlin, 1938), n. 74.

[8] Suet. *Div. Aug.* 19.

ἀγορανομήσας had used his own and hired slaves as a fire-brigade and, once illegally elected praetor, was seized with dangerous ambitions. Augustus intended to punish him, but for the moment merely made fire-watching a permanent duty of the aediles.[1] Something has gone wrong here, for under 22 B.C. Dio records, with no mention of Egnatius, the appointment of the curule aediles to this task and Augustus' gift of 600 slaves for the job.[2] Further, Velleius Paterculus gives the story of how Sentius Saturninus, sole consul of 19 B.C., forbade Egnatius—'florentem favore publico sperantemque ut praeturam aedilitati ita consulatum praeturae se iuncturum'—to stand for the consulship: this passage also has the story of the private fire-brigade.[3] The true chronology was thus, perhaps, that Egnatius was aedile in 22, praetor in 21 or 20, and then attempted to gain election to the consulship of 19 in that year. This last date is supported by Dio— Sentius was conducting the election of a colleague for himself, since Augustus had refused to take the office.[4] But Dio makes no mention here of Egnatius Rufus. The only reasonable explanation seems to be the use of two sources, firstly a non-annalistic one which described the career of Egnatius without giving a date— why Dio puts the account under 26 B.C. is not clear. The link with the preceding passage (anecdotes about incidents following the condemnation of Cornelius Gallus) is weak—οὕτω δ' οὖν οἱ πολλοὶ τὰ ἔργα τινῶν, κἂν πονηρὰ ᾖ, μᾶλλον ζηλοῦσιν ἢ τὰ παθήματα φυλάσσονται, ὥστε καὶ . . . .[5] The second, annalistic, source mentioned the appointment of curule aediles to control fires, and the riots of 19 B.C., but said nothing about Egnatius. Such a source, if there was one, might have been very brief. For instance two years, 17 and 14 B.C., get only a paragraph each in Dio.[6] The lack of a detailed chronological source might serve to explain why Dio inserts so much from subsidiary sources or from his own knowledge. He may have had no choice.

Further difficulties arise over the case of Marcus Primus and the conspiracy of Murena and Caepio. Dio records both under 22 B.C.,[7] but it should be noted that he comes to the case of Primus in the course of giving examples of how Augustus helped his

[1] 53. 24. 4–6.   [2] 54. 2. 4.   [3] 2. 92.
[4] 54. 10. 1–2.   [5] 53. 24. 4.
[6] 54. 18. 1–3 and 24. 1–25. 1. Annalistic histories could be filled out if it was required, as Tacitus knew (*Ann.* 13. 31. 1).
[7] 54. 3.

friends in court—ἐν δὲ δὴ τοῖς ἄλλοις ἐμετρίαζεν, ὥστε καὶ φίλοις τισὶν εὐθυνομένοις παραγίγνεσθαι (there is something odd here, for Augustus' intervention did *not* help Primus).[1] Thus it is not entirely certain that Dio meant to date the trial specifically to 22. The normal assumption, however, that the trial can be confidently attributed to 23,[2] has now been vigorously challenged. Murena need not be identified with the consul of 23; and the Marcellus to whose instructions Dio says Primus appealed might be M. Claudius Marcellus Aeserninus, the consul of 22[3] (though Dio was clearly thinking of the other Marcellus, and there are difficulties about chronology if all the events are to go into 22). Velleius Paterculus says that the death of Marcellus (August or later in 23) occurred 'ante triennium fere quam Egnatianum scelus erumperet, circa Murenae Caepionisque coniurationis tempus'.[4] This suggests 23 but is hardly definite enough to prove it. The date must be left open.

Dio, moreover, carries on from the trial of Primus with the sentence ἐπὶ οὖν τούτοις ὑπὸ μὲν τῶν εὖ φρονούντων ἐπῃνεῖτο, ὥστε καὶ τὸ τὴν βουλὴν ἀθροίζειν ὁσάκις ἂν ἐθελήσῃ λαβεῖν, τῶν δ' ἄλλων τινὲς κατεφρόνησαν αὐτοῦ.[5] The connexion with what goes before is weak; it looks as if Dio, finding a brief note of this grant in an annalistic source, has used it as a connecting link between the story of Primus and that of Murena and Caepio.

Dio clearly regards the Licinius Murena who prosecuted Primus and the conspirator Murena as the same person. But is this correct? Velleius calls the conspirator L. Murena;[6] Suetonius has Varro Murena.[7] An L. Terentius Varro Murena (as the brother of Terentia, the wife of Maecenas)[8] is possible; a Licinius Varro Murena is much less likely. It is possible therefore that Dio,

[1] Mr. E. W. Gray has suggested that the anomaly might have arisen because Dio was about to tell the story of Augustus' intervention in favour of Castricius, the informer who revealed the conspiracy of Murena and Caepio (Suet. *Div. Aug.* 56. 7), but, having begun the story, never finished it.

[2] e.g. R. Syme, *The Roman Revolution* (Oxford, 1939), 333, and P. Sattler, *Augustus und der Senat* (Göttingen, 1960), 63 f.

[3] K. M. T. Atkinson, 'Constitutional and Legal Aspects of the Trials of Marcus Primus and Varro Murena', *Historia* 9 (1960), 440, see especially 445; the possibility that 'Marcellus' here might be the consul of 22 was suggested by Andersen, op. cit., n. 74.

[4] 2. 93. 1.   [5] 54. 3. 3.

[6] 2. 91. 2.

[7] *Div. Aug.* 19. 1; *Tib.* 8. 1.

[8] See the stemma produced by Atkinson, op. cit. 473.

finding the conspirator referred to simply as 'Murena', assumed that he was identical with the *patronus* of Primus and, therefore, that the conspiracy must have come after the trial of Primus. He was well informed about the conspiracy, being aware that Caepio was the leader, that neither Murena's brother-in-law, Maecenas, nor his cousin, Proculeius, had intervened to save him, and of how Caepio's father freed a slave who had stayed with his son and punished another who betrayed him. In other words it can be suggested that Dio had a fairly full account of the conspiracy from a non-annalistic source, which he inserted in his history where it seemed most appropriate. From Velleius it appears that he *may* have put it a year too late.

The same pattern of chronological misplacement appears in Dio's version of the conspiracy of Cinna,[1] while that of the younger Lepidus gets a passing reference later,[2] but is not recorded in context, 30 B.C. It is difficult to believe that this succession of chronological difficulties in a basically annalistic work is a coincidence. The only, partial, objection to the theory of a separate source on conspiracies is that Dio fails to note some other minor examples listed by Suetonius.[3]

If there was a separate work on conspiracies which Dio used, it seems clear that there was also one which listed the honours and powers voted to Caesar and Augustus. It has been shown that a number of such lists as given by Dio are not firmly placed in their narrative context and further that they are not in themselves evidence that the powers or honours were actually accepted; Dio normally leaves the point obscure.[4] It might be that Dio gathered documentary material for these items, but it is not easy to believe and would be a surprising exception to his normal methods of work; it is far more probable that they came from some literary source.

Finally, it is worth noting Dio's treatment of military history under Augustus. Dio's sources were fuller than the version he

---

[1] See p. 78.

[2] 54. 15. 4.

[3] See *Div. Aug.* 19. Though the Πουπλίου τινὸς 'Ροὑφου mentioned by Dio under A.D. 6 as suspected of distributing subversive *libelli* (55. 27. 2) is probably the Plautius Rufus in Suetonius.

[4] Andersen, op. cit. 9–48. It cannot be emphasized too strongly that Andersen's important work shows that it can never be assumed without further evidence that any of the powers and honours included in these lists by Dio actually came into effect.

gives; under 19 B.C. he mentions a large number of triumphs given for minor police operations;[1] similarly, under A.D. 6:

κἂν τοῖς αὐτοῖς τούτοις χρόνοις καὶ πόλεμοι πολλοὶ ἐγένοντο . . .
οὐ μέντοι καὶ περὶ πάντων αὐτῶν ἀκριβῶς ἐπεξάξω· πολλά τε γὰρ
ὡς ἑκάστοις καὶ οὐκ ἀξιόλογα συνηνέχθη, καὶ οὐδὲν ἂν λεπτολογη-
θέντα ὠφελήσειε. τά γε μὴν μνήμης τινὸς ἄξια κεφαλαιώσας, πλὴν
τῶν μεγίστων, ἐρῶ.[2]

The implication is that he had three ways of treating military history. Some items were ignored, some were given in brief (so, in this passage, with the Gaetulians and Isaurians), and some he transmitted as he found them more or less in full. This should apply especially to the detailed treatment of the campaigns of M. Crassus in Thrace,[3] the Spanish wars,[4] the Pannonian revolt[5] and the *clades Variana*.[6] This is confirmed for the campaigns of Crassus by a note of Dio's—ταῦτα μὲν ἐν χρόνῳ ἐγένετο, γράφω δὲ τὰ ἄλλα ὥς που παραδέδοται, καὶ αὐτὰ τὰ ὀνόματα—followed by an indication of the varying names and habitations of various Balkan tribes down to his own day.[7] The most extensive treatment of all is that given to the Pannonian revolt and the defeat of Varus. Both look as if they were taken in full from Dio's source. It is significant that there is no trace of any conflict of sources in any of Dio's accounts of military operations under Augustus (compare the reference to Augustus in Rome rending his clothes on the news of Varus' disaster—'as some say').[8] For all the considerable bulk of his military history here, it is difficult not to feel that he was not especially interested; he makes little of it in either literary or historical terms—though in writing of Aelius Gallus' Arabian expedition he was given the opportunity, which as a loyal imitator of Thucydides he must have welcomed, of giving a short technical account of a 'plague'.[9]

In sum, a survey of the material in these books of Dio suggests that he did not follow one main source—and perhaps that no adequate chronological source was available. Much had to be

---

[1] 54. 12. 1–2. Compare Suet. *Div. Aug.* 38. 1.   [2] 55. 28. 1–3.
[3] 51. 23. 2–27.
[4] 53. 25. 2–26. 1; 29. 1–2; 54. 5. 1–3; 11. 2–6.
[5] 55. 28. 7–34. 7; 56. 11–17.   [6] 56. 18–22.
[7] 51. 27. 2. Compare 53. 25. 2–3 on the Salassi, Cantabri, and Astures.
[8] 56. 23. 1.
[9] 53. 29. 4–6. Compare Lucian, Πῶς δεῖ ἱστορίαν συγγράφειν, 15.

supplied from non-annalistic sources and from the writer's own knowledge and experience. Just how much Dio puts in from his own knowledge can be illustrated for a start by a simple list of the passages in which he gives information, varying from trivialities to items of major importance, on the customs and constitutional practice of his own day. It is no accident that such references, though found throughout his History, are particularly common in the books on Augustus,[1] for it is here that Dio's personal imprint on the structure and tone, and even the style,[2] of his narrative is most marked. This extremely important element, Dio's personal contribution, has to be borne in mind in considering his account of the constitution established by Augustus.

A simple rule, not always kept, has to be observed—when he uses the present tense he is speaking either specifically of his own time or, more often, of the constitution of the Empire over the whole period. When the rule is applied many of the constitutional anachronisms attributed to him disappear. We are then left with his conception of Augustus' own institutions; in this there are unquestionably some serious errors and some ambiguities. But some errors derive from the determination of commentators to see alleged *constitutional* measures in what are in fact Dio's *political* judgements.

Two examples will suffice. One is his comment on Julius Caesar's adoption of Octavian as his heir: ὡς καὶ τοῦ ὀνόματος καὶ τῆς ἐξουσίας τῆς τε μοναρχίας διάδοχον καταλείψων.[3] It has been suggested that Dio, misled by the conditions of his own time, is making a mistake here.[4] But, firstly, even in the early third century the Principate could not constitutionally be inherited; Dio cannot be making some *legal* error. Secondly the suggestion ignores the fact that Dio's statement is, in political terms, true. If Octavian had not been Caesar's heir he could not have made himself Emperor.

Similarly, such a misreading of Dio was the starting-point for von Premerstein's invention of Augustus' *cura et tutela rei publicae*

---

[1] The relevant passages are included in Appendix IV, which does not include passages from the continuous account and analysis of the Principate in Book 53 (discussed below in this chapter).

[2] See E. Norden, *Die antike Kunstprosa*[5] (Darmstadt, 1958), 395.

[3] 45. 1. 2. Compare Fr. 102. 2: [Sulla] ... τὸν Κίνναν Γναιόν τέ τινα Ὀκτάουιον διαδόχους ἀπέφηνεν and 58. 18. 1 on the adoption of Gaius and Lucius.

[4] Levi, *Tempo*, 422.

universae as a blanket grant of powers to Augustus in 27.[1] Dio has τὴν μὲν φροντίδα τήν τε προστασίαν τῶν κοινῶν πᾶσαν ὡς καὶ ἐπιμελείας τινὸς δεομένων ὑπεδέξατο.[2] To admit that Dio is referring to a grant of legal powers is to make the constitutional history of Augustus' reign unintelligible. In fact all that Dio is saying is that the settlement of 27 was an acceptance of Augustus' complete *political* control of the State.[3]

It is therefore essential to attend to this distinction in studying Dio's view of Augustus. Dio accepts the Empire as the only stable form of government, but this in no way blinds him to the gap between political realities and constitutional forms.

To Dio the Empire was a monarchy, the rule of one man. At the beginning of Book 51 he dates the beginning of monarchy firmly to Actium, the second of September 31 B.C.; Actium was not a *constitutional* but a *political* turning-point. At the beginning of 52 he returns to the subject: after 725 years of successive monarchy, democracy, and dynasties, monarchy had come back. This is merely a formal introduction to the debate of Agrippa and Maecenas; there is no need to see in it a different system of dating. Finally, Augustus' address to the Senate in January 27 B.C. was followed by a vote of double pay to the praetorians—οὕτως ὡς ἀληθῶς καταθέσθαι τὴν μοναρχίαν ἐπεθύμησε.[4] Dio's irony is heavy but to the point.

Whatever the constitutional formulae, the rule of one man had begun at Actium and continued. Thus Dio feels entitled to pass at numerous points from recording an institution of Augustus to indicating a constitutional feature of the Principate in general. It is not, however, correct to call this a static picture of the Principate,[5] if that means that Dio was unaware of changes in constitutional practice in the interval between Augustus and the early third century. He mentions changes in the distribution of the provinces,[6] and the legions,[7] the formalization of the *decennalia* of later Emperors[8] and the abandonment since Domitian of the

---

[1] *Vom Werden und Wesen des Prinzipats, ABAW* Ph.-hist. Abt., N.F. 15 (1937), 117–33.　　　　　　　　　　　　　　　　　　　　　　　[2] 53. 12. 1.

[3] See the treatment of this passage by Béranger, *Recherches*, 199 f. and 203 f. Compare also Dio's description of the power of Perennis in the reign of Commodus, 72. 9. 1 (290): ὁ Περέννιος ἠναγκάζετο οὐχ ὅτι τὰ στρατιωτικὰ ἀλλὰ καὶ τἆλλα διὰ χειρὸς ἔχειν καὶ τοῦ κοινοῦ προστατεῖν.

[4] 53. 11. 5.　　　　　　　　　　　　　　　　　　　[5] So Andersen, op. cit. 61–64.

[6] 53. 12. 7–8.　　　　　　[7] 55. 23–24. 4.　　　　　　[8] 53. 16. 3.

title 'censor';[1] he records that the *ius trium liberorum*, formerly granted by the Senate, was now in the hands of the Emperor,[2] as was the appointment of *Praefecti aerarii militaris*, once made by lot.[3] He indicates changes in the recruitment and organization of the *vigiles*;[4] and he knows that in the early Empire it was not always an exceptional honour for a man to be consul for the whole year.[5]

So it cannot be maintained that he believed, mistakenly, that the constitutional practice of the Principate had remained identical throughout. The impression that he does so results from the very close interweaving of information about Augustus and about the general constitution of the Principate, above all in Book 53. Sometimes the link is made explicit, for instance in a passage on imperial policy with regard to Emperor-worship; the passage begins with measures of Augustus, passes to developments under other Emperors, and finishes up in the present tense—μεταλλάξασι μέντοι κἀνταῦθα τοῖς ὀρθῶς αὐταρχήσασιν ἄλλαι τε ἰσόθεοι τιμαὶ δίδονται καὶ δὴ καὶ ἡρῷα ποιεῖται.[6] Similarly with the *tribunicia potestas*—Augustus and later Emperors used the power, but neither he nor they took the title of tribune.[7] More often he passes directly into the present tense and it is here that the 'anachronisms' occur. Various such points arise, for instance, in 53. 13–15, on the administration of the provinces. There are references to the provisions of the *leges Iuliae*—πλὴν εἴ τῳ πολυπαιδίας ἢ γάμου προνομία προσείη—to senators *in praetorios adlecti* (δοκούντων γε ἐστρατηγηκέναι μόνον), *quinquefascales*, consuls and praetors governing provinces, and procurators deriving their titles from the amount of their salary. Of these, the first two are explicitly put among regulations of Augustus;[8] by the third Dio has slipped into the present tense (ταῦτα μὲν οὖν οὕτως ἔχει);[9] in the fourth case the reference is not entirely clear . . . καὶ πολλοὶ καὶ στρατηγοῦντες καὶ ὑπατεύοντες ἡγεμονίας ἐθνῶν ἔσχον, ὃ καὶ νῦν ἔστιν ὅτε γίγνεται,[10] while the last is again in the present tense. The following one and a half chapters show the same mixture of temporal references, as for instance on provincial governors—ταῦτα μὲν . . . ἐνομίσθη. πέμπονται γὰρ . . . .[11] Dio is taking the opportunity to give an

[1] 53. 18. 4–5.   [2] 55. 2. 6.   [3] 55. 25. 3.
[4] 55. 26. 5.   [5] 56. 26. 1.   [6] 51. 20. 6–8.
[7] 53. 32. 6.   [8] See 13. 4 ἐκέλευσε.   [9] 13. 8.
[10] 14. 1.   [11] 14. 5.

account of the administration of the Empire. He may well have
had some predecessors—his description of the division of the
provinces is paralleled by the last chapter of Strabo,[1] who retails
what is apparently the official version, that the Emperor wished
to take on the more arduous and troublesome provinces.[2] Dio
dismisses this as a sham—the idea was to deprive the Senate of
troops. But Dio has at least something to add: he promises to record future changes, notes the subsequent subdivision of the
provinces, and describes the principles upon which the imperial
half grew. Later he gives his grounds for translating *assessor* as
πάρεδρος rather than πρεσβευτής and continues (in the present
tense) with an account of how *assessores* were appointed.[3]

Of the 'anachronisms' in 53. 13–15 two disappear, and one is
a reference to a measure passed later in the reign of Augustus.
Two remain. One is the mention of consuls and praetors governing provinces. The earliest known possible instance of a consulate
in absence is Petilius Cerealis in 70, the earliest documented case
that of P. Pactumeius Clemens, *legatus* of Cilicia and consul in
138.[4] The earliest praetorship in absence comes from the reign of
Hadrian.[5] If Dio means that such appointments were made under
Augustus he is guilty of a serious anachronism—but does he?
He normally refers to Augustus as ὁ Καῖσαρ; but this passage has
ὁ μὲν αὐτοκράτωρ ὅποι τέ τινα καὶ ὁπότε ἤθελεν ἔστελλε. He is referring to the general practice of the Principate at some (unstated)
period earlier than his own. All that can be said is that he fails to
make clear that this was not the practice under Augustus. If he is
guilty it is of vagueness rather than error.

The reference to men adlected *inter praetorios* occurs in the context of regulations by Augustus; such adlections began under
Vespasian.[6] The presence in the passage of another minor
anachronism (the provisions of the *leges Iuliae*) makes it probable
that Dio's ἐκέλευσε is merely a literary device for describing
Augustus' arrangements, not a reference to instructions issued at
a particular moment. None the less this is clearly an error.

[1] 53. 12: Strabo 840.
[2] Also in Suet. *Div. Aug.* 47. 1.   [3] 14. 6–7.
[4] See R. Syme, 'Consulates in Absence', *JRS* 48 (1958), 1. But one may note
the case of Germanicus, who entered on his consulate in 18 at Nicopolis, Tac.
Ann. 2. 53.
[5] Mommsen, *Römisches Staatsrecht*, 1³, 516 n. 2.
[6] A. Stein, *Der römische Ritterstand* (Munich, 1927), 267f.

Another anachronism, or so it seems, comes in his account of Augustus' return to Rome in 24 B.C. As he was approaching, Augustus promised a *congiarium* to the people but refused to have a formal announcement of it until the Senate had voted permission. The Senate's response was simple:

πάσης αὐτὸν τῆς τῶν νόμων ἀνάγκης ἀπήλλαξαν, ἵν᾿, ὥσπερ εἴρηταί μοι, καὶ αὐτοτελὴς ὄντως καὶ αὐτοκράτωρ καὶ ἑαυτοῦ καὶ τῶν νόμων πάντα τε ὅσα βούλοιτο ποιοίη καὶ πάνθ᾿ ὅσα ἀβουλοίη μὴ πράττῃ.[1]

As he says, Dio had noted this provision in an earlier passage, one which, however, refers explicitly to his own time[2] and accords with the principle of *princeps supra leges* which was then coming to be formally expressed.[3] Possibly, Dio does indeed read into the dispensation to Augustus the (newly established) legal principle of his own time. It is equally possible that, as he does elsewhere, Dio has recorded a vote of the Senate without making clear that it was not accepted, or not accepted in full, by Augustus. What he writes is certainly misleading, not necessarily literally false.

Dio passes from his account of the establishment of Augustus' monarchy to an explanation of how the Romans hated the name of King, and an examination of the titles and powers of the Emperors as in his own time.[4] There is an element of political interpretation here, but primarily the two chapters are simply a list and explanation of the powers held by the Emperors. Various features of it suggest that it was included for the benefit of a Greek audience (if it is not a mere truism to say that works in Greek are written for Greeks); at one point the Romans are spoken of in the third person;[5] the *tribunicia potestas* (ἥ τε ἐξουσία ἡ δημαρχικὴ καλουμένη) is explained in some detail;[6] similarly he makes clear the force of *Caesar*, *Augustus*, and *Pater Patriae*.[7] The value of the terms 'Greek' and 'Roman' with reference to Dio's time is an uncomfortable subject; but it can perhaps be presumed that, even among educated Greeks, many would know little or nothing of the historic significance of the names and titles of the Emperors.

[1] 53. 28. 1–2.   [2] 53. 18. 1 λέλυνται γὰρ δὴ τῶν νόμων.
[3] *Dig.* 1. 3. 31 (Ulpian). See A. Magdelain, *Auctoritas Principis* (Paris, 1947), 109.
[4] 53. 17–18.   [5] 17. 2.
[6] 17. 9–10.   [7] 18. 2–3.

In the same way, under 13 B.C., he mentions a *senatus consultum* enabling the appointment of *vigintiviri* from among the *equites*, and follows it with an exposition of their functions, in the present tense.[1] The explanation can hardly have been of enthralling interest to Dio's Roman contemporaries; only those unfamiliar with Roman offices could have benefited—unless the information were recorded for posterity.

The explanation of the standing constitution of the Principate is one purpose which Dio is carrying out in his Augustan books; another, which has to be distinguished from the first, is to indicate the political realities of the Principate, in both its foundation and its permanent form. Dio accepts the Empire as the only secure form of government, but this does not prevent him from writing in an ironical, not to say cynical, tone of the political structure which Augustus erected. For to Dio this political structure was a mere façade, masking the simple reality of the rule of one man.

There are many passages in which this attitude is apparent. In part he attributes duplicity to Augustus himself; he wished to have his monarchy confirmed by willing subjects to avoid the *appearance* of ruling by force[2]—re-emphasized at the end of Augustus' speech—κατηνάγκασαν δῆθεν αὐτὸν αὐταρχῆσαι—the immediate consequence was the granting of double pay to the praetorians.[3] The word δῆθεν has an important part in the account of Augustus, most notably where Dio refers to the renewals of Augustus' powers. In a summary account of them he implies, without stating, that the five and ten year terms of Augustus' powers were a sham, and moves on to the purely formal decennial festival held by later Emperors.[4] Later the irony becomes more pronounced and is clearly marked where he writes of the renewal of powers in 8 B.C., A.D. 3, and A.D. 13.[5]

Another verbal weapon is the λόγῳ μέν . . . ἔργῳ δέ which he borrowed, if it was necessary, from Thucydides. The division of the provinces was in theory to put the heavier burden on the Emperor, in fact to keep the Senate harmless.[6] In theory Augustus

---

[1] 54. 26. 5–7.   [2] 53. 2. 6.   [3] 53. 11. 4–5.
[4] 53. 16. 1–3.
[5] 55. 6. 1 τήν τε ἡγεμονίαν . . . ἄκων δῆθεν αὖθις ὑπέστη (8 B.C.); 55. 12. 2–3 (Xiph. Zon.) τὴν ἡγεμονίαν . . . ἐκβιασθεὶς δῆθεν, ὑπεδέξατο (A.D. 3); 56. 28. 1 τήν τε προστασίαν τῶν κοινῶν τὴν δεκέτιν τὴν πέμπτην ἄκων δὴ ὁ Αὔγουστος ἔλαβε (A.D. 13). Compare 46. 55. 3 on the Triumviral *quinquennium*.
[6] 53. 12. 3.

was answerable to the Senate for his expenditure, in practice he could spend the public moneys as he wished.[1]

Dio did not confine himself to the mere transmission of what other people had written about Augustus, nor did he simply impose on the early Empire the image of his own time. He has a firm and realistic view of the establishment of the Principate. Monarchy returned to Rome at the moment of final victory in the civil wars and did not await constitutional formulation. Over and above this simple fact, the important thing was the settlement of 27 B.C.; and beside this the alterations of Augustus' powers and titles in 23 B.C. and 19 B.C. were, to Dio, peripheral—27 B.C. had settled the permanent shape of the constitution.

It is therefore on the first part of Book 53 that Dio lays the greatest emphasis. Chapters 2–19 contain his version of what took place in 27, with numerous additions and explanations. A table of contents is the simplest way to indicate the character of this account:

2. 5 Abolition of Triumviral *acta* (sixth consulate).
  6–7 Augustus plans grant of power by Senate (καὶ παρ' ἑκόντων δὴ τῶν ἀνθρώπων τὴν μοναρχίαν βεβαιώσασθαι). His supporters in Senate prepared.
3. 10 Speech of Augustus.
  11 Confusion of Senate. Vote of powers. Double pay for praetorians.
12. 1 ἡγεμονία confirmed.
  2–7 Division of provinces.
    Note
    8–9 Dio to indicate future changes. List given because early division in larger units than contemporary. Reference to client kingdoms and additions to imperial section.
13. 1 Decennial powers.
13. 2–15. 1 Senatorial Governors.
    Note
    13. 3 *leges Iuliae.*
      4 *in praetorios adlecti.*
      5–6 Explanation of *proconsul* and *legatus pro praetore.*
      7–8 Transfer to present time (δέδοται).
    14. 1 Absent consuls and praetors.
      3–4 Transfer to later Emperors (ὕστερον δέ . . .), then to present tense (δίδωσιν . . .), then back (ἔπεμψαν).

[1] 53. 16. 1.

14. 5   Transfer ἐνομίσθη . πέμπονται. . . .
     5–7 Discussion of translation of *assessor*.
     7   Reference to short-lived measure by Augustus (not described).
15. 1   Imperial *legati*—present tense.
15. 2–6 Procurators.
     All in present tense except:
     15. 2   ὥσπερ τότε πρὸς τοῦ αὐτοῦ Καίσαρος ἐνομίσθη (procurators sent to both types of province).
     4–5 Augustus the first to give fixed salary.
16. 1   *De facto* control of public funds.
     2–3 Later renewals of decennial powers; decennial festival of later Emperors.
     4   Votes of laurel and oak wreaths.
     5–6 Explanation of στρατήγιον (*Praetorium*).
     6–8 Augustus' Refusal of 'Romulus'. Explanation of 'Augustus'—and Σεβαστός.
17. 1–2 Monarchy. Avoidance of title 'King'.
     3–18. 5 Magistracies, powers, and titles of Emperors.
       17. 3   Magistracies still exist, except censorship. Emperors use Republican titles to avoid appearance of δυναστεία.
       4   *Consul, Proconsul* when outside *pomerium*.
           Imperator—not only those who have triumphed but all the others.
       5–7 List of Powers.
       9–10 *Tribunicia potestas*, sacrosanctity, dating of reigns.
     18. 1   *Princeps legibus solutus* (present tense).
       2–3 *Augustus* and *Pater Patriae*.
19. 4–5 Censorship. Office abandoned since Domitian. Obscurity and untrustworthiness of Imperial history.

This table may serve to re-emphasize the extent to which Dio switches directly from the institutions of Augustus to the permanent features of the Principate. But it also shows those elements of the settlement of 27 B.C. which Dio found important. The fundamental fact was the division of the provinces; then came the methods of appointment of the administrators of both types of province, and their duties and powers. Finally the various titles and powers of the Emperors could be separated and explained—but, given the basic fact of monarchy, such things could be left to the end. He fails altogether to mention the election of magistrates; a reference to this is left to a brief survey of Augustus' administrative practice;[1] this is a biographical element—Dio gives similar surveys for Tiberius and later Emperors.

This comparative lack of emphasis on the details of Imperial power and titles reappears in the accounts of 23 and 19 B.C. The vote of *tribunicia potestas* and *proconsulare imperium* is given in a few lines;[2] Dio passes no comment except to note that later Emperors took the power, but never the office, of tribune. Similarly for 19 B.C.: the much-discussed votes are passed off in a sentence.[3] It is not necessary to dispute here the existence or character of these powers; the point is the unimportance of them to Dio. He records under 12 B.C. the renewal of Augustus' *cura morum*,[4] but does not see in it any fundamental change in Augustus' power; beyond that he is not conscious of recording anything more than the right to twelve *fasces* and of sitting between the consuls. These two passages together take up less than half the space allotted to his survey of the legions and other troops from Augustus to Septimius Severus.[5]

Dio's account of Augustus is a medley of diverse elements, among which only a very thin chronological narrative can be discerned. He attempts to keep to the annalistic convention of beginning each year with the names of the consuls, but even this scheme is not adhered to strictly.[6] Nor is there any attempt to balance the amount of space allotted to the various years. The imbalance is increased by the insertion of three set speeches, a debate, and a dialogue.[7] The conversation between Livia and Augustus (an 'edifying fiction')[8] has already been noted. Augustus' speech on the *lex Papia Poppaea* is not otherwise directly attested, though Suetonius records that an extant speech by Q. Caecilius Metellus Macedonicus, censor of 131, *de prole augenda* was read by Augustus *in toto* to the Senate and published in an

---

[1] 53. 21. 6–7.   [2] 53. 32. 5.   [3] 54. 10. 5.   [4] 54. 30. 1.

[5] 55. 23. 2–24. 8. The account of the legions is correct so far as it can be checked; there may be an error in 23. 6—see Ritterling, *RE* 12. 2 (1925), 'Legio', 1798, and A. Betz, 'Zur Dislokation der Legionen in der Zeit vom Tode des Augustus bis zum Ende der Prinzipatsepoche', *Carnuntina*, ed. Swoboda (Graz–Köln, 1956), 17, on p. 22—but the text here is disturbed.

[6] The beginning of Octavian's seventh consulate (27 B.C.) is not noted. The consuls of 25 and 18 B.C. appear awkwardly in parenthesis (53. 25. 3; 54. 12. 4). 55. 1. 1 gives the consuls for both 10 and 9 B.C.

[7] 52. 2–40, Agrippa and Maecenas; 53. 3–10, Augustus in 27 B.C.; 55. 14–21, Augustus and Livia; 56. 2–9, Augustus on the marriage laws; 56. 35–41, funeral speech of Tiberius for Augustus.

[8] R. Syme, *Tacitus* (Oxford, 1958), 404 n. 2.

edict to the people.[1] In Dio, Augustus seems to be addressing the *equites*; there is nothing to indicate that the speech is modelled on that of the censor.[2]

Both Dio and Suetonius record that Augustus was honoured with two funeral orations, one by Tiberius and another by his son, Drusus.[3] Tacitus mentions the funeral but no orations.[4] If any authentic record of Tiberius' oration survived Dio failed to follow it, for he begins with a bad mistake—τίς γὰρ ἂν δικαιότερον ἐμοῦ τοῦ καὶ παιδὸς αὐτοῦ καὶ διαδόχου τὸν ἐπ' αὐτῷ ἔπαινον ἐνεχειρίσθη; The speech in fact contains a number of elements from Dio's books on Augustus,[5] and it can be assumed that it was a composition by Dio made up to suit the occasion.[6]

The occasion on which Octavian formally laid down his powers in January 27 B.C. is amply attested in literary and epigraphic sources,[7] but no other source gives the text of Octavian's speech; Dio may have had a genuine, or fictitious, text before him, but if he had none the task was not insuperable, for among standard rhetorical motifs were *pactiones deponentium imperium tyrannorum*.[8] Dio makes clear that in his view the speech was hypocritical; in writing it he was therefore free to follow the conventions of the *controversia configurata*. The content is appropriate to the situation and requires no comment.

The essential feature of Dio's account of Augustus—one which is highly relevant to his debate between Agrippa and Maecenas—is the sense of continuity he felt between that time and his own. Dio felt himself to be living in a society whose constitution had in its main lines been settled by 27 B.C., a monarchy whose constitutional forms were mere trappings. It is normal, now, to take

[1] Suet. *Div. Aug.* 89. 5, Livy, *Periochae*, 59. Aulus Gellius, *Noct. Att.* 1. 6, gives two fragments of the speech *de ducendis uxoribus* by another Metellus, namely Numidicus, censor of 102 B.C.
[2] I have not been able to see K. Atzert, *Kaiser Augustus im Kampf gegen Ehescheu und Kinderlosigkeit. Zwei Reden aus Dio Cassius Cocceianus LVI 1. f* (Breslau, 1935).
[3] Dio 56. 34. 4. Suet. *Div. Aug.* 100. 6. [4] *Ann.* 1. 8.
[5] See, for instance, 56. 38. 2 on M. Aemilius Scaurus (51. 2. 4–5), C. Sosius (51. 2. 4) and Lepidus (54. 15. 4 f.), 41. 6 on the marriage laws, 40. 2 and 41. 6–7 on soldiers' pay (54. 25. 5–6). The speech includes some points which Dio specifically disbelieves—39. 6, Augustus was forced to renew his powers; 40. 2, Augustus took on the more difficult provinces. It does not represent Dio's own view of Augustus.
[6] On various misconceptions on Dio's part embodied in the speech see D. M. Pippidi, *Autour de Tibère* (Bucarest, 1944), 135 f.
[7] *Fasti Praenestini* (*CIL* 1, p. 312); Ovid, *Fasti* 1. 589; *Res Gestae*, 34. 1.
[8] See Quintilian, *Inst.* 9. 2. 65–67. I owe the point to Sattler, op. cit. 36.

the opposite view and to regard the successive constitutional for-
mulations as fundamental, a view which is no less a subjective
interpretation of Augustus' reign than Dio's. Interpretations of
the early Principate, however, need not be argued here; the
essential thing is Dio's attitude of mixed acceptance and indignation. It is noteworthy that he does not waste much time on
praise of Augustus. A single sentence of commendation suffices[1]
until he reaches Augustus' death, where he gives popular opinions
of him and a summary, in his customary antithetical style, of his
own. The elements of the passage had been laid down long before.[2]
He has nothing new to say in praise of the founder of the Empire;
and it is perhaps no accident that his account of Augustus' reign
ends with the story of how the Senate, forced by the mob, voted
a pay rise for dancers.[3]

Agrippa and Maecenas

The debate between Agrippa and Maecenas, against and for
Augustus' continuation in power, which Dio sets in 29 B.C., has
always attracted attention but has never been satisfactorily interpreted. The classic treatment, that of Meyer, argues the view that
the latter half of Maecenas' speech is a pamphlet directed against
the 'senatorial' policy of Severus Alexander—and as a consequence that this part of it is a later insertion, tacked on to a
formal debate on monarchy which was all the text in its first form
contained.[4]

This view, though brilliantly argued, presents considerable
difficulties. Does the text really permit the assumption that
a large part of Maecenas' speech is inserted? It is certainly the
case that there is a marked imbalance between the two speeches
in the debate; Agrippa's speech, of which some is lost at the end,
takes eight and a half pages in Boissevain, Maecenas', of which
some is lost at the beginning, has just over twenty-two. Also,
there is a marked break at chapter 18. 6–7, where Maecenas
apologizes for going on to speak at such length—and it is from
this point that the detailed proposals begin. The difficulties arise
when one considers the setting of the whole debate. It is introduced

---

[1] 53. 33. 1: καί μοι δοκεῖ ταῦθ' οὕτω τότε οὐκ ἐκ κολακείας ἀλλ' ἐπ' ἀληθείας
τιμηθεὶς λαβεῖν.

[2] Compare Tac. *Ann.* 1. 9–10. See R. Syme, *Tacitus*, 271–2, 690–91.

[3] 56. 47. 2.

[4] P. Meyer, *De Maecenatis oratione a Dione ficta* (Diss. Berlin, 1891).

at the beginning of Book 52 with a brief summary of the periods of Roman history,[1] which partially reduplicates the first paragraph of Book 51 ; it is clear that its sole purpose is to serve as an introduction to the debate and that it is not an indication that Dio hesitated between 31 and 29 B.C. as the moment of the re-introduction of monarchy. At the end of the book there remains a mere couple of pages after the debate has closed. In its present form the book takes some thirty pages in Boissevain, a normal length for Dio's books; without chapters 19–42 it would be a mere ten pages or so. So, if one wishes to believe that these chapters are an insertion, one must conclude either that the book was originally very much shorter than all the others or that there was some other material in it which was later omitted. It is not easy to see what this could have been. The remaining possibility is that Book 52 in its entirety is a later insertion, the final chapters being put in from Book 53, but this is even harder to square with what is known of Dio's method of composition.

None of these solutions could, therefore, be accepted unless there were very pressing historical reasons for relating the debate to the reign of Severus Alexander. None such can be found. On his own evidence Dio was in Rome and Italy very briefly about 223, and again during his consulship, and for a few days after it, in 229. There is no evidence that he was a close adviser of Severus Alexander, who was probably fourteen years old on the first of these occasions and still only twenty on the second ; it is not indeed certain that Dio ever met him until 229. Nor is there any reason to believe that he was in any way concerned in the politics of the reign; his δαιμόνιον had already told him to retire while he was in Bithynia before embarking on his governorships,[2] while his account of the reign is extremely brief and makes no certain mention of the 'senatorial' policy then in force.[3] Furthermore, the idea that Dio could have advised the Emperor against the 'senatorial' policy is a misunderstanding at once of the whole tenor of the speech of Maecenas and of the realities of politics under Severus Alexander. The increased influence of the Senate was due not to the virtue but the weakness of the régime[4]—

---

[1] Compare Tac. *Ann.* 1. 1.   [2] 80. 5. 2 (476).
[3] See pp. 170–1.
[4] That weakness is best seen in Severus Alexander's speech in P. Fayum 20. See C. Préaux, 'Sur le déclin de l'Empire au IIIe siècle de notre ère: à propos du P. Fayum 20', *CE* 16 (1941), 123.

and was the only way by which it could maintain itself in power.

If on the other hand it is assumed that the speech was written as it stands when Dio came to it in the course of composition, it will then date to the middle of Caracalla's reign[1] and the most probable moment of writing will be the end of 214, when Dio was in Nicomedia as the *comes* of Caracalla.[2] Certainty in such matters is impossible; but convenience and probability combine to suggest that it was at that point that the speech was written. If it was indeed read before Caracalla (a sign of considerable courage in view of its contents) it was not the only performance which a Court *littérateur* gave on the journey. There is no serious room for doubt that Maecenas' speech is in itself a propaganda pamphlet, for its entire content (with trivial exceptions) relates to the early third century and not to the time of Augustus. That it was directly aimed at Severus Alexander was put forward by Meyer and has been assumed by many others since. One may accept this conception of its character and suggest with greater probability that the addressee was Caracalla. It is even possible to guess why the two halves of the debate are not balanced. Dio was in Rome during 214 and came to Nicomedia only for the first part of the winter 214/15. He may well have begun a conventional debate but, faced with a demand to read part of his work to the court, have gathered his courage and put out his own programme for remedying the ills of his time. That this suggestion need not be pressed goes without saying.

The words which respectable senators address to bloodthirsty Emperors are not necessarily sincere, and there is a significant indication that at one point at least Dio indulged in a certain flattery of Caracalla. Maecenas is made to speak in high-flown terms (which owe something to Aelius Aristides) of a universal

---

[1] Compare E. Gabba, *Studi in onore di A. Fanfani* (Milan, 1962), 25, who suggests, on a different calculation, the end of Severus' or the beginning of Caracalla's reign.

[2] A strict calculation, taking summer 207 as the moment when composition was begun (see the Chronological Table on pp. 193–4), would put the writing of this debate in summer 215. It is clear, however, that the winter of 214/15 was the only time Dio was with Caracalla after the winter of 213/14. If the Maecenas speech is to be regarded not as the musings of an historian but as a polemical pamphlet aimed at Caracalla, which I regard as being beyond reasonable doubt, then the chronological scheme of composition, which is intended only as a guide, must be slightly adjusted.

POLITICAL AND HISTORICAL VIEWS 105

grant of citizenship, in which men would regard their own cities as villages in the territory of Rome.[1] His own attitude (as recorded later) to the *Constitutio Antoniniana*, which, it can be argued, had just been published, was rather different—it was merely a device for raising cash.[2]

The writing of such a debate may have been prompted by Dio's source, or sources, for Suetonius records that Augustus twice thought of restoring the Republic, once immediately after the fall of Antonius and once when exhausted by illness (that is in 23 B.C.). But he realized that it would be dangerous to himself to retire into private life and dangerous to the State to give it into a multiplicity of hands.[3] Both arguments are used in the speech of Maecenas.[4] The first of the occasions mentioned by Suetonius does not seem to be identical with Augustus' public 'restoration' of January 27 B.C., so it can be taken that there was a separate tradition, in which Augustus considered this step in private. Since there are fairly strong grounds for thinking that Dio used Suetonius, it may be that the whole debate is a development of this one brief reference, which would be enough to suggest the theme.

Of the two halves into which the debate falls, the balanced exchange between the two advisers and the long series of detailed proposals with which Maecenas continues, the latter is by far the more important and interesting. But the first part, as an example of Dio's thought, and art of composition, deserves consideration in its own right.

In his final summing-up of Agrippa's career Dio describes him as a fervent supporter of monarchy,[5] so it must be taken that he

---

[1] 52. 19. 6. ὥσπερ τινὰ μίαν τὴν ἡμετέραν πόλιν οἰκοῦντες, καὶ ταύτην μὲν ὄντως πόλιν τὰ δὲ δὴ σφέτερα ἀγροὺς καὶ κώμας νομίζοντες εἶναι: Aristides, *Roman Oration* 61 φαίης ἂν περιοίκους ἅπαντας ἢ κατὰ δῆμον οἰκοῦντας ἄλλον χῶρον εἰς μίαν ταύτην ἀκρόπολιν συνέρχεσθαι. The theme may, however, have been a commonplace, for it appears on a Ptolemaic papyrus from Berlin (*P. Berl.* 13045, lines 28 f.) with reference to Alexandria—αἱ μὲν γὰρ ἄλλαι πόλεις τῆς ὑποκειμέ[νης χώ]ρας πόλεις εἰσίν, Ἀλεξανδρείας δὲ κῶμαι· τῆς γὰρ οἰκουμένης Ἀλεξάνδρεια πόλις ἐστίν. See *Archiv für Papyrusforschung* 7 (1923), 240.

[2] On Dio's reference—77. 9. 5(382)—see p. 153. The view that the *constitutio* was published in the late summer of 214 is argued in 'The Date of the *Constitutio Antoniniana*', *JEA* 48 (1962), 124. It need not be denied that there is an element of interdependence (which the unkind might call circularity) in the arguments for dating the debate and the *constitutio* to this year. But arguments from coherence are often necessary and I believe that this one is sound.

[3] Suet. *Div. Aug.* 28. 1.   [4] 15. 5–6; 17.

[5] 54. 29. 3.

does not seriously attribute the anti-monarchical arguments to the historical Agrippa but simply used the name as that of a well-known friend and adviser of Augustus. The speech itself is something more than a conventional elaboration of the difficulties and disadvantages of tyranny, of the type which Dio had composed earlier. Certain of these themes are taken up again—above all, the suspicions, jealousies, and dangers which characterize the Court of a sole ruler.[1] It develops the contrast between this state, where the rich, prominent, and noble are a constant danger, and a democracy, where they are its chief glory and support.[2] But, beyond that, the speech gives an accurate account of some of the actual political difficulties and limitations which faced an Emperor. There was the enormous difficulty of collecting revenues, for the subjects were reluctant to pay, regarded the State as excessively rich, and failed to consider its expenses. Moreover, while in a democracy (as in the early Republic) the same men paid taxes and received *stipendia*, in the Empire the funds were collected from some and paid to others.[3] Again, justice had to be administered, and punishment meted out, but the suspicion of bias would be ever-present;[4] while the exercise of patronage, which might be expected to be a pleasure, would be merely invidious, giving less pleasure to those honoured than pain to those excluded.[5] In a word, monarchy was a grim and tedious burden.[6]

The first part of Maecenas' speech is largely a development of the view of democracy which Dio expresses in his own right and a recommendation, without details, of cabinet government.[7] If some fragments printed by Boissevain are in fact from the missing beginning of the speech, it opened with some general remarks about democracy and kingship—some kings have done good, some democracies harm, and it is the rulers who set the tone for their subjects.[8] The first part ends by justifying Augustus' position, throwing the blame for his entry into politics on the murderers of Caesar; fate having given him his position, it was his duty to care for the State and ensure its stability.[9] Thus far this

---

[1] e.g. 2–3, 7–8, 12–13.   [2] 8–9.   [3] 6.
[4] 7.   [5] 11–12.   [6] 10.
[7] 15. 1. See J. Crook, *Consilium Principis* (Cambridge, 1955), 18, 88–89.
[8] Fr. 110. 2–6. See Boissevain, vol. 1, p. 358.
[9] 18. 1–4. Compare Augustus' own statements in *Res Gestae*, 1, and Suet. *Div. Aug.* 28. 3.

speech is rather shorter than that of Agrippa, which it balances, and it may be that in the original design it would have continued a few chapters further in the same vein; for instance, Agrippa's arguments about taxation and the payment of troops are not answered until late in the second half of Maecenas' speech.[1] But in chapter 18 the pattern is broken and Maecenas introduces the second half of the speech with an apology for its length.

What we have in the remaining chapters is, beyond all doubt, a political pamphlet. It has little relation to the conventional oration περὶ βασιλείας, whose whole burden is moral, concentrating on the personal behaviour of the ruler. Nor is it a summary of constitutional developments in the Empire down to Dio's time, with some suggestions by the author[2]—that some of its proposals coincide with past or present practice in the Empire is hardly surprising, for Dio was not inventing a Utopia. It is a serious, coherent, and fairly comprehensive plan for coping with what Dio conceived to be the evils of his time. If it bears any resemblance to other literary works it is to the 'constitution of Romulus' in Dionysius of Halicarnassus[3] or to the *Epistulae ad Caesarem senem* attributed to Sallust; a proposal made in Maecenas' speech partially coincides with one in the Sallustian letters,[4] though there is no reason to suppose a direct connexion.

As has been shown, Dio passed through two less developed stages of political thought about the Empire, writing first moralizing speeches about tyranny and then one, in the mouth of Julius Caesar, which sketches the main elements of Imperial propaganda, as directed to the propertied classes (or, in different terms, the main demands of these classes on the Emperor). With the speech of Maecenas he comes to the fullest formal expression of his political thought.

With the foundation of the Empire the Roman upper classes had effectively sacrificed their power to make political decisions in return for the maintenance of their outward dignity and position in the State. But by the early third century their position as well as their power was threatened; on the very expedition on

---

[1] 28–29.

[2] So M. Hammond, 'The Significance of the Speech of Maecenas in Dio Cassius, Book LII', *TAPhA* 63 (1932), 88.

[3] *Ant. Rom.* 2. 7–29.

[4] Secret voting (in the imperial *consilium*) 52. 33. 4—(in the Senate) *Ep.* 2. 11. 5.

which this oration was written and perhaps read we know that
the *Praefecti praetorio* took precedence over the senators in the
Emperor's train.[1] Dio's speech, far from being anti-senatorial, is
a plea for a return to the formal practice of the early Empire; the
Emperor may regard consultation of the Senate as a formality
—*which should none the less never be omitted*[2]—provided that he respects the dignity (and the personal safety) of its members.[3]
In saying this Dio was not proposing that the Senate should be
deprived of anything which it currently possessed; on the contrary, he was proposing that something which it had virtually lost
should be restored to it. Indeed he went further than that, for the
governmental scheme he proposed gave more administrative
posts into the hands of the Senate than it had ever held under the
Empire.[4]

   This is the main, counter-revolutionary, theme of the speech,
but before it is discussed it needs to be set in the context of
Maecenas' other proposals, whose character is equally firmly
marked. Dio describes and advocates a stable, centrally governed,
sharply graded society of which the primary object is to avoid at
all costs disorder and change. Thus he does not mince his words
in recommending the persecution of those who introduce innovations in religion (among whom the Christians, though not mentioned by name, must surely be included),[5] and also those who
indulge in the black arts of divination and philosophy.[6] The same
rigidly repressive attitude is shown in his discussion of the cities
of the Empire, on whose ambitions he expresses himself sourly
elsewhere;[7] the cities were to have no popular assemblies, to
limit their expenditure on building, to have some festivals but no
horse-races, which were the occasion of expense and public excite-
ment, and to give public maintenance only to victors in the
Olympic or Pythian games. They were to have no coinage of their

[1] See p. 21.   [2] 31. 1-2.
[3] 31. 3-10; 37. 1-4.
[4] The overall tendency of the speech is recognized by J. Bleicken, 'Der politische
Standpunkt Dios gegenüber der Monarchie', *Hermes* 90 (1962), 444, which appeared when this book was ready for the press. Bleicken's discussion of the speech
is selective, not related to the rest of Dio's History, and assumes the traditional
dating to the reign of Severus Alexander. But it offers a welcome confirmation of
the interpretation given here and a fuller discussion of some points.
[5] See K. Bihlmeyer, *Die 'syrischen' Kaiser zu Rom (211-35) und das Christentum*
(Rottenburg, 1916), 105 f.
[6] 36.   [7] 54. 23. 8.

own,[1] and were not to send embassies to the Emperor, but to apply to the governor of their province. In one paragraph Dio has delineated, and attacked, the main features of public life in the rich and privileged cities of the Greek East.[2] He has only to add the necessity of repressing firmly the tendency of the cities towards disorder, ambition, and mutual rivalry.[3] His attitude to the population of Rome is hardly less forbidding: while the city was to be adorned in a style worthy of the capital, to awe her allies and abash her enemies, her people were not to come together for any sort of assembly, election, or court.[4] Dio himself testifies that in his day the *comitia* were still held for ritual purposes.[5]

What he says in a brief paragraph on the army puts the argument for a professional force and emphasizes again the importance of stability and public order.[6] To put arms into the hands of the whole population in case of need is to invite revolution, but to recruit the fittest and strongest into a standing army is to protect the people effectively and prevent the strongest themselves from turning to banditry. This last point is a clear reference to what ensued when Septimius Severus dismissed the soldiers, mostly Italians, serving in the praetorian cohorts.[7] In this chapter it is noteworthy that, although Dio was addressing the would-be aggressive son of an aggressive father, he makes no mention of the use of troops for any purpose except defence. In this, as in all else, Dio puts his emphasis on the maintenance of the *status quo*.

The two chapters in which Dio discusses the revenues of the State[8] are designed as an answer to the arguments of the speech of Agrippa concerning the hatred which tax-collection incurred. The tenor of this section is rather different from the rest in that

[1] On this proposal see T. Pekáry, 'Studien zur römischen Währungs- und Finanzgeschichte von 161 bis 235 n. Chr.', *Historia* 8 (1959), 443, on pp. 486–7. In the first half of the third century 295 cities had the right in Asia alone.

[2] 30.

[3] 37. 9–11. See Magie, *Roman Rule*, 635 and ch. 27, n. 17.

[4] 30. 2.

[5] 58. 20. 4. See Appendix IV.　　　　　　　　　　[6] 27.

[7] 74. 2. 5–6 (326). See p. 140.

[8] 28–29. See Pekáry, op. cit. 485–8—who unfortunately believes both that the debate was written about 225 (p. 468) and that Dio was in public life in 176 (p. 486). A full and valuable discussion of these chapters is given by E. Gabba, 'Progetti di riforme economiche e fiscali in uno storico dell' età dei Severi', *Studi in onore di A. Fanfani* (Milan, 1962), 5, which demonstrates in detail the contemporary relevance of Dio's proposals by reference to the current economic position and to instances of similar measures under the Principate.

the emphasis is on not repression but conciliation—though the ultimate object is the same, to allow the machinery of the State to function without disturbance. The section opens with a formal statement to the effect that (given that a citizen army is too dangerous) revenues are necessary for the upkeep of the army in all states, irrespective of their constitutions.[1] The order in which the detailed suggestions for revenue are put is of great interest. Firstly, all the public property accumulated as a result of the civil wars should be sold and the cash lent out to landholders at a moderate rate; thus the land would be cultivated and an adequate and permanent revenue ensured.[2] This is clearly a topical reference—the end of the Republic had seen precisely the *dissolution* of the *ager publicus*, but considerable confiscations had followed on Septimius Severus' wars against Niger and Albinus;[3] given the obscurity which surrounds the question of imperial and public property in this period,[4] it is allowable to suppose that it is to these properties that Dio refers. What he suggests bears a close relation to the procedure adopted by Trajan, who sold off (but did not *give* back) the properties confiscated by Domitian;[5] he too loaned large funds to landholders, though in this case the interest was directed for a special purpose, the *alimenta*—which still continued, though precariously, in Dio's lifetime.[6]

The next step should be to calculate how much came in from mines and other properties and to set off against it whatever would be needed for the army and administration and for emergencies. Only after that, to cover any gap that remained, should direct taxes be levied on produce (there is no mention of the *tributum capitis*) and indirect taxes be established. This should be done equally throughout the Empire—implicitly, though not explicitly, including Italy—and the taxes should be raised in each area by procurators, who should take in as much as was

---

[1] Compare Tac. *Hist.* 4. 74 and Ps.-Quintilian, *Declam.* 341 (ed. Ritter, p. 346, lines 27 f.).

[2] 28. 1–4.

[3] Discussed by G. Barbieri, 'Aspetti della politica di Settimio Severo', *Epigraphica* 14 (1952), 3.

[4] It seems probable that under Severus the remaining portions of *ager publicus* were, at least administratively, equated with the domains of the *patrimonium*. So O. Hirschfeld, *Die kaiserlichen Verwaltungsbeamten*[2] (Berlin, 1905), 139–43.

[5] Pliny, *Pan.* 50.

[6] See R. A. Ashley, 'The "Alimenta" of Nerva and his Successors', *English Historical Review* 36 (1921), 5.

needed for the duration of their office.[1] If this were done and if the people were assured that the money was being spent for their good—and that the Emperor was not lavishing money on himself—they would pay willingly and peacefully.[2] The hint about the Emperor's personal gratification fell on deaf ears, for a couple of years later we find Caracalla remitting the debts to the Fiscus of a Mauretanian community, in return for elephants dispatched to adorn his train and add verisimilitude to his impersonation of Alexander.[3]

What Dio proposes amounts in effect to reliance on primarily domainial revenues, that is a system of state finance where the State relies in the first instance on the income of its own properties and cash reserves. How far this reflects the actual structure of finance in the Empire we cannot tell.

The most important part of the speech concerns the recruitment, training, functions, and status of the two leading orders of the State. He does not give a great deal of space or emphasis to delineating the proper conduct of the Emperor himself. Apart from a recommendation that the Emperor should take only cases on appeal or capital cases concerning prominent private individuals, *equites*, and centurions,[4] the points are largely commonplace: he should be economical,[5] should refuse excessive religious honours,[6] should be an example to his subjects[7] and should seek their praise[8]—should be, as he sums it up in the final exhortation, κόσμιον, εὐβίοτον, εὐπόλεμον, εἰρηναῖον.[9] It is highly significant that only a single short paragraph is devoted to the imperial freedmen and other court functionaries; they are to be valued, to be rewarded or punished as they deserve—and not allowed to be too important.[10]

The main theme of the speech occupies the first seven chapters of the second half,[11] with some points later on. The first of these

---

[1] 28. 4–8.　　　　　　　　　　　　　　　　　　[2] 29.

[3] An inscription from Banasa, *AE* 1948, 109. See J. Guey, 'Les éléphants de Caracalla (216 après J.-C.)', *REA* 49 (1947), 248, and Pekáry, op. cit. 483. Dio 77. 7. 4 (381) refers to Caracalla's elephants.

[4] 33. 1–2.　　　　　　　　　　　　　　　　　　[5] 29. 2 (above); 35.

[6] 35.

[7] 34. 2. Compare Sen. *de clem.* 1. 8.　　　　　　　　[8] 38.

[9] 39. 3. Compare [Aelius Aristides] *Or.* 35 Keil (εἰς βασιλέα) 38 σοφίᾳ . . . ἀνδρείᾳ . . . εὐσεβείᾳ . . . εὐτυχίᾳ, and the catalogue of imperial virtues in a Latin inscription from Ephesus, *JOAI* 44 (1959), Beiblatt 286.

[10] 37. 5–8.　　　　　　　　　　　　　　　　　　[11] 19–26.

chapters, on the recruitment and selection of the Senate, strikes the same note of anxiety about political stability as was noted in the other themes. Senators should come from the noblest, best, and richest classes not only in Italy but throughout the Empire—and thus the potential leaders of revolt will be conciliated and disarmed. The same principle should be applied with the equestrian order: enrol as many as possible without troubling about numbers, and the populace will believe they are not slaves but participants in the Empire. It is here that Dio uses those lofty terms about universal citizenship which accord so ill with his own view of the matter.

The next chapter concerns senatorial magistracies and governorships and is a plea for the preservation of order and dignity. The aim is summed up in a sentence:

μὴ μέντοι καὶ τὰς δυνάμεις σφῶν (the magistracies) τὰς ἀρχαίας τηρήσῃς, ἵνα μὴ τὰ αὐτὰ αὖθις γένηται, ἀλλὰ τὴν μὲν τιμὴν φύλαξον, τῆς δ᾽ ἰσχύος παράλυσον τοσοῦτον ὅσον μήτε τοῦ ἀξιώματός τι αὐτῶν ἀφαιρήσει καὶ τοῖς νεωτερίσαι τι ἐθελήσουσι μὴ ἐπιτρέψει.[1]

A regular ladder of promotion was essential: they should become equestrians at eighteen, senators at twenty-five, praetors at thirty. It was essential too that magistracies should be held at Rome, a convention which, as he observes elsewhere, was not always observed in his own day.[2] His recommendation that the Emperor should appoint all the magistrates himself corresponds with the plain statement of a contemporary jurist,[3] ignoring whatever antiquarian fictions were still maintained. But here too the theme of security recurs: magistrates should be at Rome not only for the sake of tradition but to keep arms out of their hands, and they should be sent to govern military provinces only after a suitable interval in private life. Thus revolts would be avoided. Finally, the magistrates should conduct the festivals attached to their office and judge cases other than murder; they should have δικαστήρια of senators and *equites* but (apparently) use them in the manner of a *consilium* and give judgement themselves.[4]

---

[1] 20. 3. [2] 53. 14. 1. See p. 94.

[3] *Dig.* 42. 1. 57 (Ulpian) 'princeps enim, qui ei magistratum dedit'; see Meyer, op. cit. 10.

[4] 20. 5. συναγέσθω μὲν γὰρ δικαστήρια καὶ ἐκ τῶν ἄλλων βουλευτῶν τῶν τε ἱππέων, τὸ δ᾽ ὅλον ἐς ἐκείνους ἀνακείσθω. The exact meaning of this sentence is obscure.

It is where he deals with posts outside the *cursus* and with the government of the provinces[1] that Dio makes clear proposals which are not mere adaptations of existing practice, but far-reaching reforms. The vital feature of the governmental scheme which he proposes is that it has no place for the government of areas of the Empire, or the command of legions, by *equites*. Their functions are limited to the handling of state funds[2] and the holding of prefectures in Rome—of the praetorian guard, the *vigiles*, and the *annona*.[3] This Dio puts forward in an age when not only Egypt but the newly conquered province of Mesopotamia was under the rule of an equestrian Prefect. Once this revolutionary, or counter-revolutionary, element is established, the fact that there are various parallels to existing or past practice in the speech[4] is shown to be trivial.

Dio makes two major proposals which seem to be entirely his own. The first is the creation of a senatorial *subcensor* (ὑποτιμητής), salaried and appointed for life, to carry out the censorial functions of the Emperor vis-à-vis the Senate and the equestrian order.[5] There is no need to think of the Augustan boards *censoria cum potestate* to see the purpose of this proposal. To persuade the Emperor to hand over his censorial powers to an experienced senator, second in seniority to the *Praefectus Urbi*, would have been to remove at a single blow one of the main elements of his hold over the members of the Roman upper classes. Caracalla was not likely to fall into a trap of that sort.

The other proposal concerns the government of the provinces (including Italy, which was to take its place as a province).[6] It envisages a more or less uniform system in which every province was governed by a consular with two praetorian *legati*; if there was only one legion in the province, one of the *legati* was to command it and to control the affairs of the cities, while the other, the junior one, was to take the civil jurisdiction[7] and the provision of

[1] 21–25.　[2] 25.　[3] 24.　[4] See Hammond, op. cit. 91–101.　[5] 21. 3–7.
[6] 22. 1. Bleicken, op. cit. 451 n. 2, points to the functions of *iuridici* in Italy as an indication that this suggestion was based partially on actual practice, and notes that a senator *electus ad corrigendum statum Italiae* appeared in Caracalla's reign. On my dating of the speech to 214 it must precede the appointment of the senator concerned, C. Octavius Appius Suetrius Sabinus (*Albo* no. 387), to the post, which he must have held in the last year or two of the reign. It remains possible that the need for such an appointment was being discussed when Dio was writing the speech.
[7] If that is the meaning of 22. 2: καὶ αὐτῷ τά τε ἰδιωτικὰ πράγματα ... προσκείσθω.

supplies for the army. If there were two legions in the province—
he advises against having more than that, precisely the reform
which Severus had begun and Caracalla had just completed[1]—
the *legati* should command one each and have identical civilian
functions. The consular should take cases involving loss of rights
or capital punishment, except for those concerning centurions and
leading citizens, which should be reserved for the Emperor. In
other words, Dio's scheme is that the government of all parts of
the Empire should, with slight modifications, follow the pattern
which already existed in the major military provinces. It is not
clear whether he intends the creation of a smaller number of
large provinces or whether he really means that there should be
at least one legion in all the existing provinces. But the pattern
would certainly have involved on the one hand the exclusion of
equestrians from executive positions and on the other an increase
of senatorial employment in provincial and military posts. Moreover, he suggests that posts should be held for between three and
five years;[2] what evidence there is gives an average actual tenure
in this period of one and a half to two years.[3] In effect, senators
were to have more posts for a longer time. It is hardly necessary
to point out that in suggesting this Dio was running directly
counter to the main administrative tendencies of his age. None
the less, it should be added, he ends the section by reaffirming the
necessity of arranging appointments so that no senator acquires
dangerous ambitions.[4]

No such striking reform appear in his discussion of the *Praefectura Urbis*,[5] but even here he is not content with reproducing
existing practice. He suggests that the Prefect of the City should
hear appeals in capital cases from the area inside the 100th
milestone from Rome (Italy outside that limit was a province in
Dio's scheme); Severus had laid down that his jurisdiction extended to the whole of Italy.[6] More important than that is the
proposal that the *Praefectus Urbi* should hear appeals from other
magistrates and governors;[7] that was an entire novelty,[8] and
must be seen as the counterpart to his implicit denial of an

---

[1] See Ritterling, *RE* 12. 1 (1924), 'Legio', 1310. Compare p. 210.
[2] 23. 2.
[3] Barbieri, *Albo*, 554–61.   [4] 23. 3.
[5] 21. 1–2.
[6] *Dig.* 1. 12. 1 *praef.*   [7] 21. 2.
[8] See *RE* 22. 2 (1954), 'Praefectura Urbi', 2522.

important legal role to the *Praefectus praetorio*.[1] The same tendency appears here as in his views on provincial government.

In discussing the equestrian posts Dio concentrates on the Praetorian Prefecture and the handling of state funds[2] (the equestrian secretarial posts get a mere passing mention).[3] With the first he begins with a topical point—there should always be two *Praefecti*, for one was too dangerous. The reference to Plautianus, who was sole *Praefectus* at the time of his fall,[4] is unmistakable. Their *imperium* should stretch over all the troops in Italy, with jurisdiction over all except centurions and troops attached to senatorial magistrates (the *cohortes urbanae*); and should also include the imperial slaves and freedmen employed there, and other prominent persons. (There is an anomaly here, which Dio does not resolve, for elsewhere he proposes that Italy should be a senatorial province like the other parts of the Empire.) That, Dio claims, is sufficient for them to do:

ταῦτα γὰρ καὶ προσήκοντα καὶ αὐτάρκη αὐτοῖς διάγειν ἔσται, ἵνα μὴ καὶ πλείω πράγματα ὧν καλῶς φέρειν δυνήσονται ἐπιταχθέντες ἄσχολοι πρὸς τὰ ἀναγκαῖα ἢ καὶ ἀδύνατοι πάντων αὐτῶν προΐστασθαι γένωνται.[5]

This sentence is the key to the whole section. For while Dio extends the standing military command of the *Praefecti* by giving them all the troops in Italy,[6] including implicitly the legion II *Parthica*, he makes no mention of their occasional active commands outside Italy;[7] and, a far more significant omission, he deprives them of their very considerable civil jurisdiction—which becomes independent and clearly established precisely in the reign of Severus.[8] Dio is attempting to relegate the Prefecture to what was its original function, the command of the Emperor's *praetorium*; in the light of the fact that the office had already been held by Papinian and at the time of writing was held by Opellius

---

[1] See below.

[2] 23. 3–25. 5.

[3] 33. 5.

[4] L. L. Howe, *The Praetorian Prefect from Commodus to Diocletian* (Chicago, 1942), 69.

[5] 24. 5.

[6] For the extent of the Praetorian Prefect's military command see W. Ensslin, *RE* 22. 2 (1954), 'Praefectus Praetorio', 2407 f.

[7] Ibid. 2408–9.

[8] See Howe, op. cit. 32–40. Ensslin, 2412–17.

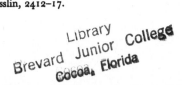

116   POLITICAL AND HISTORICAL VIEWS

Macrinus, whose rise was partly the result of his earnest application to the law,[1] this proposal is of some significance.[2]

What Dio says of the administration of public funds[3] is less
detailed and is largely devoted to outlining two principles: the
necessity of giving the *equites* concerned a fixed salary according
to rank[4] and the advantages of a division of powers—the soldiers
and the cash should be under different control. This is, therefore,
a further element in Dio's view that all the provinces should be
administered in the way that imperial ones in fact were, with
senatorial *legati* governing and commanding the troops, and imperial procurators handling the funds. He says further that there
should be in Rome an equestrian for each branch of the financial
administration with the necessary subordinates.[5] Dio does not
say what division of functions he intends, and it seems probable
that he is referring to existing practice and is not putting forward
any reform.

Nor is it clear whether there is anything original in his proposals for the education of the senatorial and equestrian classes.[6]
He lays down that they should first go together to teachers supported by the State and should then, as *iuvenes*, undergo military
training. We know of publicly supported philosophers, rhetori-
cians, and *grammatici* in Dio's time,[7] but of Augustus' elaborate
training programme for the Roman *iuventus*[8] little evidence appears in the early third century.[9] The rest of the chapter explains
the advantages of the system in creating a loyal and effective
ruling class and reducing the dangers of incompetence and in-
subordination;[10] and this concern for reducing tension between
Emperor and Senate is reflected in two later chapters where he
suggests that the Emperor should not inquire too closely into the

---

[1] 78. 11. 2 (413). Compare Herodian 4. 12. 1 τῶν δὲ ἐν ἀγορᾷ οὐκ ἀπείρως εἶχε,
καὶ μάλιστα νόμων ἐπιστήμης.
[2] Dio keeps to it consistently; in 33. 1 the *Praefectus Praetorio* is excluded from the
list of officials from whom appeals are to be heard by the Emperor.
[3] 25. 1–5.
[4] On this classification, of which the first mention relates to the reign of Claudius
(Suet. *Div. Claud.* 24. 1), see H. G. Pflaum, *Les Procurateurs équestres sous le Haut-
Empire romain* (Paris, 1950), 210 f., and *JRS* 53 (1963), 194 f.
[5] 25. 5.   [6] 26. 1–4.
[7] See *Dig.* 27. 1. 6. 5 (Paulus) and C. Barbagallo, *Lo Stato e l'istruzione pubblica
nell'Impero Romano* (Catania, 1911), 183 f.
[8] See M. Rostovtzeff, *Römische Bleitesserae*, Klio Beiheft 3 (1905), 59 f.
[9] Only Herod. 5. 7. 7.
[10] 26. 4–8.

private lives of his subjects;[1] and, while admitting the necessity
for spies and informers, he urges him to be cautious in believing
what they say.[2] The same theme reappears in a long passage on
accusations for *maiestas*:[3] reports of persons abusing the Emperor
should be ignored, for the Emperor must be above them. If
a genuine conspiracy has taken place the accused should be
brought before the Senate, and not punished excessively.

The last point, as important as any, was the question of how
and by whom executive decisions should be made and how they
should be formally expressed and presented to the world. The
basic position had been laid down in a passage from the first part
of the speech:[4] everything should be decided by the Emperor in
council with the 'best' men, in secret and with no public debate.
A passage in the second part adds that the best men should come
from both the Senate and the *equites* and that the occasion should
be used by the Emperor for testing their qualities with a view to
promotion.[5] This is in general terms no more than a description
of how decisions had been made in the Empire from its inception.
The real innovation comes when he says that the Senate should
none the less *seem* to control everything: embassies from allies,
client kings, and provincial communities should be brought before
it and, this being the vital point, all imperial decisions should be
expressed and published as *senatus consulta*.[6] All these proposals cut
right across the established practice of the Empire—and it was
precisely in Dio's lifetime that the principle was formally established that law could be made, in a number of forms, by the
pronouncement of the Emperor.[7] If Dio's suggestion had been
adopted the Senate might have been hard put to it to endorse
the whole mass of imperial legislation.[8]

Dio's purpose in writing the speech of Maecenas was to outline
a scheme by which, within a framework of rigidly established

[1] 34. 4–8.　　[2] 37. 1–4.　　31. 5–10.　　[4] 15. 1–4. See above.
[5] 33. 3. On secret voting in the *consilium* (33. 4) compare Suet. *Nero*, 15. 3.
[6] 31. 1–2. τά τε γὰρ ἄλλα καὶ σεμνὸν καὶ ἀξιόλογόν ἐστι τό τε τὴν βουλὴν πάντων
κυρίαν δοκεῖν εἶναι . . . ἔπειτα δὲ ἂν πάντα τὰ νομοθετούμενα δι' αὐτῶν ποιῇ, καὶ
μηδὲν τὸ παράπαν ἄλλο ἐπὶ πάντας ὁμοίως φέρῃ πλὴν τῶν ἐκείνης δογμάτων.
[7] *Dig.* 1. 4. 1 (Ulpian) 'quod principi placuit, legis habet vigorem. quod-
cumque igitur imperator per epistulam et subscriptionem statuit, vel cognoscens
decrevit vel de plano interlocutus est vel edicto praecepit, legem esse constat.'
Compare Gaius *Inst.* 1. 5.
[8] See, for example, the legislation of Severus and Caracalla in G. Haenel,
Corpus Legum (Leipzig, 1857), 134–56.

order and privilege, the dignity, status, and personal security of the senatorial class could be preserved and enhanced; if that were gained, the claim to political power, which had long been lost and could never be recovered, could painlessly be abandoned.

Conclusion

The long years of working through the whole of Roman history brought Dio to formulate no general historical views whatsoever. The sheer effort of note-taking and composition absorbed his energies and left no time for analysis or interpretation, and what he produced was a history whose justification lay simply in being itself, a continuous literary record which began at the beginning and went on as far as its author could take it. The opinions he expresses are therefore incidental, and largely called into existence by the demands of literary form, the need to write a suitable summing-up of the career of a historical figure, to outline the political issues which were at stake in a great battle, or to give proper expression in dialogue form to the meeting of a Roman hero and a Greek monarch. His formal statements on the transfer from the 'democracy' of the Republic to the tempered autocracy of the Empire have a certain value. But his critical faculties are awakened only when he comes to consider the birth of the particular institutions under which he himself lived. This was a question not of abstract political theory but of analysis, of seeing what was a sham and what was not. Dio, unlike some of his modern commentators, did not have to explain the fact that the Emperor's word was law in terms of some legal 'power' which he possessed. Those who live under an autocracy know what the word means: if personal security and a measure of dignity can be salvaged that is as much as can be hoped for. Dio, alone of imperial writers, expressed this aspiration, not in pious exhortations to benevolence and restraint, but in a coherent plan by which relations between the Emperor and the ruling class could be put on a secure and satisfactory footing. The plan was hopelessly reactionary and the Senate was to lose half a century later precisely the privilege which Dio most wished it to retain, the command of the legions by senators. But it is not given to all men to see those forces which make their hopes of permanence and social stability unavailing.

IV

THE HISTORY OF HIS OWN TIME

IT could be said of Dio, as of Livy, that we would willingly exchange what we have of him for what we have not. On the one hand, while Dio's history of Augustus is of the greatest value, the complex political and military events of the late Republic were a hopeless task for his narrative technique. On the other, the straight narration of early Republican history would have suited him perfectly, though the account might not have given many new facts or insights; and above all the full version of what he wrote about the obscure period of the Antonines and of his eyewitness record of the Severan age would be beyond all price.

As it is, in spite of the dire state of the text, enough remains of his contemporary history to be worth investigation. For, in spite of its fragmentary condition, Dio's account of his own time still occupies nearly 200 pages in Boissevain's edition and is thus the longest and fullest contemporary narrative we have of any period of the early Empire. Like Dio's books on Augustus, this narrative has never been studied for its own sake, and the analysis of it will have perforce to proceed on a fairly elementary level, first establishing how and when it was composed and then discussing the different sections of it in succession, with the aim of determining both the structure of the narrative and the nature of the attitudes Dio adopts in it.

Composition

The major part of Dio's History was designed to end with the death of Severus and was completed in 219; thereafter he went on adding as much as fate allowed.[1] The narrative of events from the accession of Commodus onward was probably composed in the years 218 and 219, largely perhaps while he was *curator* of Pergamum and Smyrna. For two elements of the story he was able to use pre-existing works of his own; the first was his

---

[1] 72. 23 (304–5). See pp. 28 f.

pamphlet on the dreams and portents by which Severus was fore-
warned of his ascent to the throne, and which has left its trace in
the text.[1] The second was his work on the civil wars of Severus
which, in all probability, was presented in 197 and went down to
the defeat of Albinus.[2] It was at this point that Dio was seized with
the idea of writing the whole history of Rome and it is possible
that he began at the same time to take notes of contemporary
events, preparatory to their insertion at the appropriate point. It
cannot, however, be said that there is much trace of such notes,
though the list of senators murdered by Caracalla is perhaps an
example.[3] There are no grounds for supposing that he had been
doing the same during the reign of Commodus; and in writing the
history of this reign some twenty-six years after its close he must
have relied mainly on memory. He gives his own presence in
Rome as the guarantee of his account—λέγω δὲ ταῦτά τε καὶ
τὰ λοιπὰ οὐκ ἐξ ἀλλοτρίας ἔτι παραδόσεως ἀλλ ἐξ οἰκείας ἤδη
τηρήσεως.[4]

The passage which describes the genesis of his History seems to
have been inserted (under 192/3, after the death of Commodus)
immediately on completion of the books up to the end of Severus'
reign. He was already prepared to continue, however, for in
a dream, which seems to have taken place between the death of
Severus and that of Geta,[5] Severus had told him to write down
and narrate what he saw; thus he had been led to expect that he
would write the history of Caracalla. In fact he got further, and
was able to go as far as the death of Elagabal. This much was
done in full; for the rest, up to 229 he could give only brief notes—
τὰ δὲ δὴ λοιπὰ ἀκριβῶς ἐπεξελθεῖν οὐχ οἷός τε ἐγενόμην διὰ τὸ μὴ ἐπὶ
πολὺν χρόνον ἐν τῇ Ῥώμῃ διατρῖψαι . . . κεφαλαιώσας μέντοι ταῦτα, ὅσα
γε καὶ μέχρι τῆς δευτέρας μου ὑπατείας ἐπράχθη, διηγήσομαι.[6] This
passage presents a certain difficulty, for it was not only during the
reign of Severus Alexander that Dio was largely out of Rome, but
also over the preceding four years, ever since he had been sent by
Macrinus to be *curator* of Pergamum and Smyrna in 218. None

---

[1] See 74. 3 (326–7). The connexion between this work and what Severus is
said to have written himself on the same subject in his autobiography (see Herod.
2. 9. 3; Peter, *HRR* 2. 118–20 and CLXXVIII–CLXXIX) is obscure.

[2] See p. 29.   [3] 77. 6. 1 (379).

[4] 72. 4. 2 (284).

[5] 78. 10. 1–2 (412–13). See Boissevain's comments ad loc.

[6] 80. 1. 2–2. 1 (474).

the less he was able to treat the reign of Elagabal in full; the passage must be taken to imply that it was Dio's stay in Rome in 223 or 224, however brief it was, which enabled him to collect material on the previous reign (it is not surprising to find that the account is in fact almost entirely composed of anecdotes). The few days he spent in Rome in 229 were not enough to provide full material for the reign of Severus Alexander.

The substance of his narrative was provided by personal observation. The result is largely a series of scenes in Rome— things which, he explains in an apologetic passage, he would have omitted but for the fact that he experienced them himself and knew no one better fitted to preserve the memory of them for posterity.[1] But personal observation cannot account for everything, in particular not for the wars of Severus, events in the East from the spring of 215 to the arrival of Elagabal in Rome and all the events after Dio's departure for Asia in 218. It is here that difficulties arise: how was the information obtained?

The question is of some importance, for while criticism of ancient historians has tended to concentrate on the analysis of how they used written sources, the fact that in each case *some* writer must have been the first to record a given period has at times almost been forgotten. With Dio we have the rare advantage of examining how a well-placed witness gathered and put together information on contemporary events.[2]

The Emperor's formal reports to the Senate may perhaps have helped with the campaigns of Severus, as they clearly did with the reign of Macrinus, where they are explicitly quoted and where a large part of the text is built round them. Other material from scenes at which Dio was not present looks very like current anecdotes—for instance the story of a British woman's riposte to Julia Domna.[3] Information about Elagabal's stay at Nicomedia over the winter 218/19 came explicitly from two sources, one reliable witnesses (παρ᾽ ἀνδρῶν ἀξιοπίστων πυθόμενος), the other local sources in Smyrna;[4] the contrast seems to imply that the former group were Roman, not local. Similarly, in describing the progress of a 'pseudo-Alexander' through Moesia and Thrace in

[1] 72. 18. 3–4 (300).
[2] Even here the ghost of a 'source' on the reign of Commodus (common to Dio and the *Historia Augusta*) has been raised. See p. 124.
[3] 76. 16. 5 (371).
[4] 79. 7. 4 (461).

221, he relies on the testimony of 'all those (presumably Roman officials) who were in Thrace at the time'.[1]

The possibility that Dio used any formal written sources need not be discussed, except for his reference to the autobiography of Severus: describing the death of Albinus he says λέγω γὰρ οὐχ ὅσα ὁ Σεουῆρος ἔγραψεν, ἀλλ' ὅσα ἀληθῶς ἐγένετο.[2] Also, it is perhaps not impossible that he knew the account of the *res gestae* of Severus which was written by the sophist Aelius Antipater. Dio does not mention him, but he was a Court figure and belonged to the circle of Philostratus.[3] But if any material came from such sources it was only isolated facts, for the personal and original structure of the whole narrative is beyond doubt.

Dio represents the knowledge and experience of the senatorial order in his time. His friends may have given him more than casual help, for we know from other periods how a historian's acquaintances could help him to build up the history of his time. Tacitus asked Pliny for an account of the eruption of Vesuvius, so that it might be passed down to posterity in his Histories;[4] while Cicero wrote to Lucceius to suggest that a (suitably laudatory) account of his life from 63 to 57 might form an admirable monograph, detached from the main body of the other's history.[5] Nearer Dio's time, Cornelius Fronto wrote a history of the Parthian wars of Lucius Verus, using as a basis *commentarii* with which Verus had supplied him.[6] It is possible that Dio too had the benefit of reports sent by friends who knew that he was taking notes on events as they passed. Such are the possibilities; what sort of account he actually gave and how it was constructed can only be made clear by a study of each of the reigns in turn.

Commodus

In Dio, as in Herodian,[7] the account of Commodus is introduced by emphasizing the contrast between him and his father, Marcus Aurelius. In a famous sentence Dio describes the change from father to son as the descent from a kingdom of gold to one of

---

[1] 79. 18. 2 (471) ὡμολόγητο δὲ παρὰ πάντων τῶν ἐν τῇ Θρᾴκῃ τότε γενομένων. On the episode see Appendix V.

[2] 75. 7. 3 (344). See M. Platnauer, *The Life and Reign of the Emperor Lucius Septimius Severus* (Oxford, 1918), 110.

[3] Philos. *VS* 2. 24 (Teubner ed. 109).

[4] Pliny, *Ep.* 6. 16 and 20.

[5] *ad fam.* 5. 12.

[6] Fronto, ed. van den Hout, 191, see 191–200.

[7] Herod. 1. 2–4.

iron.[1] The metaphor implicitly satirizes elements in Commodus' imperial propaganda;[2] but it does more than that, for it reveals the terms in which its author saw the period. The reign of Marcus Aurelius had been a time of constant wars, heavy expenditure and danger to the Empire—but the upper classes were treated with courtesy and tact. Commodus concluded a successful, if inglorious, treaty with the barbarians on the Danube and from that moment the frontiers of Rome suffered no serious threat until the rise of Persia, some years after Dio's phrase was written. War was replaced by civil war, and the life of senators became precarious and humiliating.

A number of serious limitations beset the study of how Dio wrote about the Emperors of his time. Dio's text is fragmentary. Except for a long section on the last years of Caracalla, the reign of Macrinus, and the first years of Elagabal, where the original text is available,[3] it is made up from the Epitome of Xiphilinus and the Excerpts of Constantine Porphyrogenitus. Even without Dio's original text for comparison it is possible to see that these two sources display here their characteristic strengths and weaknesses. The Excerpts retain much valuable material but convert Dio's uses of the first person into the third.[4] Xiphilinus omits much and also puts in some additions or explanations of his own—notably on the concubine Marcia's adherence to Christianity.[5]

Each separate section of the text as we have it can be accepted as giving a reasonable impression of what Dio wrote, but there is no way of telling how much has been lost. Xiphilinus, for instance, omits altogether the important details of Commodus' settlement with the barbarians, which are given in the Excerpts *de legationibus*.[6] Similarly, the extant text has no reference to the war of the deserters, to Maternus, or to the *classis Commodiana*, but it is difficult to believe that these were all omitted by Dio.

It would be helpful if other literary sources could be used confidently in restoration, but in fact they merely impose further

---

[1] 71. 36. 4 (279) ἀπὸ χρυσῆς τε βασιλείας ἐς σιδηρᾶν καὶ κατιωμένην τῶν τε πραγμάτων τοῖς τότε ʿΡωμαίοις καὶ ἡμῖν νῦν καταπεσούσης τῆς ἱστορίας. This passage will have been written in the reign of Macrinus.

[2] See J. Beaujeu, *La Religion romaine à l'apogée de l'Empire*, 1 (Paris, 1955), 395 f.

[3] 78. 2. 2–79. 8. 3 (404–61).

[4] See, for example, 72. 16. 3 (Xiph.) and *Exc. Val.* 322 (298).

[5] 72. 4. 7 (285). See Boissevain, ad loc.

[6] 72. 2–3 (282–4).

limitations; for both Herodian[1] and the *Historia Augusta*[2] are less reliable than Dio even in the present state of his text. This study must therefore be confined to the limited aim of discovering how and what Dio wrote about a particular Emperor; the question of its truth, still more the question of how we should now interpret the reign, must largely be left aside. Dio's picture of Commodus must be taken as an objective fact about him and men like him. In the Christian tradition the reign of Commodus was remembered as a time of peace.[3]

Dio begins by saying that Commodus was not congenitally wicked; simplicity and cowardice had combined to make him vulnerable to bad companions.[4] This contradicts the version given by the *Historia Augusta*[5] and has led some to suppose that Dio was polemicizing against a source common to both (allegedly Marius Maximus), which was also responsible for a number of similarities between the two accounts.[6] No such interpretation, which denies Dio's direct testimony that his material was derived from his own experience, can possibly be accepted. If any explanation is needed for the fact that two authorities bear a resemblance to each other the most natural assumption is that the later one owes something to the earlier. But the problem of the *Historia Augusta* is one into which sane men refrain from entering.

Commodus' agreement with the barbarians is given in full, prefaced by the view that the manpower and supplies of the Marcomanni were exhausted and that they could easily have been conquered if the effort had been made. In effect the terms seem satisfactory—and were followed by a long period in which peace was not seriously disturbed. The Marcomanni were to give up all deserters and prisoners, pay a yearly tribute of corn, and supply weapons and soldiers—though less than the 15,000 required of the Quadi. They were to assemble only once a month, under the

---

[1] See E. Hohl, 'Kaiser Commodus und Herodian', *SDAW* 1954, 1.

[2] See in general A. Momigliano, 'An Unsolved Problem of Historical Forgery: the *Scriptores Historiae Augustae*', *Journal of the Warburg and Courtauld Institutes* 17 (1954), 22; E. Hohl, 'Über die Glaubwürdigkeit der Historia Augusta', *SDAW* 1953, 2. On the reign of Commodus J. M. Heer, 'Der historische Wert der vita Commodi in der Sammlung der scriptores historiae Augustae', *Philologus*, Supp. 9 (1901), 1, and J. C. P. Smits, *Die Vita Commodi und Cassius Dio* (Leiden, 1914).

[3] Eusebius, *HE* 5. 21. 1.   [4] 72. 1 (282).

[5] *Vita Com.* 1. 7 f.   [6] Smits, op. cit. 33.

supervision of a centurion, and were forbidden to make war on certain neighbouring tribes. In return Commodus withdrew all the forts beyond the frontier. The Buri, now crushed, gave up hostages and captives—15,000 came also from 'the others' (the Marcomanni and Quadi?)—and these others were also forbidden to settle within 400 stades of the border of Dacia. Meanwhile Sabinianus brought back 12,000 Dacians who had been displaced and were off to help the enemies of Rome, promising them land in Roman Dacia.

So far Dio's account is clear and valuable. There follows a long section concerning conspiracies against Commodus and his executions of prominent persons.[1] Considered as part of an annalistic history, it is hopelessly muddled; but it may be that this section is part of a feature which is found in Dio's earlier accounts of Emperors, a collection of incidents taken out of their chronological setting, designed to illustrate the ruler's character and method of government.[2] There are no more than faint hints in the text that other aspects of Commodus were illustrated in a similar way,[3] but enough to support the inference that here, as in most of the other contemporary reigns, Dio followed the same convention that he had adopted in composing his earlier narrative of the Empire. It follows from this that all the incidents recorded in this section have to be dated by other evidence and that their appearance early in Dio's account of Commodus is no evidence that they happened early in his reign.

The section begins with a paragraph which is compressed to the point of unintelligibility (Xiphilinus has presumably excised some connecting sentences); it begins with a general reference to conspiracies and executions, carries on immediately with Dio's statement that from now on he was an eyewitness of events, mentions Commodus' arrival in Rome (probably 22 October 180)[4] and his speech to the Senate, and moves immediately to the attempt at assassination by Claudius Pompeianus.[5] When the attempt took place is difficult to decide. Herodian says that Commodus was restrained for a time by the memory of his father and shame before his friends; it was when these restraints

---

[1] 72. 4–7 (284–8).   [2] See pp. 40 and 61.

[3] See 72. 7. 4 (288) ὅτι ὁ Κόμμοδος πολλὰ ⟨μὲν⟩ πλούτου ἐπιδείγματα, πολλῷ δὲ πλείω καὶ φιλοκαλίας ἐν αὐτῇ τῇ Ῥώμῃ παρέσχετο. ἔστι δέ τι καὶ δημωφελὲς ὑπ' αὐτοῦ πραχθέν . . . .'

[4] RE 2 (1895–6), 'Aurelius' (89), 2471–2.   [5] 72. 4. 1–5 (284–5).

vanished that the conspiracy took place.[1] The *Historia Augusta* makes
Tarrutenius Paternus[2] a party to the attempt; if, when Perennis
was denounced at the *Capitolia* of 182,[3] he had already disposed of
his colleague, that provides a limiting date. Dio's interpretation
of the conspiracy is obscure, for the text has been compressed
and partly corrupted by Xiphilinus;[4] he *appears* to mean that
Lucilla, the sister of Commodus, initiated the attempt by Claudius Pompeianus Quintianus[5]—who was not only her prospective
son-in-law, but her lover and her stepson—as a way of getting
rid of her elderly husband, Claudius Pompeianus; or possibly he
means that Lucilla wished to punish her husband by getting his
son executed. Either interpretation presents obvious difficulties.
Herodian and the *Historia Augusta* introduce one Quadratus as
Lucilla's main accomplice (Herodian making him, not the young
Pompeianus, her lover),[6] which, if true, would disembarrass the
story of some of the complexities introduced by Dio. But again
the *Historia Augusta* gives as the motive of the conspiracy their
indignation at Commodus' way of life, and Herodian makes the
motive Lucilla's jealousy of Commodus' new wife, Crispina. The
story is a perfect exemplification of a dictum by Dio himself—the
truth about conspiracies is never likely to be known.[7]

At this point Dio mentions the banishment and death of
Crispina, without making clear that this took place some years
later—she is still honoured on an inscription of 187[8]—and also
carries on with the later history of Eclectus and Marcia, the
cubicularius and concubine of Quadratus ('one of those killed at
that time'—he had not been mentioned before), who were transferred to the service of Commodus.[9] The passage breaks off (or
rather is capped by Xiphilinus' insertion on Marcia's devotion to
Christianity) with an oblique reference to the fate of Commodus
and Eclectus—Marcia saw them both die violent deaths. The facts
which Dio does not state are that, after Marcia and Eclectus had
prepared the death of Commodus, he was killed with Pertinax,[10]
while she lived long enough to be killed by Didius Julianus.[11]

The next section is of particular interest in that it comes from

[1] 1. 8. 3.
[2] See Kunkel, *Herkunft*, 219 f.
[3] See p. 129.
[4] See Boissevain, 3, p. 285.
[5] *PIR*[2] C 975.
[6] Herod. 1. 8. 3–6; *Vita* 4. 1–4.
[7] 54. 15. 2–4.
[8] See Heer, op. cit. 60.
[9] 72. 4. 6–7 (285).
[10] See *PIR*[2] E 3.
[11] 73. 16. 5 (321)

the Excerpts, and can be taken as a full reproduction of Dio's text.[1] It records the deaths of Salvius Julianus and Tarrutenius Paternus, with the detail that the latter had been made a consular first,[2] but omitting the fact, found in the *Historia Augusta*,[3] that Paternus' daughter was betrothed to the son of Julianus. Mentioning that others were killed at the same time, Dio merely has 'others and a certain patrician lady'—the *Historia Augusta* supplies the names—Vitruvius Secundus the *ab epistulis*, Vitrasia Faustina, Velius Rufus, and Egnatius Capito.[4] It is clear that Dio, if he is not merely carrying out his principle of omitting details, had no more than a very general knowledge of the facts of the purge; he knew at least that Julianus was the commander of a great army, had the troops on his side and could have risen in revolt if he had wished—though he fails to say which army.[5] Here, as in a passage further on about Ulpius Marcellus, we catch a glimpse of the heroic role which the major senatorial military figures could play in the eyes of a young man of senatorial birth.

Dio's ignorance of detail in these events is probably to be explained by his absence from Rome. For in his account of how the house of the Quintilii was destroyed (here again there is a brief eulogy of two famous senatorial figures and army commanders)[6] it emerges that the news reached him while he was in Cilicia with his father. It was there, no doubt, that he learnt the story, which he retails at length, of how Sextus Quintilius Condianus, in Syria, escaped by feigning death, and of the long and fruitless search for him. He adds to it an anecdote about how a pretender to the name of Sextus appeared in the reign of Pertinax and, in Dio's presence, was shown up by his ignorance of Greek.[7]

In the next chapter Dio takes up the narrative of the wars in Commodus' reign. After a brief reference to fighting against the barbarians beyond Dacia,[8] he goes on to the war in Britain; the natives crossed the Wall and slaughtered a general and his troops, and Commodus in a panic sent out Ulpius Marcellus. The rest of the account of the war is taken up entirely with a description of Marcellus' character, generalship, and disciplinary quirks.[1] Over and above that only the simple fact that the barbarians were defeated is recorded.[2] This has all the signs of having been written down solely from memory; personalities and anecdotes about them are retained more easily than the detailed course of a campaign—if indeed Dio ever knew much about it.[3]

The British campaign brings Dio to the fall of Perennis, the Praetorian Prefect, which in his version was brought about partly by the army in Britain. He differs from the other sources in his view both of Perennis himself and of how he fell. To Dio it was the idleness and frivolity of Commodus that forced Perennis to take affairs into his own hands.[4] His fate was undeserved—except in that he had caused the death of Paternus—for he was neither ambitious nor avaricious, but had carried on affairs with wisdom and integrity and ensured the safety of Commodus and his throne.[5] The *Historia Augusta* makes of Perennis an avaricious tyrant who deliberately turned Commodus' attention to frivolities to increase his own power[6]—and this picture is supported by Herodian.[7] There is no valid way of deciding between the two versions; the arbitrary attribution of certain frontier measures to the influence of Perennis[8] will not help, and the claim that what we learn of the trial of a Christian 'senator', Apollonius, demonstrates Perennis' justice and observance of legal forms has little basis.[9] On the other hand, to escape from the difficulty by the announcement that Dio had received benefits from Perennis[10] is feeble and unconvincing. The contradiction cannot be resolved—even supposing that there could be a 'true' interpretation of the career of a political figure.

The confusion goes further with the rival accounts of Perennis' death. Herodian has a detailed description of how a figure dressed as a philosopher appeared on the stage at the *Capitolia* and

---

[1] 72. 8. 3–5 (288–9). One phrase—χρημάτων τε διαφανῶς ἀδωρότατος ἦν—comes from Thucydides 2. 65. 8 χρημάτων τε διαφανῶς ἀδωρότατος γενόμενος.

[2] 72. 8. 6 (290).

[3] The date of these operations is not certain. Commodus took the title *Britannicus* in 184, the year of his seventh salutation, H. Mattingly, *Coins of the Roman Empire in the British Museum IV: Antoninus Pius to Commodus* (London, 1940), clviii. This was certainly the year of Marcellus' victory. Mattingly also (clvii) refers the sixth salutation of 183 to Britain. The Dacian war is more probable.

[4] 72. 9. 1–2 (290).   [5] 72. 10. 1 (291).

[6] *Vita Com.* 5–6.   [7] 1. 8. 1–2; 9. 1.

[8] See G. M. Bersanetti, 'Perenne e Commodo', *Athenaeum* 29 (1951), 151.

[9] See Howe, *The Praetorian Prefect*, 96–97.   [10] So Heer, op. cit. 56.

warned Commodus against Perennis, mentioning that his sons were suborning the army of Illyricum. This was shortly followed by the arrival of soldiers from an army commanded by Perennis' son (only one is mentioned this time) bringing as evidence coins with his image. Commodus then had Perennis executed and, sending for the son, disposed of him also.[1]

It is one of the more alarming paradoxes in ancient history that two historians can produce not merely different interpretations but entirely different versions of events within their own lifetime with which they both equally claim personal acquaintance. Dio has a circumstantial account which agrees in no particular with that of Herodian. In Dio's version the mutinous British army selected 1,500 men as a delegation, who made their way unopposed to the neighbourhood of Rome and, met there by Commodus, announced, 'We have come. Perennis is plotting against you to make his own son Emperor.' The deaths of Perennis, his wife, and his two sons followed.[2]

Finally, the *Historia Augusta* seems to attempt a reconciliation of the two versions.[3] Perennis transferred the credit for the other generals' feats in Sarmatia (presumably the fighting of 183) to his son. He also replaced the senatorial *legati* of Britain by equestrians. But Commodus was informed ('prodita re per legatos exercitus') and Perennis was handed over to the soldiers for execution.

Herodian's introductory anecdote must relate to the *Capitolia* of 182,[4] when Dio was in all probability out of Rome, and there is no reason to presume that he would have heard of the incident; Perennis' fall did not come till 185.[5] Dio's account of the fall itself, however, is very unsatisfactory. The other versions centre round the Danube army and Perennis' son (or sons) who was a legate there. Dio knows of the claim that Perennis was trying to make his son Emperor, but the only incident he knows of is that involving the delegation from the British army. If any combination can be effected it is that a *vexillum* of troops on their way from Britain to the East was bribed by Cleander, or some other interested party, to shout against Perennis while being received by the Emperor—and that this incident was all that Dio really heard of the whole business. At this point he was still only about

[1] 1. 9. 2–9. [2] 72. 9. 2²–4 (290–1).
[3] *Vita Com.* 6. 1–2.
[4] Hohl, 'Kaiser Commodus', 16–17. [5] Heer, op. cit. 66.

twenty-one, and not yet in the Senate; it cannot indeed be *proved* that he was in Rome at any given moment between the beginning of the reign and 189.

The period up to that date is filled with some generalities on Commodus' way of life[1] and, again, a set of anecdotes illustrating the virtue and incorruptibility of a famous general, C. Aufidius Victorinus; two items about him, that Commodus set up a statue to him after his Prefecture of the city and that he went from the governorship of Germany to that of Africa, are confirmed by an inscription.[2]

From a noble senator Dio moves to an ignoble slave, Cleander, who rose from being sold in the market to be *a cubiculo* and finally *Praefectus Praetorio* of Commodus (or, to be exact, *a pugione*, the freedman colleague of the *Praefecti Praetorio*).[3] The dates of his rise to that office (which Dio does not mention explicitly—he has only ηὐξήθη ὥστε καὶ τοῦ Κομμόδου προκοιτῆσαι)[4] and of his fall are difficult. He could not have been appointed before December 186,[5] but appears as *a pugione* in a dedication to the consul T. Aius Sanctus[6] and was responsible for the demotion to *Praefectus annonae* of M. Aurelius Papirius Dionysius, who was still *Praefectus Aegypti* on 23 August 189.[7] Cleander's downfall, engineered in his turn by Dionysius, probably came in 190. Dio's paragraph on his period of power is a string of accusations of murder, bribery, avarice, and corruption[8]—with some details, such as his marriage to Demostratia, a concubine of Commodus, his sale of a place in the Senate to Julius Solon, a man of the lowest birth, and the scandal of twenty-five consuls in a single year, among them Septimius Severus.[9] In the course of it he goes back to mention the power wielded by Saoterus, the previous *a cubiculo*, whose influence had procured an *agon* and a temple of Commodus for

---

[1] 72. 10. 2–3 (291–2).

[2] See H. G. Pflaum, 'La Carrière de C. Aufidius Victorinus, condisciple de Marc-Aurèle', *CRAI* 1956, 189.

[3] *Vita Com.* 6. 13. is confirmed by documentary evidence. See L. Moretti, 'Due iscrizioni latine inedite di Roma', *RFIC* 38 (1960), 68.

[4] 72. 12. 1 (293).

[5] See the letter of Commodus on an Athenian inscription. A. E. Raubitschek, 'Commodus and Athens', *Hesperia*, Supp. 8 (1949), 279, on p. 288 f., and J. H. Oliver, 'Three Attic Inscriptions concerning the Emperor Commodus', *AJPh* 71 (1950), 170, on pp. 178–9.

[6] Moretti, op. cit. The year is not certain.

[7] A. Stein, *Die Praefekten von Ägypten* (Bern, 1950), 102–3.

[8] 72. 12 (293–4).   [9] Compare *Vita Sept. Sev.* 4. 4.

Nicomedia; he had been disposed of some years earlier, when Paternus was *Praefectus Praetorio*.[1]

About 189 Dio had his quaestorship and entered the Senate, and it is significant that it is at just this point that his narrative gains in force, detail and clarity. It is also, in its present form at least, considerably fuller. If the fall of Cleander can be placed in 190, then the last three years of the reign fill eleven pages in Boissevain, while the first ten years have thirteen. It is only the last part which clearly justifies the claim that Dio makes at the beginning, that henceforward he is recording events from his own observation.

His account of the fall of Cleander is, by contrast with that of Herodian, circumstantial and apparently accurate.[2] Papirius Dionysius, the *Praefectus annonae*, used a corn shortage to incite the mob against Cleander; then, at a race-meeting in the Circus Maximus, there was a demonstration (described in detail) against Cleander, after which the mob began to make for Commodus' house near the Appian way. Cleander sent troops against them, but to no avail. Finally, warned by Marcia, Commodus ordered the execution of Cleander and his son; the mob took the body, disfigured it, and carried the head round the city on a spike.[3]

Then came more murders, among them those of Julianus, the *Praefectus Urbi*, Dionysius, the *Praefectus annonae*, and Julius Alexander, whose death while in flight from his native city, Emesa, is recorded at length. Dio includes also a mention of a plague, the greatest he had experienced, and a peculiar business, the poisoning of many throughout the Empire by men armed with poisoned needles, a thing which had happened under Domitian.[4]

All the rest is devoted to Commodus' behaviour in the last three years of his life, and to his murder. First place is given to the titles which Commodus liberally took and bestowed—*Commodiana* for the city[5] (its title is also given by Dio as ἀθάνατον εὐτυχῆ κολωνίαν οἰκουμένην τῆς γῆς),[6] for the legions, and for the day on which this was voted—and *Hercules* for himself.[7] Then follows a full list of

---

[1] See Hohl, 'Kaiser Commodus', 13–14.
[2] Ibid. 19 f.; Herod. I. 12. 5–13. 6.
[3] 72. 13 (294–5).   [4] 72. 14 (295–6).
[5] This title belongs to Commodus' sixth consulate, in 190. See Mattingly, op. cit. clxxvii.
[6] 72. 15. 2 (296). The reading is not clear. See Boissevain, ad loc.
[7] Dating from 191. *RE* 2. 2478.

the months as renamed by Commodus, probably in 191,[1] and the heading of a letter to the Senate with the full titulature of his seventh consulate, in 192.[2] There is no indication in Dio of the dates at which these various titles were assumed; the purpose is purely illustrative, to show the heights which Commodus' arrogance reached.

Most of Dio's attention is however concentrated on Commodus' public performances in 192. Introducing them, Dio breaks into expostulation—οὗτος οὖν ὁ χρυσοῦς, οὗτος ὁ Ἡρακλῆς, οὗτος ὁ θεός—a form of words he had already used of the Emperor Gaius.[3] The sequence of events in this section is for once quite clear. Commodus arrived in Rome unexpectedly one day from the *suburbana*[4] and began an expensive series of shows, which led him in turn to condemnations of the rich to restore his funds. Then on his birthday (31 August) he extorted a contribution of two *aurei* each from the senators, and also from their wives and children.[5] After that, there followed the *ludi Romani* of 4–18 September,[6] during which Commodus displayed himself for the first time in public as a gladiator.[7] Dio's description of the games comes from memory; he relates how 'we' and the people had to shout "ζήσειας" each time the Emperor paused for refreshment,[8] gives other acclamations which they were compelled to make, and says that of all the Senate only the aged Claudius Pompeianus had the courage to stay away.[9] He defends this account of apparent trivialities on the ground that no one else was so well placed to record them[10]—rightly, for it is precisely for this, the quality of the personal experience undergone by members of the Senate in his time, that his contemporary history is most valuable. The crowning point of this personal record comes in an incident when

[1] 72. 15. 3–4 (297). On the date see *RE* 2. 2478; compare the list in *Vita Com.* 11. 8.
[2] 72. 15. 5 (297).
[3] 72. 16. 1 (297); on Gaius, 59. 28. 8 (Xiph.) οὗτος οὖν ὁ θεὸς καὶ οὗτος ὁ Ζεύς. It is not clear what connexion there is, if any, between Dio's usage and the somewhat similar phrase in *Vita Com.* 8. 2, 'ille Commodus, ille Felix'. See Baaz, *Philologische Wochenschrift*, 1916, 197.
[4] 72. 16. 1 (297).
[5] 72. 16. 3 (298).
[6] This seems clear from the reference to fourteen days in 72. 20. 1 (301). Everything from 18. 1 (299)—a reference to 'the first day' (see also 19. 1)—to 21. 3 (302)—'the last day'—seems to refer to these games.
[7] See Hohl, 'Kaiser Commodus', 23 f.
[8] 18. 2.
[9] 20. 1 and 2.   [10] 18. 3–4.

Commodus, after killing an ostrich, cut off its head and, advancing to where the senators sat at the games, brandished it menacingly as a sign of the fate which awaited them. The Senate's reaction to this fearsome threat deserves to be quoted:

κἂν συχνοὶ παραχρῆμα ἐπ' αὐτῷ γελάσαντες ἀπηλλάγησαν τῷ ξίφει (γέλως γὰρ ἡμᾶς ἀλλ' οὐ λύπη ἔλαβεν), εἰ μὴ δάφνης φύλλα, ἃ ἐκ τοῦ στεφάνου εἶχον, αὐτός τε διέτραγον καὶ τοὺς ἄλλους τοὺς πλησίον μου καθημένους διατραγεῖν ἔπεισα, ἵν' ἐν τῇ τοῦ στόματος συνεχεῖ κινήσει τὸν τοῦ γελᾶν ἔλεγχον ἀποκρυψώμεθα.[1]

With that Dio comes to the murder of Commodus, giving as the causes of the conspiracy Commodus' threats to Laetus and Eclectus and his plans to murder the *consules ordinarii* of 193, Erucius Clarus and Sosius Falco, and to usurp the consulship in their place.[2] He planned to make his procession, in the dual character of sole consul and *primus palus secutorum*, from the barracks of the gladiators. Other measures of self-glorification accompanied this (καὶ μηδεὶς ἀπιστήσῃ Dio is forced to add); the Emperor removed the head of the colossal statue of Helios and replaced it with one bearing his own features, refitting the statue with a club and bronze lion to represent Hercules.[3] He also put on his statue-bases inscriptions which Dio (in Xiphilinus) gives thus— "πρωτόπαλος σεκουτόρων, ἀριστερὸς μόνος νικήσας δωδεκάκις" οἶμαι "χιλίους"—Dio is quoting from memory, wrongly it seems, for the other sources give a different figure.[4]

Dio's account of the death of Commodus is brief and, as far as we can tell, factual. Once again it contrasts favourably with that in Herodian which contains mythical elements, some of which bear an unexplained resemblance to the version of Domitian's death which appears in Dio.[5] Laetus and Eclectus communicated their plans to Marcia and began, on the last night of 192, with an attempt to poison him; when this failed, they sent in a wrestler,

[1] 21. 2.
[2] 72. 22. 1–2 (302–3).
[3] 22. 3. See Heer, op. cit. 100–1. The Hercules *motif* is also reflected in a series of bronze medallions of December 192 showing the Emperor as Hercules Romanus and the refounder of Rome. See Mattingly, op. cit. clxxxii–clxxxiii.
[4] 22. 3. Compare Herod. 1. 15. 9 and *Vita Com.* 12. 11–12. See D. R. Stuart, 'The Attitude of Dio Cassius towards Epigraphic Sources', *Univ. Mich. Stud.* 1 (1904), 101, on pp. 134–7.
[5] See E. Hohl, 'Die Ermordung des Commodus', *Philologische Wochenschrift* 52 (1932), Poland-Festschrift, 191.

Narcissus, who strangled him in his bath.[1] Dio ends as usual by giving the length of the ruler's life and his reign and (after the paragraph on the composition of his History) the portents which foreshadowed his death, among them a fire which destroyed the temple of Pax and other buildings, the same one in which many books of Galen were lost.[2] If he found it necessary to sum up the character of Commodus there is no trace of it in the text.

Pertinax

In 193 and the following years Dio was in Rome, and all that he records of Pertinax and Didius Julianus derives from his personal experience; to say this is to claim not that he was present at all the scenes he describes, but that his narrative reflects what was known and felt at the time in senatorial circles. In the reign of Pertinax Dio was in favour, for it was Pertinax who designated him as praetor of the following year,[3] and an anecdote he tells under the reign of Commodus shows him with Pertinax when an impostor was being examined.[4]

With a single sentence of introduction, summing up Pertinax' character and fate—Πέρτιναξ δὲ ἦν τῶν καλῶν κἀγαθῶν, ἦρξε δὲ πάνυ βραχύν τινα χρόνον, εἶτα πρὸς τῶν στρατιωτῶν ἀνῃρέθη[5]—Dio takes up the story of the last night of 192 where he had left it and runs quickly through the arrival of Laetus and Eclectus to see Pertinax, his dispatch of an agent to see the body,[6] his secret journey to the Praetorian camp, and his speech to the soldiers. Before dawn Pertinax had arrived at the Senate[7] and greeted the senators, among whom was Dio, as well as he could in the tumult.[8] Thus Dio can record Pertinax' speech and the Senate's acclamation of him from personal recollection; there follows the vivid scene in which Senate and people, after the *damnatio memoriae* of Commodus, shouted against him, parodying the acclamations they had once had to voice in his honour.[9] Dio was not the only senator in whose memory that scene lived long.[10]

---

[1] 72. 22. 4–6 (303–4).   [2] 72. 24 (305). Galen 13 Kühn, 362.
[3] 73. 12. 2. See p. 16.   [4] 72. 6. 4–5 (287).   [5] 73. 1. 1 (306).
[6] 1. 2. E. Hohl, 'Kaiser Pertinax und die Thronbesteigung seines Nachfolgers im Lichte der Herodiankritik', *SDAW* 1956, 2, p. 6, arbitrarily identifies this unnamed agent with the P. Livius Larensis who appears in *Vita Com.* 20. 1 (Pflaum, *Carrières* no. 194).   [7] Compare *Vita Pert.* 4. 9.
[8] 73. 1. 4.   [9] 73. 2. (307).
[10] Marius Maximus also gave a verbatim report of the shouts of the crowd. *Vita Com.* 18–19.

The events of the first night and morning described, Dio goes back to give a formal introduction to Pertinax and the character of his rule, beginning with his origin and career,[1] and his extreme courtesy and accessibility to senators. The first item takes Dio on to a story about Pertinax' patron, Claudius Pompeianus, who in Commodus' reign had kept away from the city on the excuse of his age and bad eyesight; when Pertinax came to the throne his eyesight miraculously recovered and he reappeared in the Senate.[2] Then, with a brief digression on reactions to the news in the provinces—some governors thought it too good to be true and imprisoned the messengers to be on the safe side—[3] Dio comes to the other conventional item of his introduction, the portents of Pertinax' reign, all in this case stories about a race-horse called Pertinax in the reign of Commodus.[4] The last item is Pertinax' titles as Emperor, the usual ones, with the addition of *Princeps Senatus*.

From this point until his narrative of Pertinax' fall begins,[5] Dio describes a number of the Emperor's measures, not apparently in any strict chronological order. At the end he reverts to the attempt of the Senate, which was refused, to vote the titles of *Augusta* to Pertinax' wife, Flavia Titiana, and *Caesar* to his son;[6] this vote in fact took place on 1 January.[7] In the same paragraph Dio retails another measure of the first of January—Pertinax divested himself of his property, gave it to his son and daughter, and sent them off to live with their grandfather.[8]

The mutiny of the praetorian cohorts which brought about Pertinax' death was prefaced by an attempted *coup* on the part of Sosius Falco, the *consul ordinarius*, instigated by Laetus; Pertinax hastened back from Ostia, where he had been supervising arrangements for the *annona*,[9] and addressed the Senate, among whom again was Dio. Dio quotes the passage in Pertinax' speech

---

[1] See *PIR*[2] H 73. Dio's account is compressed, but accurate.
[2] 73. 3 (307–8). [3] 73. 2. 5–6 (308–9).
[4] 73. 4 (309). [5] 73. 8 (312).
[6] 73. 7. 1–2 (311). See H. Bloch, 'Die Gemahlin des Kaisers Balbinus', *Mem. Pont. Acad. Roma*, ser. 3. 4 (1938), 107, on p. 108. The title was used on documents in Egypt, probably through ignorance, and also in *ILS* 410 (Metz).
[7] *Vita Pert.* 5. 4.
[8] 73. 7. 3 (311–12). See Herod. 2. 4. 9, *Vita Pert.* 13. 4.
[9] Hohl, 'Kaiser Pertinax', 16 n. 52, claims that the incident must therefore date from after 5 March. It may well be so, but there is no proof that preparations for the *annona* were not in hand before the navigation season began.

in which he claimed to have given as large a donative to the soldiers as Marcus Aurelius and Lucius Verus had; the claim was false and Dio corrects it in detail.[1] The scene in the Senate ended with the declaration of Falco as *hostis* and Pertinax standing up and shouting, 'No senator will be killed in my reign, even justly!'

All that remained was the final tragedy, of which Dio gives an informed account, with a word of praise for Eclectus, who tried to save the Emperor (ὅθεν ἐγὼ καὶ πρὸ τοῦ ἄνδρα αὐτὸν ἀγαθὸν γεγονέναι νομίζων, τότε δὴ καὶ πάνυ ἐθαύμασα).[2] He ends as usual by giving the years, months, and days of his rule, prefacing this with a firm and apposite political judgement—Pertinax attempted to put everything to rights in a short time, not recognizing, for all his experience of affairs, that it is dangerous to attempt the rectification of everything at once and that the achievement of political stability, above all things, requires time and skill.[3]

Didius Julianus

Dio's brief account of the short reign of Julianus offers little for comment. He is undisguisedly hostile throughout—in dealing with the Emperors of his own time he makes no attempt at objectivity and claims none, distributing praise, blame, and abuse as he feels inclined.

Nor is there much trace of formal arrangement in this section. A few words on the character of Julianus—avaricious, spendthrift, and turbulent—and an incident from his past, his confinement by Commodus to his *patria*, Mediolanum,[4] bring Dio to the famous scene of the auction of the Empire (ὅτε δὴ καὶ πρᾶγμα αἴσχιστόν τε καὶ ἀνάξιον τῆς Ῥώμης ἐγένετο . . .).[5] Nothing is to be gained by attempting to reconcile the three accounts of it. Herodian's owes more to imagination than information;[6] the *Historia Augusta* agrees with Dio only so far as to establish the fact that Flavius Sulpicianus was already inside the camp and Julianus outside it.[7] Dio was not present at the scene—ἡμεῖς δὲ πυνθανόμενοι ταῦτα, ὥς που ἑκάστῳ διηγγέλλετο[8]—and his eyewitness report begins only with the moment when the senators, who had not only had their evening baths but dined, as he indignantly

---

[1] 73. 8. 3–4 (312). See Smits, op. cit. 77 n. 86.
[2] 73. 10. 2 (314).
[3] 73. 10. 3 (314).
[4] 73. 11. 2 (315).
[5] 73. 11. 3 (315).
[6] 2. 6. 8–9.
[7] *Vita Did. Jul.* 2. 6–7: Dio 73. 11. 3–6 (315–16).
[8] 73. 12. 2 (316).

observes, made their way to the *curia* jostled by the soldiers, to
hear a self-laudatory address by the new Emperor, some of which
Dio quotes verbatim.[1]

An unpleasant story follows in Dio—Julianus entered the Palatium and found dinner laid for Pertinax; while the body of his
predecessor lay within, he dined and diced.[2] The story may be no
more than the product of rumour; for a less detailed version, that
Julianus dined richly on the first night of his reign, is mentioned
as an agreed falsehood by the *Historia Augusta*.[3] The events of the
next day, as Dio recounts them, are more instructive. While the
senators went to pay their respects to the Emperor, masking their
grief—πλαττόμενοι τρόπον τινὰ καὶ σχηματιζόμενοι ὅπως μὴ κατά-
φωροι ἐπὶ τῇ λύπῃ γενώμεθα—the mob broke loose, shouted against
Julianus and, undeterred by the assaults of the troops, gathered in
the Circus Maximus and remained there for a day and a night
without food, shouting in support of Pescennius Niger, the legate
of Syria.[4] In this picture Dio emphasizes a contrast which he was
to recall later,[5] between the hypocrisy and servility which were
forced on the senators, each one of whom could be observed and
his conduct marked, and the freedom of the anonymous mob who
could make their anger or indifference felt as they wished. The
point is an important one: to ignore the political pressure which
the people of Rome could and did bring on Emperors[6] is to fail
totally to see one of the shaping forces of the Principate.

With a description of Julianus' efforts to win over the senators
and a quotation from a speech of his in the Senate,[7] Dio passes to
a sketch of the three pretenders who now arose, Albinus in Britain,
Septimius Severus in Pannonia, and Pescennius Niger in Syria.
Severus was the most important, and in describing him Dio does
not forget the aid which rhetoric could offer for the delineation
of character:

ὅτι ὁ Σεουῆρος δεινότατος ἦν τό τε μέλλον ἀκριβῶς προνοῆσαι καὶ
τὸ παρὸν ἀσφαλῶς διοικῆσαι, καὶ πᾶν μὲν τὸ κεκρυμμένον ὡς καὶ
ἐμφανὲς ἐξευρεῖν, πᾶν δὲ τὸ δυσλόγιστον ὡς καὶ ἁπλοῦν διακρῖναι,
πᾶν δὲ τὸ δυσδιάθετον ὡς καὶ ῥᾷστον ἐξεργάσασθαι.[8]

[1] 12. 3–5.   [2] 73. 13. 1 (317).   [3] *Vita Did. Jul.* 3. 8–9.
[4] 73. 13. 2–5 (317).
[5] On the reign of Macrinus, 78. 19. 5–20. 2 (424–5).
[6] As does M. Hammond, *The Antonine Monarchy* (American Academy, Rome,
1959), 321–2.
[7] 73. 14. 1–2a (318).   [8] 73. 15. 1 (319). Compare Thuc. 1. 138. 3.

The rest is taken up with Julianus' frenzied efforts to create some sort of defence for Rome against the rapid approach of Severus. The reaction of the Senate was simple—laughter.[1] For all that, they remained entirely passive in the grip of events. At first Julianus made them declare Severus a *hostis publicus*;[2] then, as he approached, he made them declare Severus his colleague on the throne.[3] Finally, when the troops went over, the consul, Silius Messala, summoned the Senate, among them Dio, and had Julianus condemned to death and Severus proclaimed.[4] All this Dio retails impassively and without comment. He ends by giving the last words of Julianus and, as usual, the length of his life and reign.[5]

Septimius Severus

Attempts to interpret the character of Severus and the importance of his reign have led scholars in widely diverse directions. We have had a military despot[6] or even a 'great bandit'[7] on the one hand and a 'Roman bureaucrat' on the other.[8] In face of this diversity, a first step can be taken by paying particular attention to what is said of him by Dio, the only man who knew Severus personally and left a judgement of him to posterity. This will not in itself help very much in considering Severus' place in the history of the Empire; but it will show how he stood with a man who was both a respectable contemporary senator and a typical representative of Graeco-Roman culture.

One avenue of approach has already been discarded—Dio did not fall into disgrace during Severus' reign. On the contrary, he secured his position at the very outset and in the course of the reign was praetor, perhaps then a provincial governor, consul, and an *amicus* of the Emperor.[9] There is in fact little justification for the view that Dio was hostile to Severus. Certain strong criticisms are indeed evoked by Severus' conduct during the civil wars and his expensive and wasteful campaigns in the East. But

---

[1] 73. 16. 3–4 (321) ἔστι δὲ ὅτε καὶ γέλως ἡμᾶς ἐλάμβανεν . . . μάλιστα δὲ ἐγελῶμεν.
[2] 73. 16. 1 (320).   [3] 73. 17. 2–3 (322).
[4] 73. 17. 4 (322).   [5] 73. 17. 5 (322).
[6] So Rostovtzeff, *SEHRE*², 401 f.
[7] A. Passerini, *Le coorte pretorie* (Rome, 1939), 182.
[8] M. Hammond, 'Septimius Severus, Roman Bureaucrat', *HSCPh* 51 (1940), 137.
[9] See Chapter I.

when Dio comes, after Severus' death, to his final summing-up of the man and his reign his judgement is very far from unfavourable.[1] He notes the Emperor's energy of body and, with a touch of condescension, of mind (παιδείας μὲν γὰρ ἐπεθύμει μᾶλλον ἢ ἐπετύγχανε, καὶ διὰ τοῦτο πολυγνώμων μᾶλλον ἢ πολύλογος ἦν). He states that, while Severus gathered funds eagerly from every source, he condemned no one for his property, and spent lavishly on necessary objects. Severus also—and here a certain note of criticism can be felt—repaired a great many old buildings and put his own name on them as if they were new.[2] None the less, he left a large reserve of funds at his death. Dio's description of Severus' daily routine in Rome is a tribute to his conscientiousness, simplicity, and devotion to duty—so great that on his deathbed he cried out 'Come, give it to me, if there is anything we have to do'. Dio did not feel as warmly about Severus as he had about Pertinax, but his words are those of a man who regarded the Emperor, if not with affection, at least with sincere respect.

In the early part of Dio's account of Severus it is possible, with all due caution, to detect three separate strands. One is clear—the residue of that pamphlet of portents which some twenty-four years earlier he had sent to the Emperor.[3] Then there are certain notably enthusiastic passages which fit ill with the generally critical tone in the first part and which may well have been put in from the second work, that on the wars and civil wars of Severus. The most obvious of these is the rapturous description of Severus' entry into Rome[4] in 193 which conflicts directly with the versions of the *Historia Augusta* ('fuitque ingressus Severi odiosus atque terribilis') and of Herodian.[5] The critical tone is resumed immediately after this. Later there is a formal *periphrasis* on the 'funeral' and deification of Pertinax[6] (followed by what may be part of Severus' funeral oration),[7] the most important political gesture of Severus' first stay in Rome. It is not improbable that this had its place in the history of Severus' early struggles; and the

[1] 76. 16. 1–17. 4 (370–2).
[2] Severus' buildings and repairs are listed by H. W. Benario, 'Rome of the Severi', *Latomus* 17 (1958), 712.
[3] See pp. 29 and 119–20.   [4] 74. 1. 3–5 (324–5).
[5] *Vita Sept. Sev.* 7. 1–3; Herodian 2. 14. 1.
[6] 74. 4. 1–5. 5 (327–9). Brief account in *Vita Pert.* 15. 1.
[7] 74. 5. 6–7 (329). See Boissevain, ad loc.

same may be true of the long set piece on the three-year siege of
Byzantium,[1] which is filled with all those dramatic details which
befit the story of a beleaguered city—divers cutting the cables of
ships, merchant ships running the blockade, women cutting off
their hair, and statues being used for defensive works.[2] If all this
was in the original work, it was not put in entirely untouched, for
Dio ends by criticizing Severus for the destruction of the walls of
Byzantium[3]—and omits to mention that he rebuilt them.[4]

Of Severus' first stay in Rome as Emperor Dio's extant text
adds nothing, except a sarcastic account of Severus' speech, in
which he promised to put no senator to death; not only was the
promise not kept, but the very senator, Julius Solon, who drew
up the *senatus consultum* which followed, was himself executed.[5] Dio
further complains of the mass of soldiers who infested and terrified the city[6]—though the extant text does not contain a detail
which he mentions in Book 46, that the soldiers terrified Severus
also and extorted a donative from him.[7] Finally there comes a rare
item of direct social observation, that Severus, by barring the
recruitment of Italians into the praetorian cohorts, forced the
youth of the country to turn to brigandage.[8]

The remains of Dio's narrative of the civil wars are too fragmentary for a coherent picture of how the subject was tackled to
emerge. Xiphilinus retains continuous accounts of the first campaign, that of Cyzicus and Issus in 194,[9] of the siege of Byzantium,
and of the defeat of Clodius Albinus in 197.[10] The changes of fortune in each battle are related in considerable detail, though no
indication is given of how the information was acquired; in the
case of the battles in Bithynia and at Issus Dio will have known the
terrain already. As with his accounts of campaigns in the body of
his history, there is no attempt to fix with any accuracy the

---

[1] 74. 10. 1–14. 6 (334–8).

[2] The intention is quite conscious. See 10. 1 οἱ δὲ δὴ Βυζάντιοι . . . πολλὰ καὶ
θαυμαστὰ ἔδρασαν and 12. 1 λελέξεται δὲ ὀλίγα καὶ τὰ ἐχόμενά τινος θαύματος.

[3] 14. 4–5. The words τῶν δὲ δὴ Ῥωμαίων μέγα καὶ φυλακτήριον καὶ ὁρμητήριον
πρὸς τοὺς ἐκ τοῦ Πόντου καὶ τῆς Ἀσίας βαρβάρους seem puzzling if written by Dio,
who could hardly have imagined barbarians in *Asia*. Were they perhaps inserted by
Xiphilinus?

[4] See Platnauer, *Septimius Severus*, 98.

[5] 74. 2. 1–2 (325).   [6] 74. 2. 2–3 (325–6).

[7] 46. 46. 7 (see Appendix III). Compare *Vita Sept. Sev.* 7. 6.

[8] 74. 2. 5–6 (326).   [9] 74. 6. 3–8. 3 (330–2).

[10] 75. 6. 1–7. 3 (342–4).

chronological sequence of events. The siege of Byzantium is covered in a single long passage with no separation of events into years; the expedition to Osroëne and Adiabene (in 195) is dated merely as having taken place during the siege.[1] A few incidents come to life in the narrative, the troops shouting 'Water, water!' in Mesopotamia,[2] the brigand Claudius coming up unrecognized to greet the Emperor,[3] and the dignified defence of a senator, Cassius Clemens, who was judged before Severus for having supported Pescennius Niger.[4] The case, it seems, took place in Syria and Dio must have received his verbatim report of it from some informant.

More interest attaches to Dio's comments on persons and events. Introducing Pescennius Niger, he says that he was a complete mediocrity and for that reason had been made governor of Syria by Commodus[5]—the best men were not always rushed through the *cursus* to take the great military commands. Of Severus' attempt to make Nisibis the bulwark of Syria he says that the sole effect was to waste money and involve the Empire in a series of wars with Parthia; written as it was in 218 or 219, this comment is not lacking in point.[6]

Meanwhile Dio was in Rome, in 194 as praetor. At the *Saturnalia* of December 196 he was an eyewitness of a demonstration in which the people protested against the continuance of civil war— 'How long shall we suffer such things?'—'How long shall we be at war?' Dio thought it must be divine inspiration—how else could tens of thousands of people have chanted slogans together?[7] The technique, if it is a conscious technique, of using popular reactions in Rome, which were vivid and forceful, as a sort of commentary or counterweight to the progress of events elsewhere is taken up again and used more fully in the reign of Macrinus.

The end of the civil wars is recounted in a tone of profound bitterness: Severus' victory brought a heavy drain on the strength of the Empire. It is here alone, on the manner of Albinus' death, that he mentions and refutes the version of events in Severus' autobiography.[8] What followed revealed that Severus was not a good Emperor. He inspected the body of Albinus with pleasure

---

[1] 75. 1. 1 (338).   [2] 75. 2. 2 (339).   [3] 75. 2. 4 (340).
[4] 74. 9. 1–4 (333–4).   [5] 74. 6. 1 (329).
[6] 75. 3. 3 (340). See Appendix III, the first passage.
[7] 75. 4. 2–6 (341–2).   [8] 75. 7. 3 (344).

and had the head sent on to Rome. Then his wrath turned from his armed opponents to the defenceless Senate and people; and he signified his change of attitude by calling himself the son of Marcus Aurelius, and (more to the point) the brother of Commodus.[1] Dio's hostility in this passage is more marked than at any other point, and it may well be that he was countering not only what Severus had written but what he had written himself in the work on Severus' wars, which in all probability was presented at this very moment, the brief stay of Severus in Rome in the summer of 197. It is likely to have contained a flattering account which Dio would later have wished to expunge—and the atmosphere of terror and oppression which made flattery necessary are well illustrated in the passage which follows. Severus came to the Senate and made a threatening speech, praising the sternness of Marius, Sulla, and Augustus, defending Commodus, and casting scorn on his audience. Dio gives extracts from it in direct speech, and was probably there himself.[2] In recording the humiliations of the Senate,[3] Dio is none the less scrupulous in giving the numbers of those freed as well as those executed.[4]

The narrative of the Parthian wars and Severus' travels in the East offers the same difficulties as that of the civil wars; the text is compressed or fragmentary and all sure indications of date are lacking. Dio begins by giving the *casus belli*, the Parthian attack on Nisibis while Severus was still engaged on the civil wars, but then moves straight to the arrival of Severus before Nisibis,[5] omitting the games given to the people of Rome[6] and the time and manner of his journey to the East.[7] Of the campaign itself he records an apparently pointless anecdote of Severus' encounter with a dangerous boar, and then moves swiftly on to the voyage down the Euphrates and the capture of Seleuceia, Babylon, and Ctesiphon,[8] which took place at some point in the winter of

[1] 75. 7. 3–4 (344). The official attachment to the Antonine house in fact appears in his titulature from the year 195. See J. Hasebroek, *Untersuchungen zur Geschichte des Kaisers Septimius Severus* (Heidelberg, 1921), 90 f.

[2] 75. 8. 1–3 (344–5).

[3] See further 75. 8. 5–74. 9. 6 (345–6).

[4] 75. 8. 4 (345). See G. Barbieri, 'Aspetti della politica di Settimio Severo', *Epigraphica* 14 (1952), 3, on pp. 6–8.

[5] 75. 9. 1–2 (346–7).

[6] *Vita Sept. Sev.* 14. 11; Herod. 3. 8. 9.

[7] See *Vita Sept. Sev.* 15. 2.

[8] 75. 9. 2–4 (347).

197/8.[1] Dio's tone is severely critical—Severus neither pursued Vologaeses nor held Ctesiphon; the only purpose of the whole operation was apparently to ravage the place, and the army had to be split into two divisions for the return march because of the scarcity of supplies.[2]

The remaining events of the Parthian war, namely the two sieges of Hatra, should probably be dated to 198; Severus was in Egypt certainly by the autumn of 199 and perhaps as early as the spring of that year.[3] On the way there he visited Syria, Palestine and, possibly, Arabia.[4] It is likely, therefore, that the first siege took place in the spring of 198 and the second, which lasted twenty days,[5] in the late summer or autumn.

Dio had given a brief description of Hatra, its barren situation and the temple of Helios,[6] and had mentioned Severus' attempt on it, in narrating the equally unsuccessful siege by Trajan.[7] Here he gives only a single sentence on the first siege, emphasizing the loss of men and materials which it involved, but describes in fuller detail the executions during its course of the tribune Julius Crispus[8] and Laetus, the defender of Nisibis, whose renown was too great for safety.[9] The second siege gets a full set-piece description which does not omit to note once again the waste of men, money, and machines.[10] The succession of disasters is vividly recounted: Arabian horsemen skirmished on the enemy's flanks and other

[1] See G. J. Murphy, *The Reign of the Emperor L. Septimius Severus from the Evidence of the Inscriptions* (Philadelphia, 1945), 21–22, 24–26. The *Feriale Duranum*, col. 1. 14–16, dates the capture of Ctesiphon to 28 January. But see *Dura Final Report*, V. 1, p. 206.

[2] 75. 9. 4–5 (347–8).

[3] K. Hannestad, 'Septimius Severus in Egypt', *Classica et Mediaevalia* 6 (1944), 194, suggests that Severus was in Egypt by the spring. But see W. L. Westermann and A. A. Schiller, *Apokrimata: Decisions of Septimius Severus on Legal Matters* (New York, 1954), 26 f., especially p. 30.

[4] Hasebroek, op. cit. 120.   [5] 75. 13. 1 (350).

[6] See A. Maricq, *Syria* 34 (1957), 289–90.

[7] 68. 31. See Appendix III.

[8] The man's crime had been to criticize the conduct of the war by quoting three lines of Virgil—*Aen.* xi. 371–3 'Scilicet ut Turno contingat regia coniunx / nos animae viles, inhumata infletaque turba / sternamur campis.' Dio gives a rather flat paraphrase—ἵνα δὴ τὴν Λαουινίαν ὁ Τοῦρνος ἀγάγηται, ἡμεῖς ἐν οὐδενὶ λόγῳ παραπολλύμεθα (10. 2). It is none the less the only formal indication that Latin poetry was something familiar to him.

[9] 75. 10. 3 (348). See also Dio's fervent praise in 75. 9. 1–2 (347). Compare *Vita Sept. Sev.* 15. 6—Marius Maximus also mentioned this execution and said that Severus later denied responsibility. The man himself is little known—*Albo* no. 323a.

[10] 75. 11. 1 (Dio's comment)—13. 1 (348–50).

Arabians who were expected to help failed to arrive. The European troops mutinied and the Syrian ones, pressed reluctantly into battle, suffered heavy losses.[1] The Emperor was disheartened; when someone claimed that given 550 European troops he could take the town, he replied, 'Where can I get as many soldiers as that?'

Severus' visit to Egypt marked the most important step in the history of the province since its absorption into the Empire. Alexandria was given a *boulē* and the other communities received some autonomous institutions.[2] Only the establishment of the Alexandrian *boulē* finds a place in the literary sources, and in Dio it appears not in the (extant) narrative of Severus' travels but in a passing reference in the reign of Augustus.[3] All that Dio has at this point is Severus' voyage up the Nile, his removal of sacred books from the temples, and his closing of the tomb of Alexander;[4] according to the *Historia Augusta* Severus used later to refer to the pleasure he had gained from antiquarian and religious interests on this journey.[5] Dio excuses himself from giving a full description of Egypt, but announces that he is qualified, after wide research, to indicate the sources of the Nile, which he does.[6]

How long Severus and his household remained in Egypt is uncertain. If the *Historia Augusta* can be relied upon, Caracalla assumed the *toga virilis* in Antioch and immediately afterwards entered upon the consulship of 202 there with his father;[7] an inscription from Rome seems to show that the imperial household made a sea-voyage in 201, perhaps that from Alexandria to Antioch.[8] From there Severus made his way back to Rome by land, visiting the armies of Moesia and Pannonia on the way, and arriving in time for the celebration of his *decennalia* in 202—which he must have celebrated not on 13 April but on 9 June, the anniversary of his arrival in Rome in 193.[9]

---

[1] On the units which took part in the Eastern Campaigns see Murphy, op. cit. 22–24.

[2] See, for example, A. H. M. Jones, *Cities of the Eastern Roman Provinces* (Oxford, 1937), 329.

[3] *Vita Sept. Sev.* 17. 2; Dio 51. 17. 3 (see Appendix III).

[4] 75. 13. 1–2 (350).   [5] *Vita Sept. Sev.* 17. 3–4.

[6] 75. 13. 3–5 (351). See p. 178.

[7] *Vita Sept. Sev.* 16. 8 (put before the visit to Egypt). See G. Downey, *A History of Antioch in Syria* (Princeton, 1961), 242.   [8] See Murphy, op. cit. 28–29.

[9] Herod. 3. 10. 1–2. See J. Fitz, 'Der Besuch des Septimius Severus in Pannonien im Jahre 202 n. Chr.', *A. Arch. Hung.* 11 (1959), 237. For this dating of

In the extant text of Dio there is no formal account of any events between Severus' journey to Upper Egypt and the celebration of the *decennalia*. Instead, there is a long section designed to illustrate the growing power of Plautianus and his abuse of it.[1] The material collected in this section covers a period of some five years, beginning with the murder of Q. Aemilius Saturninus in about 200[2] and Plautianus' theft of some sacred horses from islands in the Red Sea, which must date from the stay in Egypt.[3] It includes also incidents at Tyana and Nicaea which date from the return journey early in 202,[4] the wedding of his daughter, Plautilla, to Caracalla in 202 and his consulship in 203,[5] a case before Severus in 204, at which Dio was in the *consilium*,[6] and even, in parenthesis, a reference to some discoveries made after Plautianus had been killed in 205.[7] The evidence is not given in strict chronological order, and that this is intentional is clear when Dio later resumes annalistic treatment with the *decennalia* of 202 and a full description of the wedding of Caracalla and Plautilla.[8]

With that, the text moves straight to the fall of Plautianus, omitting any mention of the visit to Africa by Severus and the Court in, probably, 202/3[9] or of the *ludi saeculares* of 204. Plautianus' fall itself is introduced by a portent, an eruption of Vesuvius, the sound of which reached Capua,[10] and by a demonstration against him, at which Dio was no doubt present, by the crowd in the Circus Maximus.[11] Dio then continues with a long and detailed account of the circumstances which brought about Plautianus' death, including the motives of the main characters and a full narrative of various events at which he could not have been present himself; suspect as his account is, there is no way of controlling it, for Herodian's version is even less reliable.[12] The two

---

Severus' return, as against Hasebroek, op. cit. 126–8, see Fitz, pp. 250–2. The attempt by F. Papazoglou, 'Septimia Aurelia Heraclea', *BCH* 85 (1961), 162, to show that Severus returned along the Via Egnatia is quite unacceptable.

[1] 75. 14. 1–16. 5 (351–6).   [2] 14. 2. See Howe, op. cit. 70.
[3] 14. 3–4.   [4] 15. 3–5.   [5] 15. 2. See 14. 5.
[6] 16. 2–4. See p. 17.   [7] 14. 4–5.   [8] 76. 1 (357–8).
[9] Murphy, op. cit. 33–34, has 203–4. But see J. Guey, 'Lepticana Septimiana VI', *Revue Africaine* 95 (1950), 51, on pp. 55–67. The visit is mentioned by Philostratus, *VS* 2. 20 (Teubner ed. 103).
[10] 76. 2. 1 (358).   [11] 76. 2. 2–3 (358).
[12] 76. 2. 4–4. 5 (358–60): Herod. 3. 11. 4–12. 12. See E. Hohl, 'Herodian und der Sturz Plautians', *SDAW* 1956, 2, pp. 33–46.

are in direct conflict; Herodian accepts, and Dio does not, the official story that Plautianus had engineered a plot against Severus and Caracalla. This was no doubt the story which, as Dio records, was immediately afterwards recited to the Senate by the agents of Severus,[1] and Dio's version is in effect a critique of it. He begins with a brief survey of the relations of Severus' family with Plautianus; the Emperor's brother P. Septimius Geta had warned against Plautianus on his death-bed,[2] and Plautianus and Caracalla were on bad terms over Plautilla. Dio shows no hesitation in making clear that Plautianus' plot was an invention by Caracalla, who arranged that some tribunes should report to Severus that they had been entrusted with the murder, and even supplied them with written evidence. The absurdity of the thing, he says, was patent—Plautianus would never have given such an order to ten tribunes, above all not in writing, before dinner on a day in which a festival (the *ludi palatini* of 21–23 January) was being celebrated in the Palatium. None the less he makes clear that in his view Severus really believed the story, having just had a dream in which Clodius Albinus appeared and plotted against him. The rest is taken up with a circumstantial account of Plautianus' summons to the palace, the words which passed between him, Severus, and Caracalla, and his death. Dio concludes with a brief echo of a familiar moral and rhetorical theme—Plautianus had raised himself to the pinnacle of power and had ended with his body's being thrown down from the palace into the street.

The death of Plautianus meant the usual consequences for his friends and enemies. Within the framework of what appear to be several successive meetings of the Senate which followed, Dio recounts in detail the banishment, and later recall (in 212), of a prominent hanger-on, Aelius Coeranus, the suicide of another, Caecilius Agricola, and the banishment of Lipara of Plautianus' children, Plautius and Plautilla—and their execution under Caracalla. The role of the Senate was no more noble than could be expected; they voted thanks (ψηφιζομένων δὲ ἡμῶν) to Euodos, who had prepared the trap for Plautianus, and were then

---

[1] 76. 5. 2 (360).

[2] His death must fall between his consulate with Plautianus in 203 and January 205. On his career see G. M. Bersanetti, 'P. Settimio Geta, fratello di Settimio Severo', *Epigraphica* 4 (1942), 105, who suggests (p. 129) 204 as the year of his death.

reproved by Severus. Later they acclaimed the Emperor—"'πάντες πάντα καλῶς ποιοῦσιν, ἐπειδὴ σὺ καλῶς ἄρχεις".[1]

For the period between the death of Plautianus and the British expedition of 208 the anecdotal character of Dio's work is particularly marked. The material consists in sum of comments on the behaviour of Caracalla and Geta, 'rid of Plautianus as of a pedagogue',[2] eyewitness accounts of the proceedings which led to the death of various senators, and the story of the famous bandit, Felix Bulla, who held sway in southern Italy with a band of 600 men, mainly recruited from slaves who had escaped from imperial estates.[3] The literary and documentary sources do not make clear what, if anything, has been omitted from the narrative of these years—Herodian indeed states that Severus spent them peacefully in conducting public business from Rome or Campania.[4] Some have thought that the inscriptions showed a serious revolt in 207, but the evidence for it is unconvincing.[5] What Dio records, however, has its own interest in that it shows the workings of imperial politics as they were seen by an ordinary senator who was close to events but did not intervene in them. The most revealing section is the long report of how the proconsul of Asia, Apronianus,[6] was charged in his absence with *maiestas*, and of the other accusations which followed.[7] The charge was that Apronianus' nurse had dreamed that he would be Emperor and that he had used magic to bring this about. The Senate assembled to have read to it the transcript of the interrogation of witnesses, with (apparently) additions by Severus himself.[8] The testimony implicated an unnamed bald senator and an extraordinary scene ensued. Men eyed each other suspiciously, murmurs arose naming one senator or another, all except those with a good head of hair were thrown into confusion, and Dio admits to having put up his

[1] 76. 5–6 (360–1). 6. 3 ἐπὶ δ' Ἀντωνίνου ἀπώλοντο shows that the passage must have been written after the death of Caracalla (8 April 217).
[2] 76. 7. 1 (361).
[3] 76. 10 (364–5).
[4] 3. 13. 1.
[5] See Murphy, op. cit. 38–40, reviewed by M. Hammond, *AJPh* 71 (1950), 193, on pp. 194–9.
[6] Probably Popilius Pedo Apronianus—*Albo* no. 431. See Magie, *Roman Rule*, ch. 28, n. 32.
[7] 76. 8–9 (363–4). The opening sentence (. . . τὰ περὶ τὸν Ἀπρωνιανὸν ἐτελέσθη, παράδοξα ὄντα καὶ ἀκουσθῆναι) makes clear that Dio was deliberately selecting dramatic incidents for inclusion.
[8] 8. 3 notes that Severus had *not* added a certain point.

hand to feel the hair on his own head. All this took place while the
reading continued, for now a further item was added—the bald
senator had been wearing the *toga praetexta*. At once all looked
(ἀπείδομεν) at the aedile, Baebius Marcellinus,[1] who was bald.
The latter stood up and challenged the informer to recognize him.
Amid applause the informer was brought in and stood for a long
time looking round before saying, in obedience to a nod from
someone, that Baebius was the man. He was immediately dragged
off and executed, before Septimius was aware that he had been
condemned, so Dio says. The consequences of the case did not
stop at that: the accuser, Pollenius Sebennus,[2] was in his turn
accused—of malpractices in his government of Noricum—by one
Sabinus (presumably P. Catius Sabinus who also governed Noricum, before 209, and was suffect consul by 210).[3] Sebennus was
handed over to the provincials for execution and the Senate had
the spectacle (εἴδομεν) of his lying on the ground and begging for
mercy; he would have lost his life but for the intervention of his
uncle, Pollenius Auspex,[4] a savage wit, equipped to help his
friends and harm his enemies, and to mock the Emperor to
his face.

Many things are revealed in this story. Political trials continued
under the Empire as they had in the Republic—*maiestas* merely
added another weapon for use in mutual strife—and gave Emperors another means to divide and rule. Personal enmities and
alliances were the dominating factors and political power meant
the ability to ensure the safety, and property, of oneself and one's
friends. When one senator fell, some others would be gratified.
Even those who, like Dio, could see how things were done, and
were indignant, did not dare to speak out.

The expedition to Britain which occupied the last three years
of Severus' life is covered at considerable length in Dio—though,
as might be expected, he uses it largely for anecdote and description, ignoring both the detailed course of the campaigns and their
purpose. It can now be seen to have served two major ends, the
repulse of the Maeatae[5] and the establishment of a new frontier

[1] *Albo* no. 86. Nothing more is known of him.
[2] *Albo* no. 414. Barbieri makes *CIL* 3. 5537 refer to him. *PIR*[1] P 411 was justly
sceptical.
[3] *Albo* no. 126.
[4] *Albo* no. 412. See Jagenteufel, op. cit. 69–72.
[5] Referred to by Dio in 75. 5. 4 (346). See Boissevain, ad loc.

system based on Hadrian's Wall.[1] Dio, like Herodian, represents it as an excuse for removing Caracalla and Geta from the pleasures of Rome and reviving the discipline of the troops;[2] and once again he represents the actual fighting as a mere ravaging expedition attended with great difficulty and loss and little profit.[3]

He begins, after noting some omens which indicated that Severus would not return,[4] with an account of Britain and its inhabitants—the barbarians of the North, that is, for the inhabitants of the Roman province are ignored. The description of the island itself and also an account of how the voyage round it was once again accomplished appear to have dropped out,[5] though he gives the dimensions of the country and the proportion of it held by Rome.[6] What remains is his famous description of the Caledonii and Maeatae—'a strange compound of generalities and travellers' tales . . . practically worthless'.[7] Dio, as an *amicus* of Severus, might have gone on the expedition, but in the absence of first-person reports it is safe to assume that he did not. What he says about Britain must be made up from literary sources, possibly from official reports, though there is no obvious trace of these, and above all from anecdotes and stories from persons serving in the country or with the imperial household. This source must account for the retort of the British women to Julia Domna —'We satisfy our natural desires much more fittingly than you; for while we consort openly with the noblest men, you do so secretly with the lowest'[8]—and probably for Caracalla's attempts to get rid of the imperial slave, Castor, and of Severus himself;[9] the story that Caracalla in fact helped on his father's death and the report of some sayings of Severus near the end of his life are explicitly attributed to hearsay.[10]

Such details apart, Dio's information on the fighting itself amounts only to a graphic description of the army's advance through difficult country nearly to the farthest point of Scotland,

---

[1] See K. A. Steer in *Roman and Native in North Britain*, ed. I. A. Richmond (Edinburgh, 1958), 91–111.

[2] 76. 11. 1 (365); Herod. 3. 14. 1–2.   [3] 76. 13. 1–2 (368).

[4] 76. 11. 1–2 (365–6).

[5] See the reference in 39. 50. 4. (See p. 177 and Appendix III.) The description of Britain will have been between 76. 11 and 12 (366).

[6] 76. 12. 5–13. 1 (367–8).   [7] Steer, op. cit. 93.

[8] 76. 16. 5 (371).   [9] 76. 14 (368–9).

[10] 76. 15. 2, 4 (370) συνεργασαμένου τι πρὸς τοῦτο καὶ τοῦ Ἀντωνίνου, ὡς λέγεται . . . τάδε λέγεται τοῖς παισὶν εἰπεῖν . . . λέγεται δὲ . . . εἰπεῖν.

with a mention of the agreement which followed, that the barbarians should give up some land;[1] a glimpse of Severus and
Caracalla making another journey northwards to parley with the
Caledonii,[2] and a mention of the preparations for further fighting,
which were taking place when Severus died at York on 4 February
211. Dio ends with a summing-up of Severus' rule[3] (which is
effectively confined to Dio's direct experience of him in the middle
years while he was in Rome) and, as before, by giving the length
of his life and reign.[4]

Caracalla

The death of Severus, leaving his two sons as joint *Augusti*, had
an easily predictable result: they quarrelled, set up separate esta-
blishments, and finally Caracalla, after an abortive attempt in
December 211, was able to dispatch his brother, in late February
of 212—in his mother's arms, according to Dio. Dio's account of
the murder and what followed is circumstantial,[5] though there is
no indication in it of his own movements at the time; Caracalla
went straight to the praetorian camp and gained the support of
the troops with lavish gifts and promises. The next day he appeared before the Senate and announced, without excessive
formality, the return of all exiles. Even this could not please
Dio; it was simply bringing back to Rome all the worst characters[6]—an attitude which reaffirms his basic approval of Severus'
régime.

Writing about Caracalla some eight years after his accession
and two after his death, Dio described him with unabashed
hatred. For contrast he could portray Julia Domna, the Empress
who alone of all women was not allowed to mourn her own son,[7]
and the figure of Severus, who now appears as the wise and
conscientious father who did his best to educate and train his son

---

[1] 76. 13 (368).
[2] 76. 14. 3 (369). Herodian 3. 14. 9 can explain one point here—Geta had been
left behind.   [3] See p. 139.
[4] 76. 17. 4 (372). Dio is right, as against *Vita Sept. Sev.* 1. 3, in putting his birth in
145, not 146. See J. Guey, 'La Date de naissance de l'empereur Septime-Sévère,
d'après son horoscope', *BSNAF* 1956, 33.
[5] 77. 2. 2–3. 3 (374–6). Compare Herod. 4. 4. 3–5. 7.
[6] 77. 3. 3. Supported in detail by 76. 5. 5 (360)—Aelius Coeranus; 77. 17. 2
(396)—Sempronius Rufus; 78. 13. 3–4 (417)—Aelius Triccianus (on the name see
Albo no. 926); 79. 3. 5 (457)—Claudius Attalus.
[7] 77. 2. 6 (374).

—but all in vain, the boy might never have heard the word
παίδευσις and, even worse, despised 'those of us with some smattering of culture'.[1] His dislike of the Emperor evokes in Dio the
revelation of some interesting prejudices. Not only was Caracalla
obstinate, self-willed, and ignorant;[2] deeper faults were ingrained
in him, the levity, cowardice and rashness of a Gaul, the roughness and ferocity of an African, and the cunning of a Syrian.[3]

Hatred and mockery combine when Dio describes Caracalla's
self-identification with Alexander the Great, of which he gives an
account as part of his introductory treatment of the Emperor's
character,[4] though its manifestations began with the march
through the Balkans in 214. Reverence for Alexander had a long
history in Rome[5] but had never been carried to such lengths. Not
content with dressing up for the part, and with using weapons and
cups which were said to have belonged to Alexander, Caracalla,
imitating Nero,[6] formed a phalanx of Macedonians (in 214),[7]
persecuted the Peripatetics on the grounds of their supposed part
in Alexander's death,[8] and, on discovering a Macedonian called
Antigonus the son of Philip, instantly promoted him and later
adlected him *inter praetorios*.

Most of what Dio records of Caracalla's early years in Rome,
and even before he arrived there,[9] concerns, inevitably, the
executions of leading men. Dio made a list of those executed,
according to Xiphilinus,[10] and it is to these names that the narrative of the years 211–12 is attached.

The episode which is described in the greatest detail is the
escape of Cilo—L. Fabius Cilo Septiminus Catinius Acilianus
Lepidus Fulcinianus[11]—a famous figure who had been a general of
Severus in the civil wars and *Praefectus Urbi*, whom Dio introduces
with the phrase τὸν τροφέα τὸν εὐεργέτην, τὸν ἐπὶ τοῦ πατρὸς αὐτοῦ

[1] 77. 11. 2–4 (385).   [2] See 77. 11. 2–7 (385–6).
[3] 77. 6. 1a (379–80). Compare 77. 10. 2 (383).
[4] 77. 7–8 (380–1). The structure of Dio's introductory chapters on Caracalla is
analysed in *JEA* 48 (1962), 124.
[5] See A. Bruhl, 'Le Souvenir d'Alexandre le Grand et les Romains', *MEFR* 47
(1930), 202.   [6] Suet. *Nero*, 19. 4.   [7] Herod. 4. 8. 2.
[8] Their *syssitia* in Alexandria were abolished (7. 3); this was no doubt during
his visit in 215—see especially 77. 23. 3 (401).
[9] See 77. 1. 1–2 (373).   [10] 77. 6. 1 (379).
[11] *Albo* no. 213, and additions (p. 593) and Magie, *Roman Rule*, ch. 28, n. 19.
See G. Vitucci, *Ricerche sulla Praefectura Urbi in età imperiale* (Rome, 1956), 75 f.,
107–8.

πεπολιαρχηκότα, ὃν καὶ πατέρα πολλάκις ἐκεκλήκει.[1] It is characteristic of the casual (or at least the fragmentary) nature of Dio's
history of his own times that Cilo is mentioned here for the first
time. Cilo was dragged from his bath, brutally treated, and
would have been killed but for the anger of the populace and the
cohortes urbanae. Caracalla was forced to pretend that the order
had never been given and to execute those he had sent to carry it
out. Many other prominent men were less fortunate, including
the jurist, Papinian, who suffered the ultimate indignity of
execution by the axe, instead of the sword.[2]

In such an atmosphere it was perhaps not to be expected that
a respectable senator would view the Emperor's administrative
measures dispassionately; and Dio shows marked hostility to an
important measure of the Severan régime, the establishment of
a system of *mansiones* or stations along the main military roads, for
the delivery of supplies to the Court in transit.[3] Dio interprets
Caracalla's measures to this end solely as the erection of numerous
and unnecessary stopping-places for himself.[4] Similarly, Dio later
gives a contemptuous description of Caracalla, on the campaign
against the Alamanni, choosing sites for settlements[5]—archaeology
shows that these will have been *castella* and posts of auxiliaries on
the *limes*.[6] To Dio (and to those who reported it to him) this was
just another example of the Emperor's vanity and folly.

[1] 77. 4. 2–5 (377).
[2] 77. 4. 2 (377). He too plays little part in Dio's extant narrative: see 76. 10. 7
(365) and 77. 1. 1 (373)—his dismissal by Caracalla.
[3] D. van Berchem, 'L'annone militaire dans l'Empire romain au IIIᵉ siècle',
MSNAF viiiᵉ sér. 10 (1937), 117, followed by R. Mouterde, 'Une dédicace d'Apamée
de Syrie à l'approche de Caracalla et l'*Itinerarium Antonini*', *CRAI* 1952, 355
(= *IGLS* 1346), argues that Severus introduced at one blow the full system of the
annona militaris, familiar from the fourth century. His evidence, however, will not
bear the weight put upon it—see, for instance, P. A. Brunt, 'Pay and Superannuation in the Roman Army', *PBSR* 18 (1950), 50, n. 75, and L. Robert in *REA* 42
(1940), *Mélanges Radet*, 307, n. 6. Robert (*BE* 1954, no. 244) does not accept
Mouterde's interpretation of the Apamea inscription. All that can be proved is
that this period saw the irregular beginning of what became the system in the
fourth century.
[4] 77. 9. 5–7 (382–3). οἰκίας αὐτῷ παντοδαπάς, ἐπειδὴ τῆς Ῥώμης ἐξώρμησε, καὶ
καταλύσεις πολυτελεῖς ἐν μέσαις ταῖς ὁδοῖς καὶ ταῖς βραχυτάταις οἰκείοις δαπανήμασι
κατασκευάζειν ἠναγκαζόμεθα, ἐν αἷς οὐχ ὅσον οὐκ ἐνῴκησέ ποτε ἀλλ᾽ οὐδὲ ὄψεσθαι
αὐτῶν τινα ἔμελλε.
[5] 77. 13. 4 (388–9).
[6] See W. Schleiermacher, 'Der obergermanische Limes und spätrömische
Wehranlagen am Rhein', *33. Bericht der röm.-germ. Kommission 1943–50* (1951),
133, on pp. 146–7.

Hostility does, however, lead him to give an accurate and instructive account of the ways in which Caracalla set about raising cash[1]—the *aurum coronarium*, 'gifts' from communities or rich individuals, and the doubling of the *vicesima libertatis* and the *vicesima hereditatium*. On the latter tax the provision by which heirs who were close relatives were exempt[2] was removed and at the same time, since only citizens paid on legacies, the citizenship was extended to all the inhabitants of the Empire. This is all that Dio has to say on the famous question on which so much thought, and ink, has been expended.[3] It now seems clear that those subjects of the Empire who were not members of recognized communities were in fact excluded from the grant,[4] and to that extent Dio's account of it cannot be literally true. But his interpretation of it is if anything strengthened; low as it was, the limit below which legacies were not liable to tax[5] was probably high enough to exclude the possessions of the average peasant in the Empire. By extending the *vicesima hereditatium* to all members of recognized communities Caracalla will have included most people who were worth taxing. The mystery is hardly solved with that, but the opinion of the observer who, with Ulpian,[6] stood closest to the event is worth considering.[7] Another, less important, difficulty arises in the passage where Dio states that Caracalla, while giving good coins to the barbarians, gave debased ones to his own subjects.[8] The allegation is not effectively supported by the coins themselves.[9]

Of Caracalla's conduct in foreign relations and war only scattered, and largely derogatory, anecdotes are preserved in Dio.

---

[1] 77. 9. 2–5 (382).

[2] See Pliny, *Pan.* 37–40.

[3] The literature is summed up by Chr. Sasse, *Die Constitutio Antoniniana* (Wiesbaden, 1958).

[4] Em. Condurachi, 'La Costituzione Antoniniana e la sua applicazione nell'Impero Romano', *Dacia*, N.S. 2 (1958), 281.

[5] See J. F. Gilliam, 'The Minimum Subject to the *Vicesima Hereditatium*', *AJPh* 73 (1952), 397.

[6] *Dig.* 1. 5. 17.

[7] It follows from the character of this section of Dio's text that he does not date the *constitutio* to 212. In 'The Date of the Constitutio Antoniniana', *JEA* 48 (1962), 124, I attempt to show that there is no evidence for 212 and that the true date is probably 214.

[8] 77. 14. 3–4 (391).

[9] See H. Mattingly, *Coins of the Roman Empire in the British Museum V: Pertinax to Elagabalus* (London, 1950), p. xvii.

The purpose is explicitly to illustrate the Emperor's character—
τὸ μὲν οὖν σύμπαν τοιοῦτος ἦν. ἐν δὲ τοῖς πολέμοις ὁποῖος, ἐροῦμεν[1]—
and this purpose is re-emphasized in a passage which refers to the
expedition of 213: the Celtic people witnessed neither wisdom nor
courage in the Emperor, but found him deceitful, stupid, and
cowardly.[2] Even the endurance which Caracalla displayed in the
campaign of 213, and his determination to share the lives of the
troops in every detail, could be turned to good effect—he seemed
to think that victory lay in these things and not in good generalship.[3] Later Dio describes without pity Caracalla's mental tor-
ments—his remorse and dreams of Severus and Geta and the
physical sufferings which led him to seek the aid, in vain, of
Apollo Grannus, Asclepius, and Serapis.[4]

Similarly what Dio says of diplomatic relations with the East
in the early years is used entirely to illustrate the Emperor's
duplicity. The first example of treachery concerned Abgar IX of
Osroëne who was summoned by Caracalla and then imprisoned;[5]
unless the King travelled all the way to Gaul the incident must
have taken place before Caracalla's departure in the early spring
of 213,[6] probably in 212.[7] The same fate awaited the King of
Armenia and his sons; Dio is happy to note that this did not lead
to the submission of the Armenians, and rubs the point in with
a little apposite moralizing about the proper conduct of a monarch
towards his friends.[8] The culminating example of shamelessness
was Caracalla's letter to the Senate on the dispute between
Vologaeses V and Artabanus V, the sons of the deceased King of
Parthia (he had died in 207/8, though Dio does not make this
clear), which broke out in about 213.[9] The letter will then have
been sent while Caracalla was in Gaul, or perhaps on the first
part of his Eastern expedition in the following year; in it he
moralized upon the dangers which the dispute between two

[1] 77. 12. 1 (386).   [2] 77. 13. 3 (388).   [3] 77. 13. 1–2 (389–90).
[4] 77. 15. 2–7 (392–3). The visit to the shrine of Apollo Grannus was in 213 (on
the shrine see Robert, BE 1958, no. 422), that to Asclepius at Pergamum in the
autumn of 214 (see Magie, op. cit., ch. 28, n. 41) and that to Serapis in Alexandria
in 215.   [5] 77. 12. 1[2] (386).
[6] See von Rohden, RE 2 (1895–6), 'Aurelius' (46), 2446.
[7] A. Maricq, 'La Chronologie des dernières années de Caracalla', Syria 34 (1957),
297, corrects von Rohden's attribution of this incident to 216 (op. cit. 2449)
but puts it in 213, not noting Caracalla's absence from Rome.
[8] 77. 12. 1–2 (387).
[9] N. C. Debevoise, A Political History of Parthia (Chicago, 1938), 263.

brothers had brought upon the Parthian state, thus affording Dio the opportunity for some heavy irony at his expense.[1]

Amid all this the amount of concrete information on the campaign of 213 is very small; there are stories of the treacherous slaughter of the youth of the Alamanni,[2] a bought victory over the 'Cenni',[3] the suicide of the captured womenfolk of the Chatti and Alamanni,[4] and the establishment of relations with tribes as far as the Elbe by means of lavish payments.[5] That is all, and there is no way of discovering how full the original account was.

At the end of the year Caracalla returned to Rome,[6] and it is from the winter of 213/14 that various trials and executions reported by Dio seem to derive—the case of a youth who took into a brothel a coin bearing the image of the Emperor, the execution of two Vestal virgins and the suicide of a third, for transgression of the rule of chastity, and the suicide of Cornificia, the daughter of Marcus Aurelius.[7]

Xiphilinus, who is exceptionally inadequate for the reign of Caracalla, does not take up the story again until the stay of the Court at Nicomedia in the winter of 214/15. To fill the gap there is a passing reference to the journeys through Dacia and Thrace,[8] and an oblique mention of Caracalla's accident while crossing the Hellespont;[9] then there follows the celebration of games at Ilium and anecdotes about the visit to Pergamum.[10] What Dio records of

---

[1] 77. 12. 3–5 (387). Also 13. 3 (388).   [2] 77. 13. 5 (389).

[3] 77. 14. 1–2 (390). The name is probably corrupt. See Boissevain, ad loc. The report came from hearsay, see 14. 1 οὓς λέγεται ... and also a reference to a letter to the Senate 77. 13. 6 (389).

[4] 77. 14. 2 (390–1).   [5] 77. 14. 3–4 (391).

[6] This is difficult to establish with certainty. See von Rohden, op. cit. 2447, and Mattingly, op. cit. ccv. The *Liberalitas* VIIII of this year (Mattingly, ccxi and nos. 70, 71) does not formally prove that the Emperor himself was in Rome. But the *Itinerarium Antonini* (see van Berchem, op. cit. 170 f.) shows (Cuntz, pp. 18 f.) Caracalla's route beginning at Rome.

[7] 77. 16. 1–6a (393–5).

[8] See F. W. Drexler, *Caracallas Zug nach dem Orient und der letzte Partherkrieg* (Diss. Halle, 1880), 8 f., von Rohden, op. cit. 2447–8, and for the important work of constructing fortifications in Dacia, M. Macrea, 'Apararea granitei de vest si nord-est a Daciei pe timpul imparatului Caracalla', *SCIV* 8 (1957), 215. (French résumé 248–51). He suggests that it was at Porolissum that the negotiations with the Dacians, Vandals, and Quadi, referred to by Dio 77. 20. 3 (398) and 78. 27. 5 (435), took place.

[9] 77. 16. 7 (395) καὶ τὸν Ἑλλήσποντον οὐκ ἀκινδύνως διαβαλών. See *Vita Ant. Car.* 5. 8 and *CIL* 6. 2103a (*Acta Arvalium*), line 8 '[ex naufragii periculo s]alvus servatus sit'. See also p. 215.

[10] 77. 16. 7–8 (395–6). See Magie, op. cit., ch. 28, n. 41.

the winter at Nicomedia is again devoted to the illustration of
the Emperor's iniquities: his laziness, neglect of his senatorial
amici—and favour to his freedmen—and his absurd military
preparations.[1]

For the events of 215, apart from the Alexandrian massacre,
Dio's text is (and perhaps always was) brief and anecdotal. He
had left the Court in the winter and all that he records of Caracalla from now on must come from hearsay; the fragmentary
text gives us the death of another senator, some boastful remarks
from Caracalla, his behaviour in Antioch and a letter of his to the
Senate, quoted in part.[2] Of the Parthian expedition itself there is
the mere mention that it took place because Vologaeses refused
to give up Tiridates and a Cynic philosopher called Antiochus,
and that it ended when he did so.[3] More space is devoted to
Antiochus, who had once given a lesson in endurance to the
troops of Severus by rolling in the snow; but Dio believed that
all philosophers were fraudulent—φιλοσοφεῖν κυνηδὸν τὰ πρῶτα
ἐπλάττετο.[4] The same pattern emerges with the expedition of Theocritus into Armenia: the bare fact is mentioned, while a whole
paragraph is devoted to the rise of Theocritus himself from being
the favourite of Saoterus (Commodus' *a cubiculo*) to the post of
Caracalla's dancing-master, and finally chief adviser. His actual
function, it is clear from Dio's description, was that of *Praefectus
annonae* for the expedition.[5]

The real course of events, and the causes, of the Alexandrian
massacre carried out late in 215 remain a mystery, and the thing
is an object lesson in how little our sources help us to understand
particular events. Of the literary sources, Dio has a massacre of
the leading men of the city who came out on an embassy (possibly a *thiasos*), to greet the Emperor, followed by a massacre of
the population.[6] Herodian and the *Historia Augusta* have the last
item, but precede it by a massacre of the youth of the city, drawn
up for inspection.[7] A papyrus, the so-called *Acta Heracliti*, the record of a *cognitio* before Caracalla in 215, is probably, though not

---

[1] 77. 17–18 (396–7). See p. 21.

[2] 77. 20 2²–20. 2¹ (398–9).

[3] 77. 19. 1 (397) and 21. 1 (399). Tiridates was 'perhaps an Armenian prince',
Debevoise, op. cit. 264.   [4] 77. 19. 1–2 (397–8).

[5] 77. 21. 2–4 (399–400). See van Berchem, op. cit. 177–8.

[6] 77. 22. 2–23. 2 (400–1).

[7] Herod. 4. 8. 6–9. 8; *Vita Ant. Car.* 6. 2–3.

certainly, connected with these disturbances and suggests that the initial incident was the destruction by the mob of statues of Alexander—presumably ones being prepared for Caracalla.[1] It has a possible reference to the embassy mentioned by Dio[2] and a more dubious one to persons of military age[3] (which would support Herodian and the *Historia Augusta*). Another detail given by Dio—that strangers, other than merchants, were expelled from the city[4]—is confirmed by the last decree of Caracalla in the famous papyrus, P. Giessen 40, which lays down that Egyptians who had no valid reason for being in the city should be ejected.[5] One person who left Alexandria at this point was Origen, who fled to Caesarea.[6] Finally, the papyri add one entirely new dimension to the story—that Caracalla had plans, which were not fulfilled, for returning to Egypt in the spring of 216.[7]

So although the evidence is relatively rich in detail there is no hope of establishing an authoritative picture of the causes and course of the massacre against which Dio's version could be set. All that can be done is to set out the character of his version as it stands. He distinguishes four stages: first, previous provocation by the Alexandrians, who abused Caracalla, particularly over the murder of Geta; second, the arrival of Caracalla and the killing of the delegation; third, the occupation of the city and the massacre; and fourth, the expulsion of strangers. Finally he gives some measures which followed—the abolition of the *syssitia* and the establishment of cross-walls and guards in the city. He implies that he could have given more detail than this but preferred to spare the feelings of his readers.[8] There is no formal indication of the source of his information except two references to letters of

---

[1] See H. A. Musurillo, *The Acts of the Pagan Martyrs* (Oxford, 1954), xviii (text 77–79, commentary 229–32).

[2] Col. 2. 14.

[3] Col. 2. 1. See the restoration by P. Benoît and J. Schwartz, 'Caracalla et les troubles d'Alexandrie', *Études de Papyrologie* 7 (1948), 17, on pp. 26, 30.

[4] 77. 23. 2 (401).

[5] Text (*P. Giss.* 40, col. 2. 17 f.) and translation in F. M. Heichelheim, 'The Text of the *Constitutio Antoniniana* and the Three Other Decrees of the Emperor Caracalla contained in Papyrus Gissensis 40', *JEA* 26 (1940), 10. Heichelheim's view that the second half of col. 1 contains a separate edict (making four in all) of Caracalla is entirely hypothetical, as is his 'restoration' of it.

[6] *RE* 18. 1 (1939), 1039.

[7] J. Schwartz, 'Note sur le séjour de Caracalla en Égypte', *CE* 34 (1959), 120.

[8] 22. 3. καὶ ἵνα τὰς κατὰ μέρος συμφορὰς τὰς τότε κατασχούσας τὴν ἀθλίαν πόλιν παρῶ. . . . .

Caracalla to the Senate,¹ in which he claimed that the Alexandrians had deserved death and boasted of having executed them. He also tells a story about Theocritus and his clash with one Flavius Titianus, an official in Alexandria,² which must have occurred after the Court had arrived—and which shows that Dio had at least one informant in Egypt. If this was not the same source as that from which he got a story about politics in Egypt under Macrinus³ it was probably someone who was travelling with the Court.⁴ Dio gives no explanation of the massacre, beyond the motive of revenge, and he uses it to pile on instances of the Emperor's wickedness.⁵ It was yet another example of Caracalla's utter depravity and that was all that needed to be made known about it.

The Parthian expedition of 216 itself was not remarkable for great military exploits and Dio makes as little of it as he can. He gives briefly the occasion of the war, Caracalla's demand for the hand of Artabanus' daughter—a further element of his imitation of Alexander⁶—and Artabanus' refusal to hand her over;⁷ and the course of events—a rapid incursion into 'Media',⁸ the destruction of forts, the capture of Arbela and the despoiling of the royal tombs; the Parthians did not offer battle. Dio is compelled to look for colourful incidents to liven up the narrative, and inserts stories of two soldiers quarrelling over a wineskin and of the Emperor's encounter with a lion—a thing Caracalla had recorded himself in his report.⁹

¹ 22. 3 (Xiph.); 23. 2ª (Exc. Val. 392). The references might be to the same letter.
² 77. 21. 4 (400) ἐπιτροπεύων γὰρ ἐν τῇ Ἀλεξανδρείᾳ. Stein, *Praefekten*, 119–20 shows that this cannot mean *Praefectus Aegypti*. He was perhaps *idiologus*—see Pflaum, *Carrières*, 1085. ³ 78. 35 (443–4).
⁴ For what it is worth, *ILS* 1738 shows a freedman of Caracalla, who died 'on his way back to the city from the expeditions' in 217. No doubt there were other people who, like Dio, joined the Court for a time and then left it.
⁵ Especially 77. 23. 4 (401). τοιαῦτα περὶ τὴν ταλαίπωρον Ἀλεξάνδρειαν ἔδρασεν ὁ Αὐσόνιος θήρ . . . .
⁶ On the historical and political significance of Caracalla's plan for a marriage alliance between the two dynasties see J. Vogt, 'Die Tochter des Großkönigs und Pausanias, Alexander, Caracalla', *Satura: Früchte aus der antiken Welt O. Weinreich . . . dargebracht* (Baden-Baden, 1952), 163.
⁷ 78. 1. 1 (403). Herodian 4. 10. 1 f. has a different story. See Debevoise, op. cit. 265, and Magie, op. cit. ch. 28, n. 44.
⁸ See Magie, op. cit. ch. 28, n. 45.
⁹ 78. 1. 2–5 (403). The intention is again conscious—οὐδὲ ἔσχον τι ἐξαίρετον . . . συγγράψαι, πλὴν ὅτι . . . .

From this point up to the middle of the reign of Elagabal we
have a Vatican codex of Dio, very deficient in parts but retaining
a large proportion of the original text.[1] It is valuable not only for
what it contains itself, but especially because it makes clear that
the reconstructed text of the other parts of Dio's contemporary
history does not grossly misrepresent what he originally wrote.
Here too anecdotes, stories of the fortunes of individuals and the
examination of the personal conduct of Emperors, predominate.
Beginning with an account of the means by which Caracalla
tried to discover whether individual senators were favourable to
him or not, it moves on to a description of his behaviour in the
face of Parthian military preparations. Rhetoric as usual comes
to the aid of character analysis—θρασύτατος μὲν γὰρ ἀπειλῆσαί τι
καὶ προπετέστατος τολμῆσαι, δειλότατος δὲ διακινδυνεῦσαί πη καὶ
ἀσθενέστατος πονῆσαι ἦν.[2] There follows a description of the
Emperor's clothing—his light imitation breastplate, the Celtic
cloak from which his nickname was derived, and his Celtic shoes;
and, leading on from that, the demoralized and untrained state
of the army.[3]

Preparations for war were interrupted by the murder of the
Emperor, and it is here that Dio's narrative style comes into its
own. The whole thing is recorded in the greatest detail. First there
is the prophecy of his own ascent to the throne, which brought
Macrinus into danger, and made murder the only way out; then
a similar prophecy on the spot by an Egyptian called Serapion—
and the fate of the prophet; a detail from this story is attributed
to hearsay.[4] The murder itself, which took place on 8 April 217
as Caracalla stopped to relieve himself on the road from Edessa
to Carrhae, is described circumstantially, with the names of the
main participants.[5] Dio follows this up with an excursus on Caracalla's Scythian and German guard and on his supply of poisons;
the details about the poisons were later communicated to the
Senate by Macrinus, and some other facts, on Caracalla's dealings
with embassies from Scythia, were learnt from the barbarians
themselves.[6] Finally comes the customary statement of the length

[1] 78. 2. 2–79. 8. 3 (404–61). See Boissevain's discussion in vol. 3, pp. iii–ix.
[2] 78. 3. 1 (405).
[3] 78. 3. 2–5 (405–6). On Boissevain's reading in 3. 3 see p. 22, n. 5.
[4] 78. 4. 1–5 (406–7): 4. 5 ὥς φασι.
[5] 78. 5. 1–5 (407–8). See the discussion by E. Hohl, 'Das Ende Caracallas',
Misc. Acad. Berol. 2/1 (Berlin, 1950), 276. [6] 78. 6. 1–4 (408–9). See p. 22, n. 5.

of the Emperor's life and reign and a long section on various
portents and prophecies of his death, including a dream of Caracalla's at Antioch, his last words to Dio at Nicomedia, and incidents at the games in Rome to celebrate Severus' *dies imperii*,
which took place on the following day (9 April).[1]

A summing-up of Caracalla's reign was not required; in its
place there is a paragraph on the Emperor's fate after death—his
body was burned and the bones later taken to Rome and buried.
The senatorial order hated him to a man, but could not damn his
memory for fear of the troops, and he was later deified.[2] Dio closes
with a survey of the various names the Emperor had borne,
Bassianus, Antoninus, Caracalla—and Tarautas, after a gladiator
who was very small and very ugly in body and very fierce and
bloodthirsty in character.[3]

Macrinus

Dio's treatment of the reign of Macrinus is in many ways the
most important and revealing part of his contemporary history.
This is not solely because for the whole of it we have the (fairly
complete) original text. Two accidents combine to give it a force
and accuracy unknown to the rest of the narrative: the arrival of
an *eques* on the throne was a severe shock to conservative sentiment
and called forth in Dio a more analytical attitude to the conduct
of affairs than he shows elsewhere. This tendency is reinforced by
the fact that throughout his fourteen-month reign Macrinus was in
the East while Dio was in Rome. A large part of Dio's narrative
has therefore to be built up from the letters Macrinus sent to the
Senate and from the news of appointments affecting senators,
most of which were greeted with dismay. A further valuable
element which the situation brings into Dio's text is his reports of
senatorial and popular reactions in Rome, which form a commentary on the events of the reign. The treatment of Macrinus'
governmental measures and their reception in Rome therefore
occupies a high proportion of the text. The operations against
Parthia, such as they were, get only a few pages and the rest is
devoted to the rising of Elagabal, which began and came to
a successful conclusion within the space of a month.

[1] 78. 6. 5–8. 6 (409–11). For Severus' *dies imperii* see *Feriale Duranum*, col. 2. 3.
[2] 78. 9. 1–2 (412). See von Rohden, op. cit. 2450.
[3] 78. 9. 3 (412).

The life-story of Macrinus, with which Dio begins,[1] is in itself a superb illustration of the workings of politics in imperial Rome, the sort of story which must lie behind many an apparently orderly *cursus* inscription. Dio must have had personal acquaintance with Macrinus on the imperial *consilium*[2] and is able to testify that while his knowledge of the law was not profound he administered it with integrity. It was this, and contact with Plautianus over a lawsuit, which set him on the road to success, from the most obscure beginnings in Mauretania. He became Plautianus' financial agent, but, when he fell, avoided destruction by the protection of Fabius Cilo. This danger over, he was appointed *Praefectus vehiculorum per Flaminiam* by Severus, and by Caracalla first to some other procuratorial post and then quickly to that of *Praefectus praetorio*, probably in 212.[3] Success, even in gaining minor administrative posts, depended on personal contacts and political skill.

Once he has narrated Macrinus' initial moves to secure the throne,[4] Dio comes to his main point of criticism, Macrinus' handling of senatorial appointments.[5] The Empire saw the replacement of a system whereby power and position were the prerogatives of birth by one in which first power and then position went to those, irrespective of birth, who had the trust of the monarch or, if not that, military experience. The final break-up of the old pattern of status began precisely in Dio's lifetime and was revealed with ruthless clarity by Macrinus. Dio gives in detail the careers of two men who were sent to govern Dacia and Pannonia Inferior—to replace senators whom Macrinus wished to have safely by him. One was Marcius Claudius Agrippa, who began as the slave and hairdresser of a Roman lady and was then *advocatus fisci* of Severus; banished by him, he was brought back by Caracalla and made *a cognitionibus* and *ab epistulis* and finally adlected *inter praetorios*—which was effectively a demotion.[6] If the *Historia Augusta* is to be believed he took part in Caracalla's expedition as commander of the fleet.[7] The other was Aelius

---

[1] 78. 11. 1–3 (413).   [2] See *Cod. Just.* 9. 51. 1. Compare p. 21.
[3] For the full details of his career see H. von Petrikovits, *RE* 18 (1939), 'Opellius' (2), 542–3, and Pflaum, *Carrières* no. 248.
[4] 78. 11. 5–12. 7 (413–16). The latter part of the text is almost completely lost.
[5] See 78. 13. 1 (416).
[6] 78. 13. 2–4 (416–17). *Albo* no. 353 and Hohl, op. cit. 284, 287.
[7] *Vita Ant. Car.* 6. 7.

Triccianus, who served in the ranks of a Pannonian legion, was
domicurius of the provincial legate, and then Prefect of the legion
II *Parthica*.[1]

Worse was to follow, for Macrinus made his aged colleague as
Praefectus praetorio, M. Oclatinius Adventus (who himself had
claimed the throne and solemnly yielded it on grounds of age), not
only a senator but consul with himself for 218, and *Praefectus
Urbi*. He had been a *speculator* then a *frumentarius*, adding to the
indignity of service in the ranks the shame of being an executioner
and a spy; later he rose to be *Princeps peregrinorum* and to procuratorial posts. He was an easy target for Dio's sarcasm—μήθ' ὁρᾶν
ὑπὸ γήρως μήτ' ἀναγιγνώσκειν ὑπ' ἀπαιδευσίας μήτε πράττειν τι ὑπ'
ἀπειρίας δυνάμενον—unable to make a proper speech in the Senate,
on the day of the elections he had to pretend illness. The culminating insult, however, was that he became *Praefectus Urbi* before
being a senator—a disturbance of the proper order of appointments which was only to be expected of a man who claimed the
throne while only an *eques*.[2]

The theme of Macrinus' appointments continues here with the
promotion to *Praefecti praetorio* of Ulpius Julianus and Julianus
Nestor, who had damned themselves in Dio's eyes by serving as
Principes peregrinorum under Caracalla.[3] Later, Dio reverts to
senatorial appointments, notably a complicated series of transactions involving the proconsulship of Asia. Macrinus first
appointed C. Julius Asper,[4] ignoring his attempt to decline the
post; he was actually on his way when he decided to replace
him by Q. Anicius Faustus,[5] whom Severus had passed over
in drawing the lot for the consular provinces. As it was already
late in the year (217) he was given a second year, thus dis-
placing Aufidius Fronto (who had been consul as far back as
199 and was the son of a famous Antonine general, Aufidius
Victorinus).[6] He had originally drawn Africa, was rejected by the

---

[1] Dio 78. 13. 3 (417) has Δέκκιον Τρικκιανόν which is probably a textual corruption. See *Albo* no. 926 and *AE* 1953. 11.

[2] 78. 14. 4 (417–18): 14. 4 ταῦτα γὰρ περὶ αὐτὸν ὥσπερ τὰ καθ' ἑαυτόν, ὅτι τὴν
αὐτοκράτορα ἀρχὴν ἱππεύων ἔτι ἡρπάκει, ἐπηλυγασόμενος ἔπραξεν.

[3] 78. 15. 1 (418). Dio has τῶν ἀγγελιαφόρων ... ἡγουμένους. See Stein, *Ritterstand*,
165 f., Howe, op. cit. 73–74, and Pflaum, *Carrières* no. 288.

[4] On the name see *Albo* no. 285.

[5] *Albo* no. 27 and H. G. Pflaum, 'A propos de la date de création de la province
de Numidie', *Libyca* 5 (1957), 61, and Leglay in *CRAI* 1956, 294.

[6] *Albo* no. 69.

province, and now lost Asia as well. Offered the appropriate salary of 250,000 denarii in its place, he refused, saying that he wanted not money but a governorship, a remark which seems to have earned him restoration to Asia by Elagabal.[1] The story illustrates how carefully an Emperor had to proceed if he was not to antagonize a Senate which clung with desperation to the orderly regulation of honours and advancement. Yet Macrinus succeeded in breaking all the rules, as, for instance, when he first made Marius Secundus a senator and governor of Syria Phoenice and then gave him some function in Egypt, where no senator was supposed to be.[2]

The rest of the first part, up to the few pages on Macrinus' military operations, is largely concerned with scenes and reactions in Rome: first the fair hopes entertained, and rapidly dismissed, of the new Emperor;[3] then his first letter to the Senate in which he called himself *Caesar, Imperator, Severus, Pius, Felix, Augustus,* and *Proconsul*—οὐκ ἀναμένων τι, ὡς εἰκὸς ἦν, παρ' ἡμῶν ψήφισμα.[4] Dio was present when the letter was read out, as he reveals much later in recounting the portents of Macrinus' fall.[5] The accustomed titles were now duly voted to Macrinus and those of *Caesar* and *Princeps Juventutis* to his son Diadumenianus.[6] Dio's memory has failed him here, for in fact Diadumenianus did not receive these titles until the summer of 217; and he himself indicates this later in saying that the title of *Caesar* was awarded when Macrinus was passing through Zeugma on his expedition against Parthia. The *senatus consultum* will have followed then.[7]

What follows is a long and complicated account of Macrinus' reasons for neither deifying Caracalla nor damning his memory— and, as a counterpart to this, popular attitudes in Rome to the new Emperor and the old.[8] Reactions to Caracalla were hostile

---

[1] 78. 22. 2–5 (427–8). The lines (428. 9–10) on the restoration of the province are fragmentary. Magie, *Roman Rule,* 1585 queries.
[2] 78. 35. 1 (443).   [3] 78. 15. 2–4 (418–19).
[4] 78. 16. 2 (420). 17. 2–3 (421) seems to refer to contents of the same letter, with comments by Dio. But the reference may be to later letters. The version of the letter in Herodian 5. 1. 2–8 is clearly an invention.
[5] 78. 37. 5 (446).   [6] 78. 17. 1 (421).
[7] 78. 40. 1 (449). See H. von Petrikovits, *RE* 18 (1939), 'Opellius' (1), 540. Diadumenianus was in fact entitled *nobilissimus Caesar.*
[8] 78. 17. 4–20. 4 (421–25). The early part partially reduplicates what Dio had written about the end of Caracalla. See 78. 9. 1–2 (412) on Caracalla's fate after death.

and brought about, among other things, the abolition of the celebration of his *natalia* (4 April—so for the next year) but were partially repressed by fear of the soldiers. The crowd were enabled to acclaim the name of Martialis (the murderer of Caracalla) only by its resemblance to that of Mars[1]—the reference must be to the *ludi Martiales* of 12 May. But public opinion, which began by welcoming Macrinus, or rather rejoicing at the death of Caracalla, swung against him after the award to Diadumenianus of the title of *Caesar* and the name Antoninus. At the games to celebrate the *natalia* of Diadumenianus, on 14 September,[2] a popular outburst occurred; the crowd stretched out their hands to the heavens and shouted, 'He is the Augustus of the Romans; having him we have all.'[3] Their Augustus, it is clear, was Jupiter, for Diadumenianus' birthday fell during the *ludi romani* and on the day following the consecration of the temple of Jupiter Optimus Maximus. Here Dio emphasizes once again the relative freedom of expression which the crowd enjoyed—ὁ δὲ δῆμος, ἅτε καὶ ἐν τῇ ἀγωνίᾳ λανθάνων καὶ ὑπὸ τοῦ πλήθους σφῶν μᾶλλον θρασυνόμενος, μέγα ἀνεβόησεν. The soldiers now joined the current of feeling against Macrinus, as did the people of Pergamum who had lost some privileges granted by Caracalla; they abused Macrinus and were punished by a general loss of rights.[4] This information was probably obtained during Dio's *cura* of Pergamum and Smyrna which began in the following year.

Postponing a more detailed account of Macrinus' relations with the troops, Dio reverts to his correspondence with the Senate and its consequences. One of the pleasures of a new régime was the dispatch of those who had acted as informers under the old one. Macrinus could not afford to neglect the tradition, but refrained from sending a mass of evidence to the Senate, claiming that he had found none in Caracalla's archives. Instead he sent the names of three senators, laying down that they should be banished, but not executed.[5] The Senate added a name of its own, Lucilius Priscillianus, of whom Dio (who is a born prosopographer) gives a brief biography.[6] Priscillianus was renowned equally for

[1] 78. 18. 3 (422).
[2] 78. 20. 1 (424). *Vita Diad.* 5. 5 has 19 September.
[3] 78. 20. 2 (425).   [4] 78. 20. 4 (425).
[5] 78. 21. 1–2 (425–6).
[6] 78. 21. 3–5 (426). Dio has Λούκιος Πρισκιλλιανός. See *Albo* no. 337 and also Pflaum, *Carrières* no. 249.

his prowess in the arena and for the accusation of senators and *equites*; treasured for these qualities by Caracalla, he was adlected *inter praetorios* by him and made governor of Achaia—παρὰ τὸ καθῆκον, Dio again emphasizes. The Senate loathed him heartily and he was banished to an island.

The rest of the narrative, up to the rising of Elagabal, forms in effect an introduction, or series of introductions, to the fall of Macrinus. First there is an excursus on Julia Domna, her tentative relations with Macrinus (where the text is largely lost), her death, and her burial by Julia Maesa. Dio adds an unexceptionable, if unilluminating, comment—one cannot call the powerful fortunate unless they also enjoy private happiness.[1] This leads him on to the imminent death of Macrinus and he gives a number of portents which foreshadowed it; all of them, including one at the *Volcanalia* on 23 August, occurred in Rome.[2] From here Dio passes to Macrinus' operations against Artabanus, which themselves form the background to the promised analysis of the Emperor's relations with the troops. The military operations get little space; we have firstly the diplomatic preliminaries in which Artabanus was on the offensive[3] and then, largely lost, a description of the battles at Nisibis.[4] The chronology is obscure, since Dio's narrative is divided by subjects and Herodian does not help,[5] but it seems probable that the battles did not take place till the autumn of 217.[6] Though Macrinus claimed a victory, he had to pay reparations to Artabanus and his allies to secure peace over the winter; in commenting on this Dio reveals further group prejudices—καὶ γὰρ Μαῦρος ὢν δεινῶς ἐδείμαινεν.[7] Not only was Macrinus cowardly, his troops were restive and undisciplined. Then Dio states that Macrinus concealed the truth of the situation in his letter to the Senate; the implication is that he had private sources of information. He mentions also, what the documentary sources confirm, that Macrinus declined the title of *Parthicus*.[8]

[1] 78. 23–24. 2 (428–31).   [2] 78. 25 (431–2).
[3] 78. 26. 2–4 (432–3).   [4] 78. 26. 5–8 (433–4).
[5] See 4. 14. 3–15. 9.
[6] H. von Petrikovits, 'Die Chronologie der Regierung Macrins', *Klio* 31 (1938), 103, puts the battles in May (p. 104) without giving reasons. The coins, however, do not show *Victoria Parthica* till the next year. See Mattingly, op. cit. ccxxi–ccxxii. The only temporal reference in Dio is 26. 8 where the text is partly restored—τότε μὲν δὴ ταῦτα ἐγένετο, ἐν δὲ δὴ τῷ μετοπώρῳ τῷ τε χειμῶνι . . . .
[7] 78. 27. 1 (434).   [8] 78. 27. 2–3 (434–5).

With a brief note of settlements with Armenia and the Dacians[1]
Dio comes now to a full analysis of Macrinus' relations with the
troops, the prelude to the civil war of 218. Over and above their
indiscipline and intolerance of hardship, they were at once restive
over prospective decreases in pay and privileges and concentrated
for the war in dangerously large numbers. Macrinus in fact proposed to do no more than bring the pay of future recruits down to
the level established by Severus, and to leave that of soldiers already in service as it was;[2] this manœuvre, Dio believes, would
have succeeded if he had dispersed the troops to separate camps—
and put them under senatorial commanders. But it was not to be,
and the result was the death of the Emperor and his replacement
by one under whom nothing happened that was not wicked and
shameful.[3]

The narrative of Elagabal's rising opens with a detailed survey
of his family,[4] going back to his grandmother, Julia Maesa, the
sister of Julia Domna, and her consular husband Julius Avitus;[5]
of their two daughters, Soaemias was married to Varius Marcellus from Apamea, who served in procuratorial posts and was
then adlected into the Senate,[6] and was the mother of Varius
Avitus (Elagabal). Her sister, Julia Mammaea, was the wife of
Gessius Marcianus, from Arce in Syria, who also served as procurator.[7] The passage shows again Dio's interest in the persons
and careers of his contemporaries; but it is also significant that it
is precisely on this aspect, the official standing of the family, that
he concentrates. There is no sign that he regarded the family as
such as anything strange, exotic, or 'Oriental'. Roman senators
and *equites* from Syria were not an unknown phenomenon in the
early third century.[8]

In the next section, the early stages of the revolt, the text is
largely lost. A fragment mentions the initiative taken by one

---

[1] 78. 27. 4–5 (435).
[2] This appears to be the meaning of 78. 28. 3–4 (436). So A. Passerini, 'Gli
aumenti del soldo militare da Commodo a Massimino', *Athenaeum* 24 (1946), 145,
on pp. 156–7.
[3] 78. 9. 3 (436). A minor point of difficulty follows at this point. Dio 78. 30. 1
(437) refers to an eclipse which portended Macrinus' death. But the only eclipse
at about this time must have been that of 7 October 218, after his death had
occurred—see von Petrikovits, *Klio* 31 (1938), 105–6. Dio must simply have forgotten when it took place.   [4] 78. 30. 2–3 (437–8).   [5] *Albo* no. 286.
[6] See *RE* 8A (1955), 'Varius' (16), 407–10.   [7] *PIR*² G 171.
[8] See *Albo*, 440–1, 446–7, and Stein, *Ritterstand*, 405 f.

Eutychianus, who is almost certainly not to be identified with Valerius Comazon whom Elagabal later made *Praefectus Urbi*,[1] and there are clear references to the soldiers' hatred of Macrinus, to favourable omens from the god Elagabal, and to the plan to pass off the young Varius Avitus as the son of Caracalla.[2] The story becomes clear again with the entry of Varius Avitus into the camp (of the legion III *Gallica* near Emesa) on the morning of 16 May 218.[3] From then on there is a straightforward narrative, with some gaps in the text. The *Praefectus praetorio* Julianus attempted to storm the camp of the III *Gallica*, but on being addressed from the walls his troops deserted and he fled, to be captured and killed later. Meanwhile Macrinus arrived at the camp of the legion II *Parthica* at Apamea, proclaimed Diadumenianus *Augustus*, and distributed largesse to the troops and people. But on hearing of the death of Julianus he fled to Antioch and the II *Parthica* deserted in its turn.[4] How Dio came by his detailed and confident narrative of these events there is no direct indication. At this point he turns aside to describe the effects of the situation in other parts of the Empire—many messengers sent by both sides were killed and those who failed to come over quickly enough suffered for it later. The details he ignores as being uniform and trivial (the implication is none the less that he had information about events in other provinces), though what happened in Egypt is narrated in full.[5]

From Egypt Dio turns to the situation in Rome and the reception of Macrinus' letter, addressed to the *Praefectus Urbi*, Marius Maximus, in which he described Elagabal's rising in abusive terms and went on to discuss the grievances of the troops. Dio relates the contents of much of the letter, quotes part of it in direct speech, and gives an interjection by a member of the Senate;[6] a later passage describes more of the letter and of the debate which followed, in which Elagabal and his family were declared *hostes publici*. It is clear that Dio was present on the

---

[1] See Boissevain's discussion ad loc. (438), *Albo* no. 1174, *RE* 14A (1948), 'Valerius' (131), 2412–13, and D. M. Pippidi, 'Beiträge zur römischen Prosopographie des dritten Jahrhunderts', *Philologus* 101 (1957), 148. Dio's wording, 78. 31. 1 (438), Εὐτυχιανός τις, makes it difficult to believe that he is referring to a figure who was prominent in the following years.

[2] 78. 31. 1–3 (439).   [3] 78. 31. 4 (439–40).
[4] 78. 31. 4–34. 5 (440–3).   [5] 78. 34. 6–35. 3 (434–4).
[6] 78. 36 (444–5).

occasion.[1] This last section, along with some notes about earlier letters, comes rather awkwardly between the two passages in which Dio describes the battle between Macrinus and Elagabal near Antioch on 8 June.[2]

It remained only to describe how Diadumenianus, sent by his father to Artabanus for safety, was caught at Zeugma, and how Macrinus himself, posing as a *frumentarius*, got as far as Chalcedon by the *cursus publicus* before being arrested.[3] The details were perhaps learnt when Dio came to Bithynia a few years later. He inserts a valuable comment—if Macrinus could have got to Rome he would have been saved, for the Senate and people favoured him, resenting the impertinence of the Syrians, the youth of Elagabal, and the presumption of Gannys and Comazon. In summing up, Dio gives not only the conventional series of rhetorical contrasts between the former power and ultimate fate of the Emperor,[4] but also a considered reaffirmation of his judgement on the reign. Macrinus' only crime was that as an *eques* he had taken power himself; he should have selected a senator as the ruler of the Empire.[5]

Elagabal

Dio was in Asia throughout the reign of Elagabal and (unless he saw the young Elagabal while he was being reared at Caracalla's Court)[6] never had any personal experience of him. How he came by his information on the reign, which must have been written down under Severus Alexander,[7] can only be surmised. Some rumours and reports will have come to Pergamum and Smyrna; he quotes hearsay evidence from reliable sources for events which occurred during Elagabal's stay at Nicomedia over the winter of 218/19,[8] and refers obliquely to the news of Severus Alexander's nomination as Caesar (on 26 June 221).[9] For the rest he seems to have relied on verbal information gathered in Rome on his way between Bithynia and Africa.[10] In 222,

---

[1] 78. 38. 1–2 (446–7). See 38. 2 ἐξ ὧν . . . κατέγνωμεν.
[2] 78. 37. 3–4 (446) and 38. 2–4 (447).   [3] 78. 39–40. 2 (447–9).
[4] 78. 40. 3–5 (449–50).   [5] 78. 41. 2–4 (450–1).
[6] Herodian, 5. 3. 2–3. See Lambertz, *RE* 15A (1955), 'Varius' (10), 392.
[7] The first sentence of the narrative, 79. 1. 1 (453), already refers to Elagabal's death.   [8] See p. 121.
[9] 79. 18. 3 (471). For the date, *Feriale Duranum*, col. 2. 16–17. Cf. p. 23.
[10] See p. 121.

immediately after the death of Elagabal, the sophist Aelianus wrote a work entitled κατηγορία τοῦ Γύννιδος which he read aloud, apparently in public.[1] There was patently no lack of material.

An examination of Dio's narrative supports this hypothesis; it is a collection of anecdotes, many of which are profoundly obscene,[2] and which relate to all parts of the reign without regard to temporal order. There is a certain element of chronological sequence in that Dio describes the Emperor's journey to Rome, staying at Nicomedia over the winter of 218/19 and going on via Thrace, Moesia, and the two Pannonias;[3] while at the end he relates in order events from the adoption of Elagabal's cousin Bassianus, and his renaming as 'Alexander', to the death of Elagabal on 11 March 222.[4] These sections apart, however, Dio's whole account of Elagabal is designed as an illustration of character,[5] and the stories about him are therefore grouped by subjects—his murders of prominent men,[6] his religious innovations[7] and his private life.[8] His marriages—three are attested though Dio seems to suggest more—are collected in a single paragraph.[9] Thus stories relating to events in Rome, in Nicomedia,[10] and in Syria in 218[11] can be brought in at any point.

Little of this calls for comment. To Dio the whole episode was an outrage.[12] His attitude to the introduction of the god Elagabal and the Carthaginian Urania is of a traditional Roman pattern:

[1] Philos. VS 2. 31 (Teubner ed. 123).

[2] Above all, the story of Elagabal and Zoticus of Smyrna, 79. 16. 1–6 (468–70).

[3] 79. 3. 2 (456). He arrived in September 219—CIL 6. 31162 = ILS 2188 (29 Sept.).   [4] 79. 17. 2–20. 2 (470–3).

[5] See 79. 3. 2–3 (456) ἐν μέν τι καὶ σφόδρα ἀγαθοῦ αὐτοκράτορος ἔργον ποιήσας . . . ἐς δὲ δὴ τἆλλα πάντα καὶ αἰσχρουργότατα καὶ παρανομώτατα καὶ μιαιφονώτατα ἐξοκείλας.

[6] 79. 3. 4–7. 4 (457–61).   [7] 79. 11 (462); 79. 11. 3–12 (464).

[8] 79. 13. 2–16. 6 (465–70).

[9] 79. 9 (463). The wedding to Julia Cornelia Paula belongs to 219, the first wedding to Aquilia Severa to 220/1, that to Anicia Faustina to 221, and the second wedding to Aquilia Severa to 221/2. See Lambertz, op. cit. 401, and Ph. Lederer, 'A New Coin of Aquilia Severa of Alexandria', NC, 6th ser. 3 (1943), 94.

[10] 79. 6. 1–2 (460). 7. 3 and 8. 3 (461).

[11] 79. 3. 4 (457). Possibly also the revolts of . . . us Verus and Gellius Maximus in Syria belong to 218. They are normally assigned to 219 (e.g. Lambertz, op. cit. 396) but the context, 79. 7 (460–1), suggests that they took place before the events at Nicomedia.

[12] See especially his comment on the award to Comazon, of first the ornamenta consularia, then the consulship (220), and finally the Praefectura Urbis for three terms —ὅθεν που καὶ τοῦτ' ἐν τοῖς παρανομωτάτοις ἐξαριθμήσεται. 79. 4. 1–2 (457).

shock relieved by derision. The whole thing is an illustration of
how far social disintegration had gone, in that a senator could see
nothing in a four-year reign that deserved praise or even required
interpretation and understanding. It also shows that in considering the scandalous stories which collected round some earlier
Emperors we do not have to look to the later elaboration of
tradition. A fiercely hostile and fantastic conception of an Emperor's conduct can easily be the accurate reflection of contemporary rumour and belief.

Severus Alexander

In this reign also Dio was out of Rome, except for a brief
moment between his governorships of Africa and Dalmatia and
a few days after his second consulship in 229, the last event that
he records. What he relates of the reign, apart from information
about himself, amounts to very little. Beginning with the dispatch of some of Elagabal's aides—and the survival of Comazon[1]
—he passes to the appointment of Ulpian as *Praefectus praetorio*
and the entrustment to him of the main charge of affairs.[2] Then,
after the passage on his own movements, he comes to the only
events which (in Xiphilinus' text) he records from the internal
history of Rome under Alexander, the deaths of the Prefects
Flavianus and Chrestus at the hands of Ulpian and then the
death of Ulpian himself, which is related in more detail; it was
preceded by a battle between the populace and the troops in
Rome and followed by the dispatch of Epagathos, the main
culprit.[3] This is all that Xiphilinus has, except a general reference
to other risings and disorders. Zonaras, however, has a reference
to the influence of Mammaea and the senatorial council which
may perhaps come from Dio.[4] He could hardly have been unaware of political conditions in Rome, since the last phase of his
own career was a product of them.

[1] On the fact that Comazon now had yet another term as *Praefectus Urbis*, in succession to Fulvius, Dio produces for once a vivid and not inapposite simile—ὥσπερ
γὰρ προσωπεῖόν τι ἐς τὰ θέατρα ἐν τῷ διακένῳ τῆς τῶν κωμῳδῶν ὑποκρίσεως ἐσε-
φέρετο, οὕτω καὶ ἐκεῖνος τῇ τῶν πολιαρχησάντων ἐπ᾽ αὐτοῦ κενῇ χώρᾳ προσετάττετο
79. 21. 2 (473).
[2] 80. 1. 1 (473). Dio's abbreviated text can hardly help towards a solution of the
problems which surround the chronology of Ulpian's prefecture. See Howe, op. cit.
75–76; Pflaum, *Marbre de Thorigny*, 41–44; Stein, *Eunomia* 1 (1957), 4–6; Kunkel,
Herkunft, 245–6.
[3] 80. 2. 2–4 (424).   [4] See Boissevain, 3, p. 477.

All the rest of what Dio narrates about public affairs concerns the overthrow of Parthia and the rise of Sassanid Persia.[1] Dio's version is brief but apparently accurate. Artaxerxes the Persian defeated the Parthians in three battles,[2] killed the king Artabanus V and attacked Hatra, unsuccessfully. Artabanus was killed on 28 April 224,[3] and Artaxerxes was crowned in Ctesiphon in 226.[4] The attack on Hatra, the subjugation of large parts of Media and Parthia, and the unsuccessful invasion of Armenia, all noted by Dio, appear to be subsequent to the coronation. Dio gives two possible interpretations of the retreat from Armenia—ὡς μέν τινες λέγουσιν, ἔφυγεν, ὡς δ' ἕτεροι, ἀνεχώρησε. It seems clear that the story is made up from contemporary reports of what was happening in the East. These are the last historical events he records, and he ends by emphasizing the danger to the Empire of a power which claimed all that the ancient Persians had once held. The danger was all the greater because of the unreliability of the Roman armies—and with that he comes to the legions of Pannonia, the turbulence of the praetorian cohorts, and the conclusion of his own career as a Roman senator.

Conclusion

Dio was no Polybius. In writing the history of his own times he had no conscious historical theory or framework, but was simply concerned to carry on his History as far as fate would allow. The result is inevitably disappointing; Dio did not see, or did not appreciate, what can now be seen as the fundamental historical processes of the age, the growth of Christianity and the danger which threatened from the northern barbarians. Instead, he carries on doing much as he had done in describing reigns before his own time. The Emperors dominate the scene and the narrative is largely concerned with their actions, personal behaviour, treatment of the Senate, and campaigns. General judgements, in so far as there are any, tend to be reserved for the biographical introductions and summings-up for each reign.

---

[1] 80. 3. 2–4 (475).
[2] On the localities see H. Christensen, *L'Iran sous les Sassanides*[2] (Copenhagen, 1944), 87 f.
[3] So Christensen, op. cit., and R. Ghirshman, 'Un bas-relief d'Artaban V', *Monuments Piot* 44 (1950), 97, on pp. 105–7. A different chronology is proposed by B. Simonetta, 'A Note on Vologeses V, Artabanus V and Artavasdes', *NC*, 6th ser. 16 (1956), 77.
[4] Agathias 4. 24.

It is not only the Emperors who bulk large in the narrative of his own time. The reign of Commodus, the early part of Dio's public life, was dominated in the eyes of a young man by the remaining Antonine military figures, Claudius Pompeianus, Aufidius Victorinus, or Ulpius Marcellus (though it is notable that the first of the great Danubian generals, Valerius Maximianus,[1] finds no mention); the later period of Dio's life saw the rise of figures of a very different social background—Theocritus, Valerius Comazon, Adventus, Marcius Agrippa, Aelius Triccianus—men who rose from the ranks, from being household slaves or from humble posts in the imperial service. Dio analyses their careers with the fixed attention born of hatred and resentment. In between, the fortunes of ordinary senators and anecdotes of scenes in the Senate take up a fair proportion of the text.

Governmental measures, on the other hand, get relatively scant attention, and where he gives exceptionally valuable details of them—as with Commodus' settlement with the barbarians, Caracalla's financial methods, or Macrinus' senatorial appointments—it is usually with the design of emphasizing the enormity of an Emperor's actions. Similarly, the only wars within his time which get fairly full treatment, those of Severus against Parthia and Britain, are ones in which Dio was convinced of the wastefulness and folly of the operations (the siege of Byzantium was an exceptional case, presenting literary attractions of its own).

A curious feature of his work is that, while in writing about Augustus he solemnly warns the reader that the truth about events in the provinces or about conspiracies in the capital is hard or impossible to discover, he rarely seems conscious of any such difficulty in writing about his own time. He seems assured of his own knowledge of a large number of events both in Rome and outside it at which he was certainly not present; and these include episodes like the 'conspiracy' of Plautianus which were precisely of the type where, he said, the truth is always obscure. The basic stuff of his contemporary history was the general knowledge of affairs and incidents which any man in public life

---

[1] On the long inscription of his career see H. G. Pflaum, 'Deux carrières équestres de Lambèse et de Zana (Diana Veteranorum)', *Libyca* 3 (1955) 123 (pp. 135 f.) = *AE* 1956. 124. The latest treatment, quoting subsequent literature, is I. Berciu and Al. Popa, 'Marcus Valerius Maximianus, *legatus Augusti legionis XIII Geminae*', *SCIV* 12 (1961), 93 (French summary, 103–4). See also Pflaum, *Carrières* no. 181 *bis* and addenda (p. 982).

would possess. If he mentions what can be called 'documents'—the *album* of adultery cases under Severus, or imperial speeches and letters—this is only in the sense that he happened to come across them or hear them at the time; there is no indication that he felt the need to *consult* documents in the full sense of the word. About occasions on which he was not present he could still learn at the time from those who were; so homogeneous is this blend of personal and second-hand information that it is often difficult to be certain whether he was present on a given occasion or not.

Dio's contemporary history is therefore essentially reminiscence, though its form is the compound of history and biography which characterizes his account of earlier Emperors. He makes no attempt to step away from the standpoint which personal circumstance had given him, to avoid *studium et ira*, or to impose a pattern on his experience. Such limitations perhaps raise rather than lower the historical value of these books.

V

DIO AND ROME

BEHIND Dio and his History lies an important phenomenon which has not yet found its historian—the renaissance of the Greek cities and Greek cultural life which appears in the latter half of the first century, continues into the third, and reappears in the fourth. The peaceful and prosperous life of the Greek Near East under Roman rule represents the most complete development of Greek civilization in antiquity; more than that, it provides the vital cultural and economic link between the Hellenistic world and the Byzantine Empire[1] and is thus one of the basic elements in the history of the ancient world. Nothing would be more valuable than a full account of the life of the Greek world in the Roman period, with all the vast range of documentary and literary evidence that is available.

The whole civilization was centred on the cities. The peasants by whose work the cities lived[2] have left little trace in history; but there is evidence to show that, behind the international and almost uniform culture of the cities,[3] native languages (and no doubt local customs) survived, to emerge in the Byzantine age.[4] Greek city-life found its fullest expression in public entertainments and performances, from races and athletic contests to

[1] See N. H. Baynes, 'The Hellenistic Civilization and East Rome', *Byzantine Studies and Other Essays* (London, 1955), 1.

[2] The most remarkable single item of evidence on this point is a passage in Galen (Kühn 6, 749 f. = *Corp. Med. Graec.* 5. 4. 2, pp. 389 f.). The inhabitants of the cities as a matter of course removed the best crops in the autumn, to be stored up for the year. The peasants were left with inferior foods, and not much of those. In bad years it was possible to observe in them the gruesome effects of malnutrition, which Galen describes in detail.

[3] On the fringes of the Greek world, especially, there were cities where Greek and native cultures intermingled, for instance Dura-Europus on the Euphrates, Palmyra, or the northernmost Greek settlement, Tanais at the mouth of the Don. See D. B. Shelov in *Griechische Städte und einheimische Völker des Schwarzmeergebietes* (Berlin, 1961), 112 f.

[4] P. Charanis, 'Ethnic Changes in the Byzantine Empire in the Seventh Century', *Dumbarton Oaks Papers* 13 (1959), 23, gives (pp. 25–26) the fullest collection of the evidence. See also Rostovtzeff, *SEHRE²*, ch. 6, n. 1.

gladiatorial shows, a Roman innovation which found a ready public in the East,[1] and to public declamations by rhetors, the most distinctive feature of the age. The most famous rhetors held state in Athens or in the chief cities of Asia, Ephesus, Pergamum, and Smyrna; but their greatest triumphs were won when they appeared before the Emperor to represent a city or a province[2] and might hope to gain imperial favour and a prominent post in the imperial service. But rhetors, who gained power and standing, became the friends of Emperors and governors, and might dare to show an unwelcome proconsul the door,[3] were only the most prominent members of the wealthy classes in the Greek world, not a few of whom had Latin names and were descended from Italian merchants or settlers. Their great wealth was expended in distributions of bread or oil, games and shows, but above all in splendid buildings for their cities, like those of the sanctuary of Asclepius at Pergamum,[4] or the library at Ephesus.[5] In the early Empire at least, Roman rule brought little but benefit to the upper classes, for their privileged status was protected and indeed furthered,[6] and the way into equestrian and senatorial posts was soon open. For the lower classes in the cities, robbed of political power and at the mercy of the rich if bread was short, as it often was,[7] life was not always easy and the evidence gives occasional glimpses of riots and political strife in the East.[8]

The cultural milieu stretched from Egypt and Cyrene to Pontus and the Cimmerian Bosphorus and from Mesopotamia to Gaul, but the primacy was maintained by areas which had been Greek before Alexander's conquests, mainland Greece (or rather Athens

---

[1] L. Robert, *Les Gladiateurs dans l'Orient grec* (Paris, 1940).

[2] See, for example, Philostratus, *VS* 1. 21 (Teubner ed. 33-34), Scopelianus before Domitian; 1. 24 (42), Marcus of Byzantium before Hadrian; 1. 25 (43), Polemo before Hadrian; 2. 5 (77), Alexander of Seleuceia before Antoninus; 2. 7 (83), Hermogenes of Tarsus before Marcus Aurelius; 2. 32 (124), Heliodorus before Caracalla.

[3] Philostratus, *VS* 1. 25 (44-45), tells the story of how the sophist Polemo arrived at his house in Smyrna to find it occupied by the future Emperor, Antoninus Pius, then proconsul of Asia. He made him move out.

[4] See Th. Wiegand, *Zweiter Bericht über die Ausgrabungen in Pergamon 1928-32: das Asklepieion*, Abh. Preuß. Ak. Wiss. 1932, Ph.-hist. Kl. 5.

[5] See *Forschungen in Ephesos V. 1: die Bibliothek* (Munich, 1944).

[6] See especially A. H. M. Jones, *The Greek City* (Oxford, 1940), 170 f.

[7] The frequency of corn shortages can easily be seen from the indexes of *IGR* s.v. 'σιτοδεία'. See also Rostovtzeff, *SEHRE*², ch. 5, n. 9.

[8] The evidence is collected by Rostovtzeff, *SEHRE*², p. 621, n. 45. See also B. Baldwin, 'Lucian as a Social Satirist', *CQ*, N.S. 11 (1961), 199, especially 205-7.

alone) and the cities of Ionia.[1] Bithynia occupied the second rank, less prosperous and civilized than the province of Asia, but less remote and uncultured than Cappadocia or Pontus.[2] Its social structure was a microcosm of the historical development of Asia Minor in the classical period.[3] A small number of Greek colonies of the archaic and classical period lay along the coasts of the Propontis, but inland the native Bithynians, of Thracian origin, maintained their independence and defeated a force sent by Alexander. In the following age the Bithynian kings, Hellenized like the members of other eastern dynasties, founded a number of cities of Greek type and language in the interior and absorbed Nicaea, which Antigonus had founded with a population of Greeks and Macedonians. In the Roman period, from Julius Caesar to Vespasian, a number of new foundations were made, nearly all on the sites of existing Greek cities or villages. Still, in this period, Thracian and other pre-Greek names appear on some Bithynian inscriptions,[4] though there is no clear evidence that the native language persisted.[5] By the time of Augustus, Nicaea had a regular settlement of Romans,[6] and under the Empire a significant minority of Latin names appears in the inscriptions of the Greek cities;[7] some a result of Italian settlement, others of the acquisition of Roman citizenship.

Geographical and military factors dictated that half a century after Dio's death Nicomedia, and half a century after that Byzantium across the Straits, should become the capital of the eastern half of the Empire. But, if Bithynia was never so important as a centre of Greek civilization as it was in Roman administration, there were still a number of individuals from the province

---

[1] Note Dio's significant comment (63. 7. 1) on Tiridates' return journey from Rome in 66—καὶ εἶδε καὶ τὰς ἐν τῇ Ἀσίᾳ πόλεις, ὥστε καὶ ἐξ ἐκείνων τὴν τῶν Ῥωμαίων ἀρχὴν καταπλαγῆναι καὶ ἰσχύος ἕνεκα καὶ κάλλους.

[2] That Bithynia was joined by the Romans to Pontus as a single province was an administrative convenience which reflected no social or historical unity. The province was called 'Pontus et Bithynia'; Dio 53. 12. 4 calls it Βιθυνία μετὰ τοῦ προσκειμένου οἱ Πόντου.

[3] For what follows see A. H. M. Jones, *Cities of the Eastern Roman Provinces* (Oxford, 1937), 148 f., C. Bosch, *Die kleinasiatischen Münzen der römischen Kaiserzeit II. 1. Bithynien 1* (Stuttgart, 1935), 89 f., and G. Vitucci, *Il regno di Bitinia* (Rome, 1953), 121 f.

[4] See Bosch, op. cit. 93, n. 122.

[5] Though Charanis, op. cit. 26, notes evidence for the survival of the native language in neighbouring Mysia.

[6] Dio 51. 20. 6.   [7] Bosch, op. cit. 93, n. 120.

who gained fame in literature or rhetoric. Dio of Prusa, the rhetor and philosopher, was the most prominent; while from Nicomedia there was the historian, Flavius Arrianus, a well-known
sophist, Quirinus,[1] and an obscure one, Aelius Samius Isocrates.[2]
In Nicaea, so far as we know, there were no rivals to Dio.[3]

The formative influence of the wider Greek culture is manifest
throughout Dio's work. It is not a matter merely of the prevalence
of rhetorical forms, his attempt to follow the canons of Atticism,
or his imitation of Thucydides, fashionable in contemporary
history-writing.[4] He was familiar with the standard philosophical
justifications of monarchy and Empire[5] and could introduce the
themes of popular philosophy, as in the dialogue of Cicero and
Philiscus[6] or in a curious early fragment, also part of a speech, in
which he develops the contrast between beasts, men, and gods.[7]
There are also certain items of abstruse learning. If we can trust
his own affirmation, he had studied the early geographical literature on Britain, and he feels able to pour contempt on those
scholars who had endlessly debated about whether it was an
island or not—καὶ πολλοῖς ἐφ' ἑκάτερον, εἰδόσι μὲν οὐδὲν ἅτε μήτ'
αὐτόπταις μήτ' αὐτηκόοις τῶν ἐπιχωρίων γενομένοις, τεκμαιρο-
μένοις δὲ ὡς ἕκαστοι σχολῆς ἢ καὶ φιλολογίας εἶχον, συγγέγραπται.[8]
It is curious that history does not seem to record any such debate,
for the fact that Britain was an island was known already to
Pytheas of Massilia in the fourth century B.C.[9] To Dio, however,
the thing had only been established with the expansion of Roman
power, first by Agricola and then by Severus. It seems to have
been Severus' expedition which aroused his interest in the question, and the fact that he did not go there himself did not deter
him from inserting a colourful and notoriously inaccurate description of the island in the relevant place.[10]

---

[1] Philos, VS 2. 29. The name should perhaps be Quirinius.

[2] See Not. d. Scavi 5–6 (1944–5), 79, BE 1949, no. 233, and J. Keil, JOAI 40 (1953), 21.

[3] We know only of a grammaticus of the first half of the first century A.D., Epitherses, and his son Aemilianus, a rhetor. See RE 6 (1909), 221, 'Epitherses' (2).

[4] See Lucian, Πῶς δεῖ ἱστορίαν συγγράφειν 2, 15, 18, 19, 26; and F. J. Stein,
Dexippus et Herodianus rerum scriptores quatenus Thucydidem secuti sint (Diss. Bonn,
1957).   [5] See pp. 78 f.

[6] See pp. 50–51.   [7] Fr. 30. 2–4 (87–88).

[8] 39. 50. 3–4. Compare 66. 20. 1 (155) and see Appendix III.

[9] See J. O. Thomson, History of Ancient Geography (Cambridge, 1948), 144 f.

[10] 76. 12 (366–8). See p. 149.

The same wide reading is claimed where he discusses the origin
of the name Dyrrachium[1] or gives his account of the source of the
Nile (ὃ δὲ δὴ περὶ τοῦ Νείλου πολλαχόθεν ἀκριβώσας ἔχω, δικαιό-
τατός εἰμι εἰπεῖν)[2]—the answer was the marshes at the foot of
Mt. Atlas.[3] The passage ends with a sentence which accurately
mirrors the intellectual position of a Greek under Roman
rule:

καὶ θαυμάσῃ μηδεὶς εἰ τὰ τοῖς ἀρχαίοις Ἕλλησιν ἄγνωστα ἐξηυρή-
καμεν· πλησίον γὰρ οἱ Μακεννῖται τῇ Μαυρετανίᾳ τῇ κάτω οἰκοῦσι,
καὶ πολλοὶ τῶν ἐκεῖ στρατευομένων καὶ πρὸς τὸν Ἄτλαντα ἀφ-
ικνοῦνται.

—yet another question which Greek theorists had debated had
been solved, or appeared to be solved, by the physical might of
Rome. There was still a place, however, for the cultural *snobisme*
of a Greek. He records the story of a *pantomimus* called Theocritus,
the favourite of Saoterus and dancing-master of Caracalla, who
failed to win applause in Rome; ejected from there he went to
Lugdunum where the boorish inhabitants were delighted.[4] Dio
does not seem to have liked Gauls, and a couple of passing references indicate that he conceived them to be typically brutal,
unstable, and treacherous.[5]

Dio's learning was not limited to geography. Pompey's capture
of Jerusalem in 63 B.C. afforded an opportunity for a fairly
detailed and accurate digression on Jewish religion.[6] It was the
Sabbath[7] and the institution of the seven-day week which chiefly
interested him, and he devotes to it an excursus[8] which is in fact
an accurate account of the (probably Hellenistic) planetary week
in which each of the seven days was named after a god.[9] If there
was in reality any connexion between this and the Jewish week,
in which the days other than the Sabbath had no names, it was
very ancient and obscure. Of the two explanations that Dio gives

[1] 41. 49. 2–3. [2] 75. 13. 3–5 (351).
[3] In this he follows the view put forward by King Juba. See Thomson, op. cit.
267.
[4] 77. 21. 2 (399–400). On the imperial school of *pantomimi* and their performances
in Rome, Italy, and the western provinces see M. Sordi, 'L'epigrafe di un pantomimo recentemente scoperta a Roma', *Epigraphica* 15 (1953), 104.
[5] See Fr. 50. 2–3. Fr. 57. 6ᵇ (perhaps part of a speech—see Boissevain, ad loc.).
[6] 37. 16. 5–17. 3. See Appendix IV.
[7] See also 49. 22. 4–5 and 65. 7. 2 (140). [8] 37. 17. 4–19. 3.
[9] See Boll, *RE* 7. 2 (1912), 'Hebdomas', 2547–78.

of the construction of the *hebdomas*, one is precisely that which
had been given by Vettius Valens in his *Anthologies*.[1]

An interest in the Jews and Jewish custom[2] might naturally
have led to a similar interest in Christians, but it is one of the
curiosities of Dio's History that they are never so much as mentioned, and this in an age in which Christianity was beginning to
loom large in the attention of the ruling powers.[3] Given Dio's repressive views on religious innovation[4] one might even surmise
that his references were so hostile that Christian excerptors and
epitomists simply omitted them; but it is clear that in his account
of the 'miracle of the rainstorm' which saved a Roman army on
the Danube under Marcus Aurelius he gave simply the official
version—that the miracle was brought about by Arnuphis, an
Egyptian *magus*—and did not mention the Christian claim.[5]
Similarly, with the burning of Rome in 64 he gives a straightforward account in which Nero's guilt is not questioned[6] (had he
blamed the Christians in his text, we could have expected some
comments from Xiphilinus here also). The thing remains a
mystery, but it is difficult to believe that his total silence about
Christianity was not deliberate.

By contrast it is clear that he was an unquestioning adherent of
traditional pagan belief and observance. His literary career began
with a book, or pamphlet, on the dreams and portents by which
Severus learnt that he would ascend the throne.[7] The purpose
was no doubt diplomatic but the subject-matter was to him
a reality. Although he expresses himself in guarded terms on the
meaning of portents,[8] they bulk large in his work, even in the
account of his own time.[9] Dreams play an even more important
part, for it was τὸ δαιμόνιον (the neutral term by which he desig-
nates any divine force or intervention) which appeared to him in
his sleep, encouraged him to write his second work, on the civil

---

[1] 1. 10. Περὶ ἑπταζώνου ἤτοι σαββατικῆς ἡμέρας ἀπὸ χειρός.

[2] Dio's numerous references in Boissevain, vol. 4 (ed. Smilda), Index s.v.
'Iudaei', 'Iudaea'.

[3] See K. Bihlmeyer, *Die 'syrischen' Kaiser zu Rom (211–35) und das Christentum*
(Rottenburg, 1916).

[4] 52. 36.

[5] 71. 8 (259–60). See the comments by Xiphilinus which follow in the extant
text. Cf. J. Beaujeu, *La Religion romaine à l'apogée de l'Empire*, 1 (Paris, 1955),
342–7.

[6] 62. 16–18 (55–57).   [7] 72. 23. 1 (304). See pp. 29, 119–20.

[8] Fr. 57. 22.   [9] Index s.v. 'prodigium'.

wars of Severus, and thereafter heartened him in moments of doubt and difficulty.[1] He gives us one example of a dream which he had in the reign of Caracalla. It was that he was standing on a hill near Severus who was reviewing his army when, turning to Dio, the Emperor bade him come closer so that he might see and hear everything, and record it.[2] There is no special reason to doubt that Dio actually had this dream, which is of a well-known type, a χρηματισμός or *spectaculum* in which a god or prominent figure announces or prescribes what is to happen;[3] and this being so something more is revealed—Dio could not have dreamed thus, or at least would not have recorded it, if Severus had not been to him a respected and authoritative figure. Dio, in common with his time, made no attempt to rationalize his dreams;[4] to him they were significant events in his life whose nature required no elucidation.

Dreams take us back to an earlier episode in Dio's life, when he was in Cilicia with his father. Shortly before, a senator, Sextus Quintilius Condianus, the son of one of the brothers Quintilii, had been to the temple of Mallos to inquire of the oracle, which prophesied by dreams. The dream he had during the incubation, of a child strangling two serpents and a lion pursuing a fawn, he portrayed on a votive tablet at the temple. Later, when Condianus had departed to Syria, Dio came to examine the tablet and attempt to interpret the dream, but before he could do so news came of the murder of the Quintilii.[5]

The passage is important, for with the revival of Greek culture went the final flourishing of the pagan cult centres; the hundred years from the mid-second to the mid-third century saw the height of their prosperity, followed by a sharp decline.[6] Dio went not only to the temple at Mallos. We find him (it seems) visiting the famous Nymphaion at Apollonia and testing the prophetic powers of the river Aoos; you take some frankincense, he explains,

---

[1] 72. 23. 2–4 (304). In this Dio had respectable literary antecedents; Pliny, *Ep.* 3. 5. 4 records that Pliny the Elder had begun his twenty books on the German Wars *somnio monitus* while on military service in Germany.

[2] 78. 10. 1–2 (412–13).

[3] See E. R. Dodds, *The Greeks and the Irrational* (Berkeley and Los Angeles, 1951), 107.

[4] Ibid. 121.

[5] 72. 7. 1–2. (287–8); Condianus in Syria—72. 6. 1 (286). Cf. p. 15.

[6] See J. Geffcken, *Der Ausgang des griechisch-römischen Heidentums* (Heidelberg, 1920), ch. 1.

and murmuring what prayer you will, throw the frankincense bearing it on to the river—if the river accepts it the prayer will be granted, if not, not; and so for all subjects except death and marriage, on which no questioning of the oracle is permitted.[1] At the sanctuary of Hierapolis in Phrygia he tried a different sort of experiment, testing the asphyxiating vapours of the cavern there by bending over himself and seeing the fumes and also by sending birds over it. According to Dio and others it killed all living things except eunuchs.[2] He probably did not actually visit the two temples of *Ma* at Pontic and Cappadocian Comana, but he describes their antiquities and did some research on the intriguing question of how a Tauric wooden statue had come to (Pontic) Comana; no clear answer could be found—οὐ δύναμαι τὸ σαφὲς πολλῶν λεγομένων εὑρεῖν.[3]

Such evidence of Dio's attachment to Greek cult centres is valuable, and not the less so for the contrast it affords with his silence about the western, Latin, provinces. Apart from Britain, where there was fighting during his lifetime, no features of these provinces, over and above some details of geography or nomenclature,[4] are discussed at all. There is nothing to show that he ever went further west than Rome and Africa Proconsularis.

Such was Dio's mental horizon; and what went to balance it on the Roman side is confined to constitutional matters, not only his massively reactionary programme for setting to rights the government of his own day but also various digressions on constitutional antiquities, and passing references to contemporary constitutional and legal practice.[5] The digressions cover the history of the tribunate,[6] the censors,[7] a note on precedence in the Senate,[8] and an explanation of the place of portents in the constitution, brought in to explain why Clodius brought in a law to prevent any of the magistrates watching the heavens on the day of his

---

[1] 41. 45. See p. 14.   [2] 68. 27. 3 (215–16).

[3] 36. 11. 1–2. Dio describes both temples as being in 'Cappadocia'; that is he uses the geographical term used in Roman administration. On the temples see Magie, *Roman Rule*, ch. 8, n. 13, ch. 9, n. 9.

[4] See, for example, Fr. 56. 2 (Zon. 8. 21. 5); 57. 2. 3; 46. 50. 4–5; 46. 55. 5. It is worth noting 49. 36. 5–6 where Dio states that the correct expression is Παννόνιοι (ὥσπερ που καὶ αὐτοὶ ἑαυτοὺς καὶ Ῥωμαῖοί σφας καλοῦσι) as against Παίονες (as τῶν δὲ δὴ Ἑλλήνων τινὲς τἀληθὲς ἀγνοήσαντες . . . σφας προσεῖπον).

[5] See Appendix IV.

[6] Zon. 7. 15. 1–10 (Boissevain, vol. 1, pp. 47–50).

[7] Zon. 7. 19. 6–9 (67–68).   [8] Zon. 7. 19. 10.

case against Cicero—περὶ οὗ διὰ πλειόνων ἀναγκαῖόν ἐστιν εἰπεῖν, ὅπως σαφέστερος τοῖς πολλοῖς γένηται.[1] There is nothing to show that these discussions were derived from Dio's 'source'; that on the tribunes, for instance, is a full description of the office, with translation and explanation of the terms,[2] and a sketch of its history from its inception down to the late Republic—ending with a reference to men giving up the Patriciate in order to qualify for it.

To announce baldly that Dio was 'not a Greek but a Roman'[3] is to show a certain misconception of the historical situation. While there existed an undercurrent, perhaps a strong undercurrent, of anti-Roman feeling among Greeks, on cultural and patriotic grounds,[4] it was clearly not universal; and to be a loyal servant of the régime, and to be identified with it, was not to cease to be a Greek. It is true, admittedly, that even among those Greeks who were honoured and privileged by the state, evidence of a certain tension between the two ways of life can be detected. Apollonius of Tyana meets in Rome a youth from Messene whose father, rather than educate him as a Greek, had sent him to Rome to study law,[5] and in the fourth century Libanius complained that ambition led the youth of Antioch to the law in preference to Greek culture;[6] while Philostratus says of Herodes Atticus that he was more anxious to be a great extempore orator than to be known as a consular and descendant of consulars.[7] None the less, it should be observed, Herodes allowed the consulship to be thrust upon him, and one of the most striking features of the period is the way in which Greek families, and even individuals, manage to retain a professional standing in rhetoric or poetry or history while winning high office in Rome.

[1] 38. 13. 3–6.
[2] See Vrind, De Cassii Dionis vocabulis, 20.
[3] E. Gabba, 'Storici greci dell'impero romano da Augusto ai Severi', RSI 71 (1959), 361, on p. 378.
[4] See H. Fuchs, Der geistige Widerstand gegen Rom in der antiken Welt (Berlin, 1938), especially 14 f. and notes.
[5] Philos. VA 7. 42. 'ὁ πατὴρ ... ὄντα γάρ με Ἀρκάδα ἐκ Μεσσήνης οὐ τὰ Ἑλλήνων ἐπαίδευσεν, ἀλλ' ἐνταῦθα ἔστειλε μαθησόμενον ἤδη νομικά.'
[6] See Palm, Rom, Römertum und Imperium, 84–85. On Greeks studying Roman law see, for example, the inscriptions quoted by Kunkel, Herkunft und soziale Stellung, 264 no. 8, 269 no. 41, and in general L. Hahn, Rom und Romanismus im griechisch-römischen Osten (Leipzig, 1906), 201 f., and Marrou, History of Education, 257 f.
[7] Philos. VS 1. 25 (Teubner ed. 47).

One may think of a rhetor from Antioch on the Maeander, a high priest at Sardis and the father of senators,[1] or of an Athenian inscription in which T. Flavius Glaucus, a poet, rhetor, and philosopher—and also *advocatus fisci*—honoured his distant relation, Q. Statius Themistocles, the descendant of philosophers, consulars, and Asiarchs.[2] That is a fine example of the system at work. But its greatest glory was reserved for the cities of Asia, and one may note, for instance, an inscription from Pergamum in honour of Claudius Charax, which gives his career, including the suffect consulship of 147, ending with the words τὸν ξυγγραφέα: he wrote histories of which some fragments remain, and was a major benefactor of his city.[3] Flavius Damianus, the sophist, who was himself descended from a rich and famous family,[4] married into the leading family of Ephesus, the Vedii Antonini, who were perhaps descended from Italian settlers.[5] His descendants, as Philostratus notes, all entered the Senate.[6] In many cases it was precisely a man's reputation as a sophist which gained him power and rank in the Roman hierarchy; Dionysius was honoured at Ephesus with an inscription calling him sophist, rhetor, and *procurator Augusti*;[7] at the end of his life Adrianos was appointed *ab epistulis graecis* by Commodus,[8] while Aelius Antipater, who was the son of an *advocatus fisci* and the grandson of an Asiarch,[9] gained the same post under Severus, was the teacher of Caracalla and Geta, and was then adlected *inter consulares* and made legate of Bithynia.[10]

[1] Robert, *BE* 1959, no. 172.
[2] See J. H. Oliver, 'Two Athenian Poets', *Hesperia*, Suppl. 8 (1949), 243, stemma at p. 248.
[3] See *FGrH* 103 and Chr. Habicht, 'Zwei neue Inschriften aus Pergamon', *Ist. Mitt.* 9–10 (1959–60), 109.
[4] Philos. *VS* 2. 23.
[5] See J. Keil, 'Vedii Antonini', *RE* 15A (1955), 563 f., with Robert, *BE* 1959, no. 381, and F. Miltner, 'Vorläufiger Bericht über die Ausgrabungen in Ephesos', *JOAI* 44 (1959), Beiblatt 243; ins. nos. 3–4 (257–66). R. Syme, 'Who Was Vedius Pollio?', *JRS* 51 (1961), 23, suggests (p. 28) that the name might have been assumed in honour of P. Vedius Pollio when a local family gained the citizenship, or have been transmitted through a freedman of Pollio.
[6] See the stemma in Keil, op. cit. 565.
[7] Keil, *JOAI* 40 (1953), 6.　　　[8] Philos. *VS* 2. 10 (Teubner ed. 93–94).
[9] His father, P. Aelius Zeuxidemus Aristus Zeno, *advocatus fisci* in Phrygia and then in all Asia, *PIR²* A 281; grandfather, P. Aelius Zeuxidemus Cassianus, *PIR²* A 282.
[10] *VS* 2. 24. See *Albo*, no. 4 and Pflaum, *Carrières*, no. 230. Note also Heliodorus, from Arabia (*PIR²* H 54), who was made *advocatus fisci* at Rome.

The historical significance of the appearance of Greeks in the Roman Senate is a subject of the greatest difficulty and also, above all in view of the creation of a separate Eastern Senate a century after Dio's death, of the greatest importance. It is possible to produce statistics showing the steadily increasing number of so-called 'Orientals' and other provincials who came into the Senate and the results are, at first sight, impressive.[1] A closer look dispels that illusion, for the question immediately presents itself, what is a provincial? Senatorial statistics, for instance, represent the sons and descendants of a senator from the provinces as being themselves provincials. But for such an assumption to be well founded we must know, in each case, at least that they retained strong connexions with the province. Then there are other types of ambiguity involved. To take a prominent example from Dio's time, there is a certain temptation, for the sake of drama, to regard Septimius Severus as a native African brigand, hostile to Rome and to Graeco-Roman culture; but while the attempt to represent him as a 'Roman bureaucrat' has no validity,[2] it has to be admitted that his ancestors on his father's side had held equestrian rank for nearly a century[3] while those on his mother's side were, in all probability, descended from Italian settlers.[4] In other words he was, in social origin, a standard representative of the provincial *bourgeoisie*.[5]

Italian emigration is an important factor also in considering Greek senators. It has been shown that of 69 senators from Asia Minor up to the reign of Commodus whose *patria* is known, 55 come from Roman colonies or places where settlements of Italians are attested;[6] the majority have names with no specifically Greek elements. Fifteen of them come from Pisidian Antioch alone. This

---

[1] See M. Hammond, 'The Composition of the Senate A.D. 68–235', *JRS* 47 (1957), 74.

[2] M. Hammond, 'Septimius Severus, Roman Bureaucrat', *HSCPh* 51 (1940), 137. See the effective dismissal by T. Pekáry, 'Studien zur römischen Währungs- und Finanzgeschichte von 161 bis 235 n. Chr.', *Historia* 8 (1959), 473, n. 220.

[3] J. Guey, 'L'Inscription du grand-père de Septime-Sévère à Leptis Magna', *MSNAF* 82, N.S. 2 (1951), 161.

[4] P. Romanelli, 'Fulvii Lepcitani', *Archeologia Classica* 10 (1958), 258.

[5] It may none the less be true that, as the *Historia Augusta* claims, Severus' sister could barely speak Latin (*Vita Sept. Sev.* 15. 7) and he himself spoke with an African accent to the end of his life (19. 9). His written Latin could be extremely elegant—so Ulpian, *Digest* 1. 16. 6. 3, quoting a letter of Severus and Caracalla on *xenia*.

[6] Habicht, op. cit. 121 f. Places listed by Magie, *Roman Rule*, 1615–16.

demonstration is striking and important, but care must be used before anything positive is deduced from it. Nicaea was among the places with a settlement of Romans,[1] and from that one might conclude that a Nicaean senator called Cassius Apronianus was not a Greek by descent. The fact is that the question of origin and descent is not necessarily relevant for considering the significance of an individual or a class of men in a given historical setting. Cultures can be absorbed and shed very easily within a few generations, or even a lifetime. It is worth remembering the lines of Statius about a man who was perhaps the ancestor of Septimius Severus—

> non sermo Poenus, non habitus tibi,
> externa non mens; Italus, Italus.[2]

On the other side, the elder Seneca describes an orator from Smyrna called L. Cestius Pius, who must have been of Italian descent, as *homo graecus*—and makes clear that his Latin was not without faults.[3] Similarly, if the Vedii Antonini of Ephesus were descended from immigrants, they were none the less leading figures, as benefactors and provincial dignitaries, in a Greek milieu, as well as holders of senatorial posts. The first holder of the chair of rhetoric in Athens, P. Hordeonius Lollianus, whom an inscription from Ephesus describes as τὸν σοφιστήν, ἀμφοτέρων ῥητῆρα δικῶν μελετῇσί τε ἄριστον,[4] was himself the descendant of Italian immigrants.[5]

The lines are too blurred for statistics as such to be other than misleading. Even within the class, if it can be called one, of Greek senators there are various distinctions to be made, both local and social, before any meaningful results can emerge. Dio would have looked askance at any classification which put him with Syrians,[6] let alone with the Egyptians who began to arrive in the Senate during his lifetime.[7] Some Greek senators were the descendants of local dynasts,[8] others came from the rich *bourgeoisie* of the Greek cities, who held magistracies and high-priesthoods

---

[1] Dio 51. 20. 6.
[2] *Silvae*, 4. 5. 45–46.
[3] *Contr.* 7. 1. 27. See *PIR*² C 694.
[4] Keil, *JOAI* 40 (1953), 9.
[5] *PIR*² H 203.
[6] See p. 151.
[7] See *Albo* nos. 6 and 7, where Dio's references are given. For his attitude to Egyptians in general see 42. 34. 2 and to the Alexandrians 65. 8. 4–7 (142–3).
[8] See R. Syme, *Tacitus* (Oxford, 1958), 510–11, and Habicht, op. cit. 124–5.

in their provinces;[1] others had served in equestrian posts[2] or in the Emperor's household; and others, still rare in Dio's lifetime, came up from the lowest ranks of the army.[3]

Two factors are clearly of importance in considering the social composition of the Senate. One is the simple question of wealth.[4] Those rich enough to support public life had to be sought where they could be found, and the map of the local origins of senators is in a sense simply the map of prosperous city life within the Empire (it is significant that no British senators appear in the first three centuries). We badly need a full survey of senatorial incomes and their relation to the economy of the various parts of the Roman world. The other factor is the personal influence and personal contacts of the Emperor: cases of promotion from within the imperial service apart, Emperors were constantly being confronted with delegations manned by sophists and prominent citizens from the cities and provinces of the Empire and were thus brought into contact with men whom it might be useful, or necessary, to conciliate. On their own journeys they needed the aid of local plutocrats for the entertainment and supply of the Court, and of whole armies—as they did indeed for the regular payment of taxes. It is doubtful therefore whether we should speak of the 'policy' of an Emperor in the recruitment of the Senate, let alone say that Emperors were 'guided by a hope of increasing the efficiency of the government by a supply of competent men with a knowledge of local conditions'.[5] Those who seem to choose are not often as free (or as high-minded) as they may wish to appear, and the pressure for high positions in Rome which Greeks exercised as early as Trajan is illustrated by a well-known passage of Plutarch: Chians, Galatians, and Bithynians clamoured for office, feeling each stage in the *cursus* to be yet too low.[6]

It is as yet impossible to assess realistically the effect, if any, of the entry of Greeks into the Senate. A full study of the workings of power, patronage, and influence under the Empire has still to

[1] See A. Stein, 'Zur sozialen Stellung der provinzialen Oberpriester', 'Ἐπιτύμβιον H. Swoboda (Reichenberg, 1927), 300, and Barbieri, *Albo* 544–9.

[2] A. Stein, *Der römische Ritterstand* (Munich, 1927), 195 f. and *Albo*, 540 f.

[3] e.g. P. Valerius Comazon, *Albo* no. 1174.

[4] Rightly emphasized by Habicht, op. cit. 125.

[5] C. S. Walton, 'Oriental Senators in the Service of Rome', *JRS* 19 (1929), 38, on p. 63.

[6] Plut. *de tranqu. anim.* 10 (470 c); compare Philostratus, *VA* 5. 38.

be written, and without such an analysis generalizations can be no more than hopeful speculation. A number of isolated points must suffice instead. It has long been recognized that Greek senators tended to hold governorships predominantly in Greek-speaking lands;[1] the same pattern can be seen in the quaestorship[2] and to some extent in the military tribunate, where appointments tend to divide between the Danube and the Greek provinces; only one Greek senator in the century up to 230 can be found serving as tribune on the Rhine,[3] and none, so far as is known, in Britain. It was clearly more convenient that men should govern provinces with whose language and customs they were familiar.[4] The only danger might be if a man governed the province from which he himself came, and this was forbidden after the revolt of Avidius Cassius.[5] It is quite incorrect, however, to see this revolt as the first sign of separatism and of the split between the Eastern and Western Empires.[6] Avidius gained support in the East, particularly in some communities;[7] so also had the Italian, Vespasian, and so did another Italian, Pescennius Niger. It is a fair generalization that any army in the Empire which revolted gained the support of at least some of the communities near it.

A far more significant pattern in Dio's time lay in the extent to which it was typical of Greek senators that, while their careers were passed in Rome and various provinces, their families remained rooted in their native cities.[8] Whether or not, as Herodian records, Caracalla and Geta actually proposed to divide the Empire, with Geta removing the Greek senators to Antioch or Alexandria,[9] the conception was realistic in social terms— and approximates to what happened in the fourth century. The

---

[1] See Walton, op. cit., and P. Lambrechts, *La Composition du Sénat romain de l'accession au trône d'Hadrien à la mort de Commode (117–92)* (Antwerp, 1936), 202–7. Lambrechts' title for this section, 'Les sénateurs orientaux gouverneurs de leurs pays d'origine', is a misnomer; he in fact lists Greek senators governing Greek provinces; also H. G. Pflaum, 'Principes de l'administration romaine impériale', *Bull. de la Fac. de Lett. de Strasbourg* 35 (1958), 184 (overstated).

[2] See p. 15.

[3] Ti. Flavius Claudianus, from Antioch in Syria, military tribune of XXII *Primigenia Pia Fidelis* at Mainz, *CIL* 13. 11801. See *PIR*² F 236.

[4] The principle is expressed by Philostratus, *VA* 5. 36. φημὶ δεῖν πέμπειν . . . ἑλληνίζοντας μὲν Ἑλληνικῶν ἄρχειν, ῥωμαΐζοντας δὲ ὁμογλώττων καὶ ξυμφώνων.

[5] Dio 71. 31. 1 (272).

[6] So Lambrechts, op. cit. 202.

[7] SHA *Vita Avid. Cass.* 6. 5; 9. 1; *Vita M. Ant. Phil.* 25. 8.

[8] See pp. 9 f.   [9] Herod. 4. 3. 5–9.

historically significant feature of it is not the possibility of a division in the Empire but the implicit and unquestioned assumption
that the Greeks in their Eastern capital would form a Senate on
the Roman model.

What was most essentially Roman was Roman law and it is worth
examining the role of Greeks in its development and practice.
In the development of Roman law the Severan age was both the
definitive moment of its formulation and the period at which the
participation of Greeks is most marked;[1] and the participation of
these, and other non-Italians, did not bring any significant change
in principles or practice.[2] The formulation of the law was largely
the work of men who held equestrian posts and served in the
imperial *consilium*; it is significant therefore that the only senator
of this period who is known for certain as the author of a legal
work is M. Cn. Licinius Rufinus, from Thyatira in Lydia.[3] He
too may have descended from Italian immigrants, for there was
a settlement at Thyatira,[4] but that, as we have seen, proves
nothing to the point; an inscription from Thyatira calls Licinius
Rufinus the founder and benefactor of his city,[5] and it is a legitimate inference that he was in the full sense a native of the place,
in culture and background a Greek.

It is not clear how much law a governor or magistrate had to
know himself, though jurisdiction was a major part of the work of
anyone who ascended the *cursus*; in the field of private law Dio
mentions only that the *lex Falcidia* of 40 B.C., regulating inheri-
tances and legacies, was still in effect.[6] Greek senators can be
found as *praetores urbanus, peregrinus*, and *tutelaris*;[7] there do not seem
to be any examples of *praetores de fidei commissis, pupillaris, hastarius*,
or *de liberalibus causis*. On the other hand the son of the first
Egyptian to enter the Senate became *iuridicus per Flaminiam et
Umbriam*.[8] We do not hear of the sons of senators undergoing

---

[1] So Kunkel, *Herkunft*, 311.   [2] Ibid. 317.

[3] See L. Robert, *Hellenica* 5 (Paris, 1948), 29–34; Kunkel, op. cit. 255–6 is in-
complete.   [4] Magie, *Roman Rule*, 1616.

[5] Robert, op. cit. 31.   [6] 48. 33. 5.

[7] *Praetor urbanus*, M. Pompeius Macrinus Neos Theophanes (*PIR*[1] P 475)—on
this family and its long and close attachment to Rome, see p. 12; C. Iulius C. f. Fab.
Severus—*RE* 10 (1917), 820–2. *Praetor peregrinus*, M. Sentius Proculus—*Albo*
no. 851. *Praetor tutelaris*—a number of instances, including Claudius Pompeianus,
PIR[2] C 970 (from Ulpian, *Fr. Vat.* 232).

[8] *Albo* no. 7. A possible parallel is an *ignotus* (from Lydia?) in *ILS* 8842—
iuridicus of Tarraconensis, Apulia, Calabria, and Lycaonia.

a formal legal training—what they learned had to be picked up *ad hoc* by observation and experience, as part of the technique of government. Any Greek senator who held a magistracy or governed a Western province must have been able to take cases in Latin—and it is of interest that an inscription from Rome has a dedication by M. Aurelius Papirius Socrates, the father of a senator,[1] to someone described as 'Latinae linguae facundissimo in causis';[2] it was worth recording. Dio himself mentions that he had practised in the courts in Rome and must of course have spoken in Latin.[3] In the Greek provinces cases could be heard in Greek, and we are fortunate to have two inscriptions from Dio's time, one of a case before Caracalla in Syria[4] and another of an administrative hearing by imperial procurators in Phrygia,[5] in which the protocol is in Latin while the proceedings are in Greek.

How far Roman law itself had taken root in the Greek provinces by the early third century it is not possible to say;[6] most of the νομικοί who are attested in these provinces were probably concerned with local law.[7] An inscription from Petra, however, reveals a man who seems to claim a knowledge of Αὐσονίων . . . θεσμῶν,[8] while A. Servilius Maximus, described as *iuris prudens* and νομικός, from Apamea[9] and M. Aristonicus Timocrates at Smyrna, who was learned in the law and an advocate at the tribunal of the provincial governors, no doubt concerned themselves with both systems of law.[10]

The details here escape us. But there can be no doubt that for the leading families in the Greek East, posts in the Roman governmental hierarchy were the objects of ambition and the crown of

---

[1] *PIR²* A 1568. See Kunkel, op. cit. 222–4.

[2] *CIL* 6. 1357.   [3] 73. 12. 2 (316).

[4] W. Kunkel, 'Der Prozeß der Gohariener vor Caracalla', *Festschrift H. Lewald* (Basel, 1953), 81.

[5] W. H. C. Frend, 'A Third-century Inscription relating to *Angareia* in Phrygia', *JRS* 46 (1956), 46. See Robert, *BE* 1958 no. 469, and T. Zawadski, 'Sur une inscription de Phrygie relative au *cursus publicus*', *REA* 62 (1960), 80. Compare the inscription from the Dobrudja now republished by I. Stoian, 'De nouveau sur la plainte des paysans du territoire d'Histria', *Dacia* 3 (1959), 369, where the *subscriptio* of the governor is given in Latin.

[6] See the discussion of *Reichsrecht* and *Volksrecht* in H. F. Jolowicz, *Historical Introduction to the Study of Roman Law²* (Cambridge, 1952), 542–7.

[7] See Kunkel, *Herkunft*, 354 f. See also L. Robert, *Hellenica* 1 (1940), 62, n. 9.

[8] *IGR* 3. 1383. On this expression see Robert, *Hellenica* 5 (1948), 34 n. 3.

[9] *CIL* 3. 14188² = *IGR* 3. 16.   [10] Kunkel, op. cit. 267.

social prestige—as witness the large number of inscriptions claiming relationship with senators and consulars.[1] To gain these they
must have acquired not only Latin but certain governmental
skills and attitudes of mind. What Dio represents—and with him
a whole class, or series of classes, of men—is the fusion of two
traditions, of Greek civilization and Roman government. How
far a Greek from Asia Minor who became a senator in the second
century A.D. can be regarded as a 'Roman' is something which
the facts of his career will not necessarily tell us—though there is
a significant difference in outlook between Dio and Arrian, who
was the priest of Demeter and Kore at Nicomedia and Archon
at Athens.[2] To be a Roman in Dio's time, when only one senatorial family, the Acilii Glabriones, survived from the Republic,
was to have a certain attitude to history, to identify oneself with
an historical tradition going back to the Republic and beyond,
and to look at history from Rome outwards.[3] What no amount of
research on the prosopography of Greek senators will make clear
is revealed, for Dio at least, in the pages of his History.

It is in these terms that Dio is a Roman. He does not set out to
prove anything about Rome or to compare her Empire with the
less glorious and stable empires of the past;[4] there is no need for
him to protest about the greatness of Rome,[5] to praise her capacity for absorbing foreign skills,[6] or indeed to discuss her at all.
His identification with Rome is complete and unquestioned, and
just as hostility is unthought of, so praise is superfluous. Those
expositions of the glory of Rome which were perhaps to be
expected are confined to a passing reference where he explains
that it was the power and glory of the city which made democracy
impossible,[7] and a Thucydidean oration, put into the mouth of

[1] They are too numerous to quote. Perhaps the most striking is that of an old
Lycian lady, Marcia Tlepolemis, μάμμη συγκλητικῶν (*IGR* 4. 912). See the stemma,
*PIR*² 3, p. 230.

[2] *PIR*² F 219. E. Gabba, 'Storici greci . . .', *RSI* 71 (1959), 361, makes the contrast but oversimplifies Dio's position (see above).

[3] Note the speech by Septimius Severus, recorded by Dio 75. 8. 1 (344), in
which he invoked the names of Marius, Sulla, Pompey, Caesar, and Augustus.

[4] Compare Aelius Aristides, Εἰς 'Ρώμην, 14–58, and the commentary by J. H.
Oliver, *The Ruling Power: A Study of the Roman Empire in the Second Century after
Christ through the Roman Oration of Aelius Aristides*, Trans. Am. Phil. Assoc., N.S. 43. 4
(Philadelphia, 1953), 911–26.

[5] Compare Appian, *Prooimion* 1–44.

[6] As Arrian, *Tactica*, 33. Compare Athenaeus, *Deip.* 273 d–f.

[7] 44. 4. 2.

Julius Caesar, where he outlines the successive conquests and
military glories of the Republic.[1] The identification is perhaps
only self-conscious in the speech of Maecenas, where he recommends lavish adornment of Rome along with rigorous economy
in the provincial cities.[2] With this he accepts in full the mili-
taristic traditions of the Roman ruling class; in a vivid passage
he describes how, under Nero, people from the provinces could
sit and watch with shame the descendants of those who had
conquered their native lands performing in the arena.[3] It is
consonant with this that his only comment on the destruction of
Corinth and Carthage is to note that both places later flourished
as Roman colonies.[4] To Dio the Greeks of the classical age (οἱ
ἀρχαῖοι Ἕλληνες) were men of learning—if one knew more than
they did, it was a matter for comment[5]—though he does note
Flamininus' fear that the Greeks 'might resume their ancient
courage'.[6] Roman attitudes are predominant; he accepts the
traditional truisms about Asiatic luxury[7] and its counterpart, the
pristine vigour of the northern barbarians—until it was ruined
by hot baths.[8] On the other hand he has no comment to make on
the Kings of Bithynia,[9] an instructive contrast with the philosopher who talked of Alexander as 'mv Emperor',[10] with Appian, to
whom the Lagids were 'my kings',[11] and with Arrian, who wrote
the history of Bithynia down to its absorption by Rome.[12]

Dio thus took as his own the political and national traditions
of the Roman state, while retaining unimpaired the cultural outlook of the Greek world in which he was born. These facts might
allow us to regard him as a symbol of the process that brought
about a Roman Empire ruled from Byzantium, which survived

[1] 38. 37. 3–38. 4.   [2] 52. 30. See pp. 108–9.
[3] 61. 17. 4–5. καὶ εἶδον οἱ τότε ἄνθρωποι τὰ γένη τὰ μεγάλα, τοὺς Φουρίους τοὺς
Ὁρατίους τοὺς Φαβίους τοὺς Πορκίους τοὺς Οὐαλερίους . . . καὶ ἐδακτυλοδείκτουν γε
αὐτοὺς ἀλλήλοις, καὶ ἐπέλεγον Μακεδόνες μὲν 'οὗτός ἐστιν ὁ τοῦ Παύλου ἔκγονος',
Ἕλληνες δὲ 'οὗτος τοῦ Μομμίου', Σικελιῶται 'ἴδετε τὸν Κλαύδιον' . . . .
[4] Zon. 9. 31. 9 (See Boissevain ad loc. 1, 320). Compare the reference to the
destruction of Corinth and Carthage in *Orac. Sib.* 4. 105–6.
[5] 75. 13. 5 (351) on the sources of the Nile, quoted above.
[6] Fr. 60 μὴ οἵ τε Ἕλληνες . . . τό τε φρόνημα τὸ παλαιὸν ἀναλάβωσι.
[7] Fr. 64. 1. Compare 48. 30. 1 and the speech of Marcus Aurelius in 71. 25. 1
(266).
[8] Fr. 94. 2. Compare the speech of Boudicca, 62. 6. 2–5.
[9] See Fr. 57. 58, Fr. 69.
[10] Philos. *VS* 2. 1. (Teubner ed. 65).
[11] *Prooim.* 39.   [12] *FGrH* 156, fr. 14–29.

for a thousand years after the western part had passed away. An age may be revealed in the historians it produces, and it is hardly an accident that, as the millennium of Rome approached, it was two senators who wrote in Greek, Dio and Asinius Quadratus,[1] who composed histories of Rome going right back to the foundation of the city. Their Christian contemporaries, Hippolytus and Sextus Iulius Africanus, could go back further, to the creation of the world. But the victory of that outlook was still to come.

[1] See *Albo* no. 59, and *FGrH* 97. He wrote a Roman History of fifteen books in Ionic dialect, from the foundation to the reign of Severus Alexander, and called it, prematurely, Χιλιετηρίς. A benefactor of Ephesus and honoured at Olympia, he was quite possibly, though not certainly, of Greek origin.

CHRONOLOGICAL TABLE OF DIO'S LIFE AND WRITINGS

This table sets out the conclusions as to the dates of Dio's life and the composition of the History argued in Chapters I and II and Appendixes II and III. Only the dates of Dio's praetorship, appointment as *curator* of Pergamum and Smyrna, and second consulship can be regarded as certain. The dates at which Dio wrote the individual books of his History between 207 and 219 have been slightly adjusted to allow for the view that Book 52 was written at the end of 214; those which would emerge from a strict calculation are given in brackets beside them. These calculations are of course schematic and solely intended as a guide.

LIFE		WRITINGS
c. 163/4	Birth	
180	Comes to Rome	
182–3	With father in Cilicia	
183–8	? Post in Vigintivirate	
	? Military Tribunate	
189?	Quaestor. Enters Senate	
191?	Tribune	
193	Appointed Praetor for 194 by Pertinax	
	Summer	Pamphlet on Dreams and Portents presented to Severus.
194	Praetor	
196	In Rome during *Saturnalia* (December)	
197	Summer	Work on Civil Wars of 193–spring 197 presented to Severus. Preparation for Roman History begun.
198–204	? Praetorian governorship	
205 or 206	Suffect consul	
207	Summer	Reading for Roman History completed. Composition begun. Books 1–4 written. (1–4)
208		5–11 (5–11)
209		12–18 (12–17)
210		19–25 (18–23)
211		26–32 (24–30)
212		33–39 (31–36)
213		40–45 (37–42)

LIFE		WRITINGS	
214	December. With Caracalla at Nicomedia	46–52(Maecenas' speech).	(43–49)
215	Returns to Rome	53–58	(50–55)
216		59–63	(56–61)
217	In Senate for receipt of Macrinus' letters	64–69	(62–68)
218	In Senate	70–75	(69–74)
	May or June. Made *curator* of Pergamum and Smyrna by Macrinus. Leaves Rome		
218/19	Winter. At Pergamum		
219	First half of year	76–77	(75–77)
? 219–22		78–79 (Caracalla and Macrinus).	
221	At Pergamum and Smyrna		
222	Goes to Bithynia		
222/3	Returns to Rome		
? 222/3		80 (Elagabal).	
223	Proconsul of Africa		
224–6	Legate of Dalmatia		
226–8	Legate of Pannonia		
229	Consul II *ordinarius* with Severus Alexander		
	Returns to Nicaea		
229 or after		Postscript on Severus Alexander.	

APPENDIX I

XIPHILINUS' AND ZONARAS' EPITOMES OF DIO BOOK 54

THE references to Xiphilinus follow those used by Boissevain in his text of Dio and in the text of Xiphilinus which he prints in vol. 3, pp. 479 f. Zonaras is cited by page and line in the Teubner edition by Dindorf, vol. 2 (1869).

I have had to use my discretion in abbreviating Dio (an object lesson in the difficulty of the task). Passages are quoted in Greek at some points where Dio is followed literally, or almost literally, by one or both of his epitomizers. Where no entry appears in the Xiphilinus- or Zonaras-column opposite an entry in the Dio-column the material has been entirely omitted in the epitome. Conversely, where an entry appears in one of those columns with none in the Dio column, material has been added from another source.

DIO 54	XIPHILINUS 90-95	ZONARAS 10. 33-34
1. 1-2. Consuls of 22, portents, plague, famine.		440. 29-31. Plague and famine.
1. 3. Offer of dictatorship, attack on Senate house; mob take fasces, offer dictatorship and *cura annonae*.	90. 27. Offer of dictatorship. 90. 29. Fasces.	440. 32-441. 4. Offer of dictatorship, attack on Senate house, mob approach Augustus, offer dictatorship and *cura annonae*.
1. 4. Aug. accepts *cura*, appoints two senators, refuses dictatorship, tears clothes.	90. 29. Tears clothes.	441. 5-7. Accepts *cura*, refuses dictatorship, tears clothes.
1. 5. τήν τε γὰρ ἐξουσίαν καὶ τὴν τιμὴν καὶ ὑπὲρ τοὺς δικτάτορας ἔχων, ὀρθῶς τό τε ἐπίφθονον καὶ τὸ μισητὸν τῆς ἐπικλήσεως αὐτῶν ἐφυλάξατο.	90. 30-32. ὀρθῶς τό τε ἐπίφθονον καὶ τὸ μισητὸν τῆς κλήσεως φυλαττόμενος· τὴν γὰρ ἐξουσίαν καὶ τὴν τιμὴν ὑπὲρ τοὺς δικτάτωρας εἶχε.	441. 8-10. ὀρθῶς γὰρ καὶ συνετῶς τὸ μισητὸν τῆς ἐπικλήσεως ἐφυλάξατο καὶ ἐπίφθονον, ὑπὲρ τοὺς δικτάτωρας ἔχων τὴν ἐξουσίαν καὶ τὴν τιμήν.
2. 1. Offer of censorship. Aug. appoints Aemilius Lepidus and Munatius Plancus—		

DIO 54	XIPHILINUS 90–95	ZONARAS 10. 33–34
2. 2. the last *privati* to be censors.		
2. 3. Aug. carries out many censorial functions—		
2. 3–5. measures of Aug.		
3. 1–3. Case of Marcus Primus.	91. 1–11. Marcus Primus (little abbreviated).	
3. 4–8. Conspiracy of Murena and Caepio.		441. 10–13. Conspiracy (no names). Participants flee, soon killed.
4. 1–4. Cyprus and Gall. Narb. given to Senate. Dedication of temple of Jupiter Tonans.		
5. 1–3. War against Cantabri and Astures.		
5. 4–6. Ethiopians invade Egypt. Gaius Petronius' expedition into Ethiopia.	91. 11–27. (Almost verbatim.)	
6. 1. Aug. goes to Sicily. Riots over consular elections. ... ὥστε καὶ ἐκ τούτου διαδειχθῆναι ὅτι ἀδύνατον ἦν δημοκρατουμένους σφᾶς σωθῆναι.	91. 27–31. Aug. to Sicily. Riots at consular elections. ... [ ] ὅτι ἀδύνατον ἦν δημοκρατουμένους σωθῆναι.	441. 14–17. Aug. to Sicily. Riots at consular elections. ... ὡς κἀντεῦθεν δειχθῆναι ὅτι ἀδύνατον ἦν δημοκρατουμένους αὐτοὺς σωθῆναι.
6. 2. Place as consul left for Aug. Refuses. Disputed between Q. Lepidus and L. Silvanus. Aug. summoned.		441. 17–19. Disturbances. Aug. summoned.
6. 3. Lepidus and Silvanus to Aug. Dismissed. Aug. orders further elections. Lepidus finally elected.		
6. 4. Aug. angry. Unable to go to Rome. Puts Agrippa in charge.	91. 31–92. 1. Aug. angry. Unable to go to Rome. Sends for Agrippa.	441. 19–24 (Almost verbatim transcription of Dio.)
6. 5. Agrippa summoned, made to divorce wife, marry Julia, sent to Rome. Maecenas' advice.	92. 1–6. Gives Julia as wife to Agrippa. Sends to Rome. Maecenas' advice.	441. 24–442. 1. (Almost verbatim transcription.)

DIO 54	XIPHILINUS 90–95	ZONARAS 10. 33–34
6. 6. Agrippa τὰ μὲν ἄλλα οἰδοῦντα ἔτι εὑρὼν κατεστήσατο, expels Egyptian rites, bans election of *Praef. Urbis* because of riots.		442. 1–3. Ἀγρίππας οὖν οἰδοῦντα εὑρὼν ἐν τῇ Ῥώμῃ τὰ πράγματα κατεστήσατο.
7. 1. Aug.'s measures in Sicily: makes Syracuse and other cities colonies, crosses to Greece.		442. 3–4. Measures in Sicily, crosses to Greece.
	92. 6. Crosses to Greece.	
7. 2. Sparta given Cythera and *Syssitia*. Athens deprived of Aigina and Eretria.	92. 6–10 Sparta honoured, Athens loses Aigina.	
7. 3. (Statue of Athene moves, portent.)		
7. 4. ὁ δ' οὖν Αὔγουστος τό τε Ἑλληνικὸν διήγαγε καὶ ἐς Σάμον ἔπλευσεν, ἐνταῦθά τε ἐχείμασε.		442. 4–5. καὶ τὸ Ἑλληνικὸν διαγαγὼν ἐς τὴν Σάμον ἔπλευσε κἀκεῖ χειμάσας,
Spring 20 B.C.—to Asia, measures there and Bithynia,		442. 6–7. In spring crosses to Asia, measures there and Bithynia.
7. 5. Imperial and public provinces alike. Some get grants, some increased taxes.		
7. 6. *Libertas* of Cyzicus removed for flogging to death of Roman, similarly Tyre and Sidon.	92. 11–12. *Libertas* of Cyzicus and other cities removed for harming Roman citizens.	442. 7–10. (Almost verbatim transcription.)
8. 1. Phraates fears attack, returns standards and prisoners.	92. 12–15. Phraates fears attack, returns standards and prisoners.	
8. 2. Aug celebrates as victory.	92. 15–16. Aug. celebrates as victory.	
8. 3. Sacrifices, dedication of temple of Mars Ultor, entry to city on chariot.	92. 16–18. Sacrifices, and entry on chariot.	
8. 4. Honours voted to Aug.		

DIO 54	XIPHILINUS 90–95	ZONARAS 10. 33–34
8. 5. Julia gives birth to Gaius. Honours and games.		442. 10–11. Julia gives birth to Gaius.
9. 1. Aug. rules provinces as before, allies left with own laws; οὐδ' ἠξίωσεν οὔτε ἐκείνῳ τι προσθέσθαι οὔτε ἔτερόν τι προσκτήσασθαι, ἀλλ' ἀκριβῶς ἀρκεῖσθαι τοῖς ὑπάρχουσιν ἐδικαίου.	92. 19. ἐπῃνεῖτο δὲ καὶ ἐφ' οἷς οὐκ ἠξίου ἔτερόν τι προσκτήσασθαι, ἀλλ' ἀκριβῶς ἀρκεῖσθαι τοῖς ὑπάρχουσιν ἐδικαίου (no context).	
9. 2–5. Aug.'s disposition of client kingdoms (named and given in detail).	92. 20–24. Client kingdoms (one sentence, no details).	442. 11–12. Client kingdoms (ἐθνῶν ἡγεμονίας τισὶ δεδωκώς).
9. 6. Portent of Tiberius' rule.		
9. 7. Aug. returns to Samos for winter, rewards Samos with *libertas*.		442. 12–13. ἐπανῆλθεν εἰς Σάμον, κἀκεῖ καὶ αὖθις ἐχείμασε καὶ πολλὰ διῴκησεν.
9. 8. Numerous embassies, including Indians—	92. 24 – 93. 2. Embassies, Indians, gifts, tigers, armless boy, Zarmarus (précis of Dio's account).	442. 14–16. Embassies, Indians' gifts, tigers.
9. 9. their gifts, tigers, armless boy.		
9. 10. Suicide of Indian Zarmarus.		
10. 1–2. Gaius Sentius consul. Riots at elections. Embassy to Aug. Appoints Cn. Lucretius consul, comes to Rome himself.		442. 16–20. Riots at consular elections. Aug. hastens to Rome and appoints consul.
10. 3. Various honours voted to Aug., some accepted.		
10. 4. Preparations for greeting Aug. Enters city by night. Honours for Tiberius and Drusus.	93. 3–7. Preparations for greeting Aug. Enters by night.	442. 20–24. Preparations for greeting Aug. Enters by night.
10. 5. *Cura morum* for five years and consular power for life.		442. 24–26. *Cura morum* for five years and consular power for life (précis of Dio's paragraph).

DIO 54	XIPHILINUS 90–95	ZONARAS 10. 33–34
10. 6–7. Aug.'s measures, *leges Iuliae*.		
11. 1–7. Agrippa in Sicily and Gaul. War in Spain. Anecdotes of Agrippa's character.		
12. 1–5. Miscellaneous measures of 18 B.C.		
13–14. *Lectio Senatus*.	93. 6–8. τὴν δὲ βουλὴν αὖθις εἰς βραχύτερον συστέλλων τε καὶ ὁρίζων.	
15. 1–3. Many conspiracies against Aug. and Agrippa. Dio's observations on difficulty of discovering truth.	93. 9–10. Many conspiracies against Aug.	442. 26–27. Some conspiracies against Aug. and Agrippa.
	93. 10–12. καὶ πολλοὺς ἠνάγκαζεν ἑαυτοὺς διαχρήσασθαι· ⟨ἐν οἷς⟩ καὶ Μουρήνας ὁ παρρησιασάμενός ποτε πρὸς αὐτόν.	
15. 4. ἄλλους μέν τινας ἐδικαίωσε, hated Lepidus because of son's conspiracy [in 30 B.C.], 15. 5–6. did not execute but subjected him to humiliations.	93. 13–14. ἄλλους μὲν οὖν τινας ἐδίκασε, καὶ τὸν Λεπίδου υἱόν. Lepidus humiliated (some verbal transcription).	442. 27–31. ἄλλους μέν τινας ἐδικαίωσε, Lepidus hated because of son's conspiracy, not executed but humiliated (some verbal transcription).
15. 7–8. Anecdotes of Antistius Labeo.	93. 20–26. Second anecdote, almost verbatim.	
16. 1–2. Provisions of *lex Iulia* on marriage.		442. 31 – 443. 7. Provisions in full, almost verbatim.
16. 2–5. Moral legislation. Story of Aug.'s embarrassment in Senate over advice to Livia.	93. 26–30. Moral legislation, embarrassment of Aug.	
16. 6. Aug. judging case of adulterous marriage.	93. 31–94. 6 Aug. judging case, almost verbatim.	
16. 7. Aug.'s ruling on engagements to 10-year-old girls.		443. 7–13. (Full transcription, almost verbatim.)

DIO 54	XIPHILINUS 90-95	ZONARAS 10. 33-34

17. 1–4. Various measures of Aug.

17. 4–5. Anecdote of saying by dancer Pylades.

    94. 6–10. Anecdote in brief, saying verbatim.

18. 1. Consuls of 17 B.C. Birth of Agrippa's son Lucius. Adopted, with his brother Gaius, by Aug. and made his successors.

    443. 13–17. Birth [ὁ δὲ Ἀγρίππας καὶ ἕτερον υἱὸν ἐκ τῆς Ἰουλίας ἐγείνατο] of Lucius. Adoption of Gaius and Lucius, made successors.

18. 2–3. Various measures of Aug.

19. 1–2. Consuls of 16 B.C. Aug. leaves for Gaul—desire to avoid political tensions of Rome.

19. 3. (Alternative reason for departure.) Aug.'s relations with Maecenas' wife Terentia.

    94. 10–13. Adds from Dio ch. 19. 6: τῷ δὲ Μαικήνᾳ διὰ τὴν γυναῖκα οὐκέθ' ὁμοίως ἔχαιρεν then describes relations with Terentia (no context).

19. 4–8. Various measures of Augustus.

20. 1–6. Campaigns in Alps, Noricum, Dalmatia, Spain, Macedonia, Thrace, and on Rhine.

21. 1. Consuls of 15 B.C.

21. 2–8. Exactions of Aug.'s procurator Licinus in Gaul.

    94. 14 – 95. 9. (Story given with very slight abbreviation.)

22. 1–5. Campaigns of Drusus and Tiberius in Raetia.

    95. 10 f. τὸν δὲ δὴ Τιβέριον καὶ τὸν Δροῦσον τῆς γυναικὸς αὐτοῦ παῖδας ὁ Καῖσαρ ἐπὶ τοὺς πολεμίους ἔπεμπε, καὶ κατεστρέφοντο οὗτοι τούς τε παριστρίους αὐτῷ βαρβάρους καὶ τοὺς παρωκεανείους Κελτούς. Xiphilinus

DIO 54	XIPHILINUS 90–95	ZONARAS 10. 33–34
	here abandons Dio's order and mentions Drusus' death and Tiberius' accession, the adoption of Gaius and Lucius (Dio, ch. 18. 1, above), Aug. wearing a breastplate in the Senate (12. 3), and isolated points from 35. 2–3, 30. 4, and 27. 4.	
23. 1. Death of Vedius Pollio. Recorded because of his wealth and brutality.	96. 11–16. Death of Vedius. Reasons given (uses first person, different construction).	
23. 2–6. Man-eating lampreys, story of Aug. at dinner. Property inherited from Pollio.	96. 16–97. 6. (Account in full with slight verbal changes.)	443. 17–32. Story of Aug. at dinner only (no context).
23. 7. Aug. founds cities in Gaul and Spain, restores *libertas* of Cyzicus, aids Paphos, giving title *Augusta*.	97. 6–8. πόλεις μέντοι συχνὰς ὁ Καῖσαρ ἄλλῃ τε πανταχῇ καὶ κατὰ τὴν Ἰβηρίαν καὶ Γαλατίαν ἀπῴκισεν.	
23. 8. Dio's reasons for recording these measures.		
	97. 9–12. Dedication of temple of Quirinus (from Dio, ch. 19. 4).	
24. 1. Consuls of 14 B.C. Aediles resign, then resume office.		
24. 2–3. Fire in Rome, and rebuilding. Campaigns in Pannonia and Alps.	(Xiphilinus omits the rest of Book 54.)	
24. 4–8. Settlement of affairs of Bosporan kingdom.		
25–27. Aug.'s return to Rome and various measures.		
28. 1–2. Consuls of 12 B.C. Agrippa given		

DIO 54	XIPHILINUS 90–95	ZONARAS 10. 33–34
trib. pot. for five years and *imperium maius* for campaign in Pannonia. Pannonians keep quiet, Agrippa returns to Campania, falls ill.		
28. 3. Aug. returns from Athens, finds Agrippa dead, brings body to Rome.		444. 1–3. Ἀγρίππας δὲ νοσήσας ἐν Καμπανίᾳ ἀπέθανεν· οὗ ὁ Καῖσαρ παραγενόμενος τό τε σῶμα αὐτοῦ εἰς τὴν Ῥώμην ἐκόμισε.
28. 3–5. Funeral oration by Aug. (with discussion of why the body was covered with a shroud). Agrippa buried in Aug.'s private tomb.		444. 3–5. Funeral oration, burial in Aug.'s tomb.
29. 1–3. Summing-up of Agrippa's career and character: . . . τά τε ἄλλα ἄριστος τῶν καθ᾽ ἑαυτὸν ἀνθρώπων διαφανῶς γενόμενος, καὶ τῇ τοῦ Αὐγούστου φιλίᾳ πρός τε τὸ αὐτῷ ἐκείνῳ καὶ πρὸς τὸ τῷ κοινῷ συμφορώτατον χρησάμενος.		444. 7–14. Summing-up: . . . τά τε γὰρ ἄλλα ἄριστος τῶν καθ᾽ ἑαυτὸν ἀνθρώπων ἐγένετο καὶ τῇ τοῦ Αὐγούστου φιλίᾳ πρὸς τὸ ἐκείνου καὶ πρὸς τὸ κοινῇ συμφέρον ἐκέχρητο.
29. 4. Legacies to people of Rome.		
29. 5. Legacies to Aug.		
29. 5–8. Public regret, and portents.		
30. 1–5. Aug.'s *cura morum* renewed. Various measures.		
31. 1. With death of Agrippa, need for partner in Empire. Aug. reluctantly chooses Tiberius — Agrippa's son is too young.		444. 14–18. Agrippa's death, need of partner, Tiberius (some verbal transcription).
31. 2. Tiberius divorced from his pregnant wife,		444. 18–20. Divorce and re-marriage (less detail,

DIO 54

married to Agrippa's widow Julia, and sent off to Pannonia.

31. 3. Tiberius defeats Pannonians.

31. 4. Celebration of victory in Rome.

32-33. Drusus' victories in Germany.

34. 1-2. Celebrations in Rome and elsewhere.

34. 3. Tiberius defeats Pannonians and Dalmatians.

34. 4. Dalmatia entrusted to Emperor.

34. 5-7. Lucius Piso quells disturbances in Thrace.

35. 1. Census, *lectio Senatus*, ruling on senatorial quorum.

35. 2. ἐπειδή τε ἀργύριον αὖθις ἐς εἰκόνας αὐτοῦ καὶ ἐκείνη καὶ ὁ δῆμος συνεσήνεγκαν, ἑαυτοῦ μὲν οὐδεμίαν, Ὑγιείας δὲ δημοσίας καὶ προσέτι καὶ Ὁμονοίας Εἰρήνης τε ἔστησεν.

35. 2-3. Aug. receives contributions of people on 1 Jan., makes gifts of larger amounts to senators and the rest.

35. 4-5. Death of Aug.'s sister Octavia, buried in tomb of Julii. Funeral orations by Aug. and Drusus. Senators wear mourning. Body carried by in-laws, honours voted, not all accepted.

36. 1-2. Various measures of Aug.

36. 2-4. Campaigns of Tiberius and Drusus. They return to Rome.

XIPHILINUS 90-95

ZONARAS 10. 33-34

some verbal transcription).

444. 20-22. εἶτα διά τε τούτου καὶ διὰ τοῦ Δρούσου καὶ διὰ Πείσωνος Λουκίου πολλὰ τῶν ἐθνῶν ὑπηγάγετο.

444. 22-25. ἀργύριον δὲ τῆς τε βουλῆς καὶ τοῦ δήμου εἰς εἰκόνας αὐτοῦ συνενεγκότων, ἑαυτοῦ μὲν οὐδεμίαν ἔστησεν, Ὑγιείας δὲ δημοσίας καὶ Ὁμονοίας καὶ Εἰρήνης εἰκόνας εἰργάσατο.

444. 26-30. Contributions on 1 Jan., Aug.'s gifts (abbreviated, some verbal transcription).

444. 30-445. 2. Death of Octavia, funeral orations by Aug. and Drusus, Senate assumes mourning.

APPENDIX II

THE DATE OF DIO'S FIRST CONSULSHIP

THE orthodox view is that Dio was consul for the first time under Septimius Severus. From this it would follow that in his later posts he was consular *curator* of Pergamum and Smyrna, proconsul of Africa, and then went on to be imperial legate of Dalmatia and Pannonia. The other view is that he was consul for the first time in 223 or 224, under Alexander Severus;[1] on this assumption he was a praetorian *curator* (which was far more common) and legate of the legion III *Augusta* in Numidia, also a praetorian post. A further consequence of this view is that he was out of favour under Severus and Caracalla and that this affected both his attitude to them and his political views in general.

Recent writers on the *Fasti* of North Africa have simply assumed that Dio was the proconsul of Africa.[2] The question does not yet admit of such high-handed treatment; the argument is delicately balanced and it will be necessary to take the evidence for each of the relevant offices in turn. The most important passage on the consulate occurs in Dio's summing-up of the character of Severus and his rule:

(Severus) ἐνεκάλει μὲν τοῖς μὴ σωφρονοῦσιν, ὡς καὶ περὶ τῆς μοιχείας νομοθετῆσαί τινα· καὶ διὰ τοῦτο γραφαὶ αὐτῆς ὅσαι πλεῖσται ἐγένοντο (τρισχιλίας γοῦν ὑπατεύων εὗρον ἐν τῷ πίνακι ἐγγεγραμμένας).[3]

This has been taken to mean that 3,000 was the *total* of prosecutions under Severus, and therefore that Dio saw the list after Severus' death.[4] There is some difficulty about this view, for it is not clear that lists of prosecutions were filed, or in what form; the only records of this sort we know of are the *commentarii principum*, which included information on delations and trials,[5] but it is difficult to believe that

---

[1] E. Gabba, 'Sulla "Storia Romana" di Cassio Dione', *RSI* 67 (1955), 289. The two views are tabulated by A. Wirth, *Quaestiones Severianae* (Diss. Leipzig, 1888), 54 f.

[2] E. Birley, 'The Governors of Numidia, A.D. 193–268', *JRS* 40 (1950), 60 ignores Dio. B. E. Thomasson, *Die Statthalter der römischen Provinzen Nordafrikas von Augustus bis Diokletian* (Lund, 1960) 2, 118–19, lists him, without discussion, as proconsul of Africa.

[3] 76. 16. 4 (371).

[4] So Gabba, op. cit. 289–90, and M. Platnauer, *The Life and Reign of the Emperor Lucius Septimius Severus* (Oxford, 1918), 4 n. 4.

[5] References collected in Furneaux's edition of Tacitus' *Annals* (Oxford, 1896), I, 19–20.

'ὁ πίναξ' could refer to these. A far more convincing interpretation was given by Mommsen[1]—the πίναξ contained the list of cases *pending* at the moment;[2] confirmation comes from a papyrus which has a reference to accusers who left defendants *in albo pendentes*.[3] The only obscurity about this interpretation is that there is no obvious connexion between being (suffect) consul and seeing the album of prosecutions, since the consuls did not preside at the *quaestio de adulteriis*. The passage might, however, indicate that these cases were taken in the Senate, where the consuls presided.[4]

Dio makes two other passing references, using the first person plural, to consuls and *consulares*. In Book 43 he notes that in his own time all consuls held office for only two months. The *ordinarii* gave their names to the year but otherwise there was no distinction—οὐδὲν διαφέρομεν ἀλλήλων.[5] The sudden use of the first person is awkward and might be due to a subsequent correction of the text. But the other passage, in Book 60, seems perfectly normal—not only Emperors but also *consulares* were now carried in litters—οὐχ ὅτι οἱ αὐτοκράτορες ἀλλὰ καὶ ἡμεῖς οἱ ὑπατευκότες διφροφορούμεθα.[6] If these passages are not subsequent additions they will have been written in about 213 and 216 respectively.[7]

So far, the evidence points all the same way, though not quite conclusively. The next point is the *cura* of Pergamum and Smyrna to which Dio was appointed by Macrinus.[8] Praetorian *curatores* are far more frequent than consular ones, but some consulars with this post are known, for instance an anonymous *curator* of Pergamon[9] and Rutilius Pudens Crispinus, consul between 235 and 238 and later *curator* of some Italian towns.[10] The *cura* therefore proves nothing.

The nub of the whole question is the post held by Dio in Africa. Two arguments have been used to oppose the orthodox view. The first is that if Dio was proconsul of Africa and then went on to govern imperial provinces this was a unique case and therefore unacceptable.[11] The second, put forward by Vrind[12] and accepted by Gabba, rests on the terminology in which Dio describes his African post.

The first argument cannot be formally sustained. Cases where men governed imperial provinces after the proconsulates of Africa or Asia

---

[1] Th. Mommsen, *Römisches Strafrecht* (Leipzig, 1899), 220 n. 5; 696 n. 2.
[2] The formula is given in *Dig.* 48. 2. 3 *praef.* (Paulus).
[3] *BGU* 611, col. 2. 14. On the text see J. Stroux, 'Ein Gerichtsreform des Kaisers Claudius', *SBAW* Ph.-hist. Kl. 8 (1929).
[4] The point is discussed, and left open, by Mommsen, op. cit. 696 n. 2.
[5] 43. 46. 5–6.   [6] 60. 2. 3.
[7] See the Chronological Table, pp. 193–4.   [8] 79. 7. 4 (461).
[9] *Albo* no. 551.   [10] *Albo* no. 1147.
[11] Gabba, op. cit. 292.
[12] G. Vrind, op. cit. 158 f.

are rare, but can be found. There are two first-century examples,
Ti. Plautius Silvanus Aelianus, proconsul of Asia soon after 54 and
later legate of Moesia Inferior and Tarraconensis,[1] and (in a period of
civil war) C. Fonteius Agrippa, proconsul of Asia in 68, legate of
Moesia in 69.[2] From the second century we have Bruttius Praesens,
suffect consul in 118 or 119, proconsul of Africa in 133 or 134, legate
of Syria in 135–7, and *consul ordinarius* in 139.[3] These cases are certain
and there are others which are less certain,[4] though none in either
category from the Severan period. The orthodox view cannot therefore be ruled out on this count, though it would make Dio's career
a rarity, unique so far as we know among his own contemporaries.
But, whichever solution is adopted, Dio's career did not follow any
known rules.

Vrind's view rests on the expression Dio uses in speaking of his
African post—τὴν ἐν τῇ Ἀφρικῇ ἡγεμονίαν[5]—as opposed, that is, to τῆς
Ἀφρικῆς ἄρχειν or ἡγεμονεύειν which he uses of the proconsulship.[6] The
force of the distinction, as Vrind sees it, is that ἄρχειν with the genitive
denotes the government of a region, while the use of the preposition
ἐν indicates the carrying out of a function within an area. Dio was
therefore legate of the legion III *Augusta* in Numidia, a post which
was not, technically, the governorship of the area.[7] The whole basis of
the argument is removed, however, if Numidia had become a full
province not, as Vrind tried to prove, under Severus Alexander but
under Septimius Severus. Recent attempts to demonstrate that the
change took place in the long command of Q. Anicius Faustus (196
or 197–201)[8] are not entirely conclusive; but an inscription of Ti.
Claudius Subatianus Proculus, legate in 208/10, refers to him as *leg.
Augg. pr. pr. prov. splend. Numid.*[9] and, while this will not help to date
the actual moment of the change, it does make clear that by the early

---

[1] R. Hanslik, 'Prosopographische Bemerkungen', *JÖAI* 41 (1954), 159, on
p. 163.

[2] A. Stein, *Die Legaten von Moesien* (Budapest, 1940), 29 f.

[3] H. G. Pflaum and G. Ch. Picard, 'Notes d'épigraphie latine', *Karthago* 2
(1951), 89 = *AE* 1952. 94; Thomasson, op. cit. 2. 66–68. Compare R. Syme,
'Pliny's Less Successful Friends', *Historia* 9 (1960), 362, on pp. 374–6.

[4] T. Pomponius Proculus Vitrasius Pollio, Hanslik, op. cit. 161–3. See H. G.
Pflaum, *CRAI* 1956, 195–6, and Thomasson, op. cit. 2. 84. L. Venuleius Apronianus
Octavius, Hanslik, op. cit. 166–70 and *RE* 15A (1955), 822. C. Aufidius Victorinus,
H. G. Pflaum, 'La Carrière de C. Aufidius Victorinus, condisciple de Marc-
Aurèle', *CRAI* 1956, 189–200. L. Hedius Rufus Lollianus Avitus, *PIR²* H 40.

[5] 49. 36. 4; 80. 1. 2–3 (474).

[6] See Vrind, op. cit. 158 n. 390.   [7] Op. cit. 141–52.

[8] M. Leglay, 'Inscriptions de Lambèse sur les deux premiers légats de la province de Numidie', *CRAI* 1956, 294; H. G. Pflaum, 'A propos de la date de création de la province de Numidie', *Libyca* 5 (1957), 61. See Thomasson, op. cit. 1. 86.

[9] *AE* 1911. 107 = *ILS* 9488 (Cuicul).

220's the province of Numidia as such was in being. The change in status was but slight, for the legate of III *Augusta* had always in effect carried out the functions of a governor. Tertullian, writing in 211–13, can still call him the *praeses legionis*,[1] while Dio in his own passage on the separation of the legion and the province in A.D. 39 does not seem to be aware of any alteration since that date.[2]

The orthodox view must be accepted. It is possible to be reasonably sure that Dio's career, though not according to pattern, was not so odd that some thirty years elapsed between his praetorship and his suffect consulate. Given, therefore, that Dio's first consulate was in the reign of Severus, is it possible to date it more closely? The primary passage on the consulate makes clear that it could not have been very near the end of Severus' reign; Severus was for a time, Dio says, very strict over adultery cases; then, meeting with little response, lost interest. All these phases must (presumably) have been gone through before Severus' departure to Britain in 208 and after his return from the East in 202—perhaps indeed after his visit to Africa in 202–3. The relevant period is therefore from the latter half of 203 to 207. Calculating from Dio's proconsulship, a post which was normally at this period held some 15–17 years after the consulate,[3] and which he took up about 223, one arrives at 206–8. The interval might have been lengthened by the fact that Dio was ill for a time before he went to Africa. The supposition that he was consul in 205 or 206 cannot be far wrong.[4]

[1] *Ad Scap.* 4.

[2] 59. 20. 7 (Gaius) δίχα τὸ ἔθνος νείμας ἑτέρῳ τό τε στρατιωτικὸν καὶ τοὺς Νομάδας τοὺς περὶ αὐτὸ προσέταξε· καὶ ἐξ ἐκείνου καὶ δεῦρο τοῦτο γίγνεται. Written in about 216.

[3] Thomasson, op. cit. 1. 31.

[4] This would make him consul in his early forties and thus be in accordance with the normal pattern. See M. Hammond, *The Antonine Monarchy* (American Academy in Rome, 1959), 291.

APPENDIX III

REFERENCES IN THE HISTORY TO DATABLE EVENTS WITHIN DIO'S LIFETIME

36. 6. 2. Nisibis . . . καὶ νῦν μὲν ἡμετέρα ἐστὶ καὶ ἄποικος ἡμῶν νομίζεται. Nisibis, which was probably taken by Lucius Verus, became a colony in A.D. 196. See RE 17. 1 (1936), 737. Dio notes the conferment of the title colonia in 75. 3. 2–3 (340) and complains that the 'bulwark of Syria' was merely a cause of continual wars against the neighbouring Medes and Parthians. This passage in its turn offers confirmation that the main bulk of Dio's History, up to the death of Severus, was written before the rise of Persia (224).

39. 50. 4. Britain. προϊόντος δὲ δὴ τοῦ χρόνου πρότερόν τε ἐπ᾽ Ἀγρικόλου ἀντιστρατήγου καὶ νῦν ἐπὶ Σεουήρου αὐτοκράτορος νῆσος οὖσα σαφῶς ἐλήλεγκται. Dio makes a further reference to Agricola in the appropriate place, giving the story of how some deserters sailed round the island (66. 20. 1–2: Tac. Agric. 28). 76. 12. 5 (367) shows that the (partly missing) account of Britain, which he attached to the narrative of Severus' campaigns in 208–11, also related how the fact that Britain was an island was again proved. The expression νῦν ἐπὶ Σεουήρου αὐτοκράτορος must mean 'recently, in the reign of Severus'; Book 39 should have been written in 212 or 213.

40. 14. On the Parthian Empire. This passage confirms that the main body of the text was written before the 220's. Parthia is described, largely in the present tense, as a powerful enemy of Rome from 54 B.C. up to and including the moment of writing. The passage should have been written in 213, when diplomatic relations on the Eastern frontier were already tense (see p. 154).

46. 46. 4. Σεουῆρος γὰρ αὐτοκράτωρ πρῶτος Πλαυτιανὸν ὑπατικαῖς τιμαῖς τιμήσας, καὶ μετὰ τοῦτο ἔς τε τὸ βουλευτικὸν ἐσαγαγὼν καὶ ὕπατον ἀποδείξας, ὡς καὶ δεύτερον ὑπατεύσαντα ἀνεκήρυξεν, καὶ ἀπ᾽ ἐκείνου καὶ ἐφ᾽ ἑτέρων τὸ αὐτὸ ἐγένετο. Plautianus was consul ordinarius (nominally bis) in 203 and was killed in 205 (PIR² F 554). 58. 14. 1 has another reference to Plautianus, comparing Sejanus' power to his. On the comparison see E. Köstermann, 'Der Sturz Sejans', Hermes 83 (1955), 350. The main chronological interest of the passage lies in the last clause, the reference to nominal consules bis after Plautianus. The list of consules ordinarii in the following

years (see A. Degrassi, *I Fasti Consolari dell'Impero Romano* (Rome, 1952), 57 f.) does not reveal any before Q. Maecius Laetus in 215 (on his career see *Albo* no. 341, Stein, *Praefekten von Ägypten*, 110–11, and Pflaum, *Carrières* no. 219). The next was M. Oclatinius Adventus (*Albo* no. 1117 and Addenda, and Pflaum, op. cit. no. 247) in 218. Dio in 78. 13. 1 (416) refers to this with the words ὅπερ ἐπὶ τοῦ Σεουήρου ἀρξάμενον καὶ ὁ υἱὸς αὐτοῦ ἐπεποιήκει. See also Stein, *Ritterstand*, 249 f. If Dio's use of the plural (ἑτέρων) is to be taken literally, 46. 46. 4 must date from not earlier than 217 (when Adventus was designated consul). The suggested scheme would put the writing of it in about 214. A single clause at the end of a sentence does not, however, seem sufficient reason for abandoning the scheme; and it has to be inferred that the clause is an addition, put in when Dio was confronted with yet another disruption of the established system of senatorial advancement. If the plural could be regarded as rhetorical, then the passage could have been written as it stands in 214.

46. 46. 7. The troops who came with Severus to Rome in 193 terrified him and the Senate with demands for money, which he satisfied. In the extant text Dio says that the city was crowded with troops— 74. 2. 3 (325)—but does not mention this donative. Compare SHA, *Vita Sept. Sev.* 7. 6, which also cites the parallel between the demands of Octavian's troops and those of Severus.

49. 36. 4. Description of the Pannonians. Dio gives his authority for it—ταῦτα δὲ οὐκ ἀκούσας οὐδ' ἀναγνοὺς μόνον, ἀλλὰ καὶ ἔργῳ μαθὼν ὥστε καὶ ἄρξας αὐτῶν, οἶδα—and goes on to mention his governorships of Africa, Dalmatia, and Upper Pannonia. This section at least must date from after the completion of the whole work. It is tempting to suggest that all that was inserted after 228 was Dio's reference to himself. The sentences before and after it can be read straight through—θυμικώτατοι γὰρ . . . εἰσί. / ὀνομάζονται δὲ οὗτως . . . . If this is so, Dio is not being entirely candid, for what he wrote about the Pannonians will have been written prior to any personal acquaintance with them—and this is perhaps hinted at in the expression οὐκ ἀκούσας οὐδ' ἀναγνοὺς μόνον . . . . It may be however, though it is less probable, that the whole passage (49. 36. 2–6) is an insertion and with it also the description of Siscia (49. 37. 3–4) which Dio will have known as legate of Pannonia. In either case this is the only example of a whole passage inserted a good number of years after the original composition of the work.

51. 17. 2–3. Severus allowed Alexandria to have a council, and Caracalla even admitted Alexandrians to the Senate. The Alexandrian

council dates from Severus' visit to Egypt in 199–201 (see p. 144).
The Alexandrian senators are Aelius Coeranus and his son P.
Aelius Coeranus (*Albo* nos. 6 and 7). The father was *a libellis* of
Severus and Caracalla, was exiled in 205, recalled by Caracalla and
made a senator. Dio 76. 5. 3–5 (360) says he was exiled for seven
years (so was recalled in 212) and was consul without having held
any previous office. The year of his consulship is unknown (Degrassi,
Fasti, 59—212 or a little later?). 51. 17. 2–3 will perhaps have been
written towards the end of 214, some two years after Coeranus'
adlection, and does not mention his consulship. This date is supported by 17. 3 which says of Augustus' other regulations for Egypt
καὶ νῦν ἰσχυρῶς φυλάσσεται. One of them was the prohibition on the
entry of senators into Egypt (17. 1), a rule which Macrinus, in
217/18, ceased to observe—78. 35. 1 (443).

53. 17. 1–2 and 8. The Empire should properly be called a μοναρχία,
even if two or three men hold power simultaneously. This can
hardly fail to be an allusion to the joint rule of Severus, Caracalla,
and Geta in 209–11. See also 48. 1. 2.

55. 24. 2–4. Dio's survey of the legions from Augustus to his own time.
One forward reference is explicit—Severus created three new legions,
I and III *Parthica* stationed in Mesopotamia and II *Parthica* in
Italy. There is another which is concealed but more important—
Galba created τό τε πρῶτον τὸ ἐπικουρικὸν τὸ ἐν τῇ Παννονίᾳ τῇ
κάτω. The territory of Brigetio, with the legion I *Adiutrix* which was
stationed there, was transferred from Upper to Lower Pannonia by
Caracalla in 214. See Ritterling, 'Legio' 1393, Reidinger, *Statthalter*, 141, G. Alföldy, 'Megjegyzések egy brigetiói szarkofágfelirathoz (*CIL* 3. 4327)', *Arch. Ért.* 86 (1959), 70–72 (German
summary, 72) and A. Betz, 'Zur Dislokation der Legionen in der
Zeit vom Tode des Augustus bis zum Ende der Prinzipatsepoche',
Carnuntina, ed. Swoboda (Graz–Köln, 1956), 17, on p. 23. Dio
should have written this passage in 215 and it is therefore closer to
the event than any of his other references.

68. 31. 2. Trajan's siege of Hatra—not taken by Severus either.
Severus made two attempts on Hatra, both probably in 198.
75. 10. 1 (348); 11. 1–12. 5 (348–50). See p. 143.

APPENDIX IV

REFERENCES IN THE HISTORY TO CONTEMPORARY INSTITUTIONS AND CUSTOMS[1]

Fr. 26. 1. Condemnation of Capitolinus—his house destroyed, property confiscated, and name erased from statues—καὶ νῦν δὲ πλὴν τῆς κατασκαφῆς πάντα γίγνεται ἐπὶ τοῖς τῷ κοινῷ ἐπιβουλεύουσιν.

Fr. 39. 7. Senatorial dress—— ᾗ κατ᾽ ἀγορὰν χρώμεθα.

36. 50. 3. Pompey's foundation of Nicopolis—καὶ εἰσὶ καὶ νῦν, Νικοπολῖταί τε ὠνομασμένοι καὶ ἐς τὸν Καππαδοκικὸν νομὸν συντελοῦντες. (For this use of νομός compare 48. 12. 5, 53. 26. 3 and 60. 17. 3.)

37. 15. 1. Ἀραβίων μὲν τῶν νῦν τοῖς Ῥωμαίοις δουλευόντων (the Nabataeans).

37. 16. 5–17. 3. On Jews and Jewish customs, in present tense. Refers to proselytes, Jewish community in Rome, contemporary freedom of worship, monotheism, Sabbath (excursus on origin of Sabbath follows, 17. 4–19. 3. See p. 178). Compare 65. 7. 2 (140) ἐν αὐτῇ τῇ τοῦ Κρόνου ἡμέρᾳ, ἣν μάλιστα ἔτι καὶ νῦν Ἰουδαῖοι σέβουσιν.

37. 20. 2. Pompey's arrangements in Asia—ὥστε καὶ δεῦρο αὐτοὺς τοῖς ὑπ᾽ ἐκείνου νομισθεῖσι χρῆσθαι.

37. 28. 1–3. Garrison and flag on Janiculum during *comitia centuriata*. Custom explained.

37. 46. 4. Interval for lunch in gladiatorial shows.

38. 47. 2. Caesar's legions (58 B.C.) named πρὸς τὴν τῶν καταλόγων τάξιν . . . ὅθενπερ καὶ νῦν ὁμοίως τὰ νῦν ὄντα τὰς ἐπικλήσεις ἔχει.

40. 18. 1–2. Description (present tense) of legionary eagle.

41. 49. 2. Dyrrachium ἐν τῇ γῇ . . . νῦν δὲ καὶ τότε γε ἤδη Μακεδονίας νενομισμένη κεῖται.

43. 46. 5–6. On suffect consuls. Compare 48. 35. 2–3, which contains a reference to *suffecti* in the present tense, and 56. 26. 1.

47. 18. 3. New Year oaths. Also 57. 8. 4; 59. 9. 1; 60. 4. 6.

---

[1] Omitting the systematic description and analysis of the Principate in 53. 12–21, also a number of passages in the present tense referring to geographical points, national character, or existing public buildings. No attempt has been made to provide a full commentary.

48. 33. 5. *Lex Falcidia*—πλείστην καὶ νῦν ἔτι ἴσχυν ἐς τὰς τῶν κλήρων διαδοχάς . . . ἔχων.

48. 45. 8–9. Emperors granting right to wear gold ring to individual *liberti*.

49. 30. Description of *testudo*.

51. 17. 1–3. Augustus' regulations for Egypt (no senator allowed to govern or even set foot there—compare Tac. *Ann.* 2. 59. 4). τὰ μὲν ἄλλα καὶ νῦν ἰσχυρῶς φυλάσσεται except Severus' permission for Alexandrian council and Caracalla's introduction of Alexandrians into Senate (see Appendix III).

52. 42. 6. Senators forbidden to leave Italy, except for Sicily and Narbonensis, without Emperor's permission.

53. 20. 4. Greeting to Emperor 'σοι καθωσιώμεθα'.

54. 4. 3–4. Bells carried by night watchmen in Rome.

54. 18. 2. Festival of *Honos* and *Virtus* moved ἐς τὰς νῦν ἡμέρας—15–17 July? See K. Latte, *Römische Religionsgeschichte* (Munich, 1960), 236.

54. 23. 8. Cities giving themselves honorific titles.

54. 26. 6–7. Account of *vigintiviri*.

54. 32. 1. Festival at altar of Augustus at Lugdunum.

54. 34. 2. *Augustalia*.

55. 2. 5–6. *Ius trium liberorum* granted by Emperor (formerly voted by Senate).

55. 3. 3. Names of senators inscribed on *album*—καὶ ἐξ ἐκείνου καὶ νῦν κατ' ἔτος τοῦτο ποιεῖται.

55. 8. 7. *Magistri vicorum*.

55. 22. 4. Separate places of Senate and *equites* in *circus*. See 60. 7. 4.

55. 23. 2–24. 8. Survey of legions and auxiliaries up to and including the present.

55. 25. 3. *Praefecti aerarii militaris* selected by Emperor (formerly chosen by lot).

55. 26. 5. *Vigiles* now recruited from soldiers, not *liberti*, still paid from *aerarium*.

56. 46. 5. *Ludi Palatini* established by Livia.

57. 15. 4. . . . ἔν τε σκιμποδίῳ καταστέγῳ, ὁποίῳ αἱ τῶν βουλευτῶν γυναῖκες χρῶνται. Compare 60. 2. 3 ἐν σκιμποδίοις, ὁποίοις αἱ γυναῖκες ἔτι καὶ νῦν νομίζουσιν.

57. 22. 5. (Xiph.) Those under *aquae et ignis interdictio* forbidden to make wills.

58. 20. 4. Elections to magistracies decided by Emperor and Senate. καὶ μετὰ τοῦτο ἔς τε τὸν δῆμον καὶ ἐς τὸ πλῆθος οἱ προσήκοντες ἑκατέρῳ, τῆς ἀρχαίας ὁσίας ἕνεκα, καθάπερ καὶ νῦν, ὥστε ἐν εἰκόνι δοκεῖν γίγνεσθαι, ἐσίοντες ἀπεδείκνυντο.

59. 9. 5. . . . πρὶν ἄρξαι τινὰ ἀρχὴν δι' ἧς ἐς τὴν γερουσίαν ἐσερχόμεθα.

59. 20. 7. Gaius' appointment of *legatus leg. III Augustae* in Africa. καὶ ἐξ ἐκείνου καὶ δεῦρο τοῦτο γίγνεται. See p. 207.

60. 2. 3. From Claudius, not only Emperors ἀλλὰ καὶ ἡμεῖς οἱ ὑπατευκότες διφροφορούμεθα. See p. 205.

60. 3. 3. Emperors from Claudius on guarded by soldiers at dinner— also 61. 34. 2 (16)—searching of guests abandoned by Vespasian.

60. 21. 5. No more than one acclamation as *Imperator* allowed from each war.

68. 5. 1. . . . ἄνδρα πρεσβύτην ἐν ἱματίῳ καὶ ἐσθῆτι περιπορφύρῳ, ἔτι δὲ καὶ στεφάνῳ ἐστολισμένον, οἷά που καὶ τὴν γερουσίαν γράφουσι . . . .

69. 9. 4. Hadrian's military regulations ὥστε καὶ νῦν τὰ τότε ὑπ' αὐτοῦ ταχθέντα νόμον σφίσι τῆς στρατείας εἶναι. See p. 67.

APPENDIX V

THE PSEUDO-ALEXANDER OF A.D. 221

DIO is the only source for one of the most curious incidents in the history of the early third century, the appearance of a 'pseudo-Alexander' in Moesia in 221. The passage in which he describes the pretender's exploits[1] deserves a full discussion on its own. Translated, it runs as follows:

> Just before this a *daemon*, calling himself Alexander of Macedon and resembling him in appearance and dress, set off from the region of the Danube —having arisen there in some way—and travelled through Moesia and Thrace conducting Bacchic rites, with 400 men equipped with wands and faun-skins but doing no harm. All those who were then in Thrace attest that accommodation and provisions were provided for him at public expense. Not a soul, neither governor nor soldier nor procurator, nor the magistrates of the local communities, dared to withstand him or say anything against him, and he travelled as far as Byzantium in a sort of formal progress, travelling by day and with announcements of his coming in advance. From there he crossed to Chalcedon, carried out some rites at night, made a hollow wooden horse and disappeared.

The mysterious appearance of a pretender to the name of Alexander five and a half centuries after his death seems at first sight incapable of explanation. But the story can be understood, I believe, if one looks back a few years to the journey Caracalla made through Moesia and Thrace in the first half of 214. Setting out from Rome he travelled to the Danube on the normal route to the East and then made a detour into Dacia.[2] From there he returned, probably, to Viminacium and inspected the camps along the Danube.[3] If it is correct that we should recognize a route in the *Itinerarium Antonini* as that of Caracalla on this occasion, he travelled down to the mouth of the Danube, took the road which led down the west coast of the Euxine to Marcianopolis, and then branched inland to join the main route from Sirmium to Byzantium.[4] It was at the moment when he entered Thrace, so Hero-

---

[1] 79. 18. 1–3 (471). For the date see p. 23.
[2] SHA, *Vita Ant. Car.* 5. 4 'dein ad orientem provectionem parans omisso itinere in Dacia resedit'. See D. van Berchem, 'L'Annone militaire dans l'Empire romain au IIIᵉ siècle', *MSNAF*, viiiᵉ sér. 10 (1937), 117, on pp. 172 f.
[3] Herodian 4. 8. 1.
[4] So van Berchem, op. cit. 172–3. The route is that given by the *Itinerarium Antonini*, 217⁵–231³ (Cuntz, *Itin. Rom.* 32–33). While the interpretation remains

dian says, that he began to imitate Alexander (εὐθὺς Ἀλέξανδρος ἦν), not only setting up statues of him in many cities but also imitating him in his dress and recruiting a phalanx from Macedonia.[1] Dio describes his setting up of statues, his formation of a phalanx of 16,000 Macedonians, and his assumption of armour of the type used by Alexander.[2] He also mentions that Caracalla gathered elephants to aid his imitation of Alexander—'or rather of Dionysos'—and describes the favour he showed to a Macedonian tribune called Antigonus the son of Philip.[3]

It was also no doubt his desire to imitate Alexander which led Caracalla to cross over into Asia not by the normal route to Chalcedon but over the Hellespont. His accident during the crossing—his ship capsized and he had to be rescued by his *Praefectus classis*—is intelligible if, like Alexander, he had insisted on both steering the ship himself and making a sacrifice to Poseidon in midstream.[4] At Ilium, Caracalla, like Alexander, carried out sacrifices to commemorate the Trojan wars.[5] From there he paid a visit to Pergamum, to seek the aid of Asclepius, and to some other cities in the province of Asia, and returned to Nicomedia for the winter.

It might thus be suggested that the appearance of a pseudo-Alexander is not entirely unintelligible. The pseudo-Alexander was in reality, so to speak, a pseudo-pseudo-Alexander. He was imitating Caracalla imitating Alexander.

If this is correct, the pseudo-Alexander no doubt followed Caracalla's actual route, from the mouth of the Danube. Like Caracalla he imitated the appearance and clothing of Alexander. He had not, however, like Caracalla, the facilities to have himself transported across the Hellespont, but was forced to use the normal crossing, to Chalcedon. Once on the opposite shore he carried out some ceremonies, but in the wrong place, and made a wooden horse, then as always the most striking element in the story of the Trojan war.

Whether the Dionysiac rites and the Bacchants who accompanied the pseudo-Alexander were part of the imitation of Caracalla is not at all clear. Tradition related that Alexander had celebrated the rites of

---

probable, it must be pointed out that the text of the itinerary gives the positions of two legions, I *Iovia* and II *Herculia*, which were created by Diocletian, and puts V *Macedonica* at Oescus—to which it returned after the abandonment of Dacia. See Ritterling, *RE* 12 'Legio', 1581.   [1] 4. 8. 1–2.

[2] 77. 7. 1–2 (380).   [3] 77. 7. 4–8. 2 (381).

[4] On Alexander's crossing Arrian, *Anab.* 1. 11. 5–6; Plut. *Alex.* 15. 7. For Caracalla's, SHA, *Vita Ant. Car.* 5. 8; Dio 77. 16. 7 (395).

[5] Alexander: Arrian, *Anab.* 1. 11. 6–12. 1, Plut. *Alex.* 15. 8, Aelian, *Var. Hist.* 12. 7, Diodorus 17. 17. 2–3. See H. U. Instinsky, *Alexander der Große am Hellespont* (Godesberg, 1949). Caracalla: Dio loc. cit., Herodian 4. 8. 4–5. See Magie, *Roman Rule*, ch. 28, n. 41.

Dionysos on a number of occasions, perhaps annually,[1] but of the
literary sources only Dio states that Caracalla identified himself with
Dionysos—ἐλέφαντας πολλοὺς συμπεριήγειτο, ὅπως καὶ ἐν τούτῳ τὸν
Ἀλέξανδρον, μᾶλλον δὲ τὸν Διόνυσον μιμεῖσθαι δόξῃ. Elephants were
a prominent motif in the symbolism of a ruler as Neos Dionysos[2] and
Caracalla himself is given the appellation Neos Dionysos in an inscription, probably from Pergamum, which dates to the years 198–209.[3]
An Emperor who identified himself as Neos Dionysos might, like
Hadrian, take part in the rites which formed his own cult, but it is
not attested in every case.[4] Attractive though the possibility is, it
cannot therefore be assumed, in the absence of a direct statement,
that the provincials would have seen Caracalla celebrating Bacchic
rites as he travelled through Thrace. It is safer to regard the Bacchants who followed the pseudo-Alexander as a local element. The
worship of Dionysos was popular over the whole area of Thrace and
the west coast of the Euxine, especially in the Dobrudja[5]—precisely
the area, it seems, from which the pseudo-Alexander arose.

More significance attaches to another feature of the pseudo-
Alexander's progress, as Dio describes it, the fact that he was supplied
with lodging and provisions by the communities through which he
passed (καὶ καταγωγαὶ καὶ τὰ ἐπιτήδεια αὐτῷ πάντα δημοσίᾳ παρ-
εσκευάσθη). For elsewhere Dio recounts with indignation how stopping-
places had to be made ready for Caracalla's journeys on all the roads,
even those on which he never travelled and never intended to travel,[6]
and further expostulates about the provisions exacted from communities and individuals (of whom he himself seems to have been one)
for the maintenance of Caracalla at Nicomedia over the winter of
214/15.[7] An inscription from Apamea in Syria seems to show a *mansio*
being prepared for Caracalla's arrival on this same journey; and if it
cannot be accepted that the whole system of the *annona militaris* was a
Severan creation,[8] it is clear enough that the provision of *mansiones*,
for the court at least, was an important feature of the régime.

The business of supplying soldiers, armies, or the court on the

[1] See A. Piganiol, 'Les dionysies d'Alexandre', *REA* 42 (1940), 285.
[2] See F. Matz, 'Der Gott auf dem Elefantenwagen', *Akad. Wiss. Lit. Abh.
Geistes- u. sozialwiss. Klasse* (Mainz, 1952), no. 10.
[3] *CIG* 6829 = *IGR* 4. 468.
[4] J. Beaujeu, *La Religion romaine à l'apogée de l'Empire*, I (Paris, 1955), 199–200—
Hadrian did participate—and 307–9—Antoninus probably did not.
[5] See D. M. Pippidi, 'Dionysische Inschriften aus Histria aus dem II.–III. Jh.
u. Z.', *Dacia* 3 (1959), 391. Note also the Thracian revolt of 11 B.C., led by a priest
of Dionysos, described by Dio 54. 34. 5.
[6] 77. 9. 5–7 (382–3). See p. 152.
[7] 77. 18. 3 (397). See p. 21.
[8] On the theory put forward by van Berchem, *L'Annone militaire*, see p. 152.

march was, moreover, one of the main causes of tension between state and people under the Empire; a number of documents illustrate the exactions of official travellers and the complaints of subject com-munities.[1] Dio's account of the pseudo-Alexander's progress can thus be added to the other evidence, in that it illustrates neatly the way in which communal experience of what was demanded when a real Emperor passed came into play with the appearance of a false one.

There is still much that we cannot hope to understand in the story Dio tells. But if the resemblance between the progresses of Caracalla and the pseudo-Alexander can be accorded the significance I attach to it, then the story can be related to the evidence we have con-cerning other appearances of pretenders at intervals during the early Empire. The case which most resembles that being discussed is that of a pretender who claimed to be another Alexander, the son of Herod the Great, executed by his father in 7 B.C. Shortly after Herod's death in 4 B.C. the pretender appeared in Crete and, receiving supplies from the Jewish community there, sailed to Melos, where he was given an escort (of the local Jews, possibly) and went on to Dicaearchia. He arrived in Rome with a royal escort and regalia and was welcomed by large crowds of Jews, only to be unmasked by Augustus.[2]

Here we have a clear political motive, which is lacking in the incident of 221. But the *form* of the movement is the same, a pseudo-royal progress in which the pretender assumes the outward appearance of the man whose identity he claims, and is given an escort and ap-propriate supplies and honours. Another, less close, parallel is afforded by the *falsi Nerones*, who appeared on three occasions between 69 and 89. Here, as in the case of the Jewish Alexander and in the cases to be noted below, the claim is to the identity of a royal person who has met a sudden death and might otherwise still be alive.[3] The first 'Nero'—who was a slave from Pontus, or a freedman from Italy (Tacitus does not know which)—arose in Greece in 69 and, gaining credence by his skill at singing and playing the lyre, gathered a band of deserters and beggars and set sail with the hope of reaching the Syrian legions.

[1] The relevant documents are listed by T. Zawadzki, 'Sur une inscription de Phrygie relative au *cursus publicus*', *REA* 62 (1960), 80. See also P. Herrmann, *Ergebnisse einer Reise in Nordostlydien*, Denkschr. Öst. Akad. Wiss. Ph.-hist. Kl. 80 (1962), no. 19. The complaint of the Histrian peasants has now been republished by I. Stoian, 'De nouveau sur la plainte des paysans du territoire d'Histria', *Dacia* 3 (1959), 369, and is of particular interest in the present connexion, since the inscription itself, though not the proceedings recorded in the extant part of it, seems to date from the Severan period—and also derives from the area in which the pseudo-Alexander arose.

[2] Josephus *BJ* 2. 101–10, *AJ* 17. 324–38.

[3] Dio of Prusa, *Or.* 21. 10, states that most people believed that Nero was still alive. See R. Syme, *Tacitus* (Oxford, 1958), 518.

Carried by storms to the Aegean island of Cythnus, he won over some soldiers on their way back from the East and set up a base, despoiling merchants and arming the slaves who were with him. Many turned to him in the hope of revolution ('rerum novarum cupidine et odio praesentium'). But the end was swift—though Tacitus does not indicate how it came.[1]

Then, under Titus, there came another, one Terentius Maximus, claiming that he, Nero, had escaped the soldiers sent to kill him and had lived in obscurity in the meantime. He too resembled Nero in appearance and in his skill on the lyre and as a singer. He gained a following in Asia and made his way toward the Euphrates gathering support on his way. At the end he fled to Parthia where he was unmasked and killed.[2] Finally, in 88/89, yet a third arose, this time supported by Parthia, and nearly brought about war between the two empires.[3]

In 34 a false Drusus arose in the Cyclades and crossed to Asia. Again he relied on personal resemblance to the dead man and was welcomed and escorted by the cities. He aimed to reach Syria and would have won over the legions, but was recognized, arrested, and sent to Tiberius.[4]

Finally there is the case of Clemens, a slave of Agrippa Postumus who appeared in A.D. 16 masquerading as his master, was greeted by large crowds in Rome and met the usual end—he was trapped, questioned, and executed.[5]

These cases cannot be fully discussed here. But they do suffice to provide something resembling an intelligible pattern against which to set the story of the pseudo-Alexander. Their common features can also help to illuminate a little the question of popular conceptions of monarchy, and reactions to individual monarchs, in the ancient world. For they show both that the personal appearance and habits of a monarch could be well known to the population over a wide area and that, when a pretender arose, the movement naturally took the form of a royal progress, with an escort and greetings from communities along the route. The progress of the pseudo-Alexander, indeed, seems to reflect something more specific than this, namely the impact made on the subject population by the passing of an Emperor through their midst, along a particular route and at a certain moment, seven years before.

[1] Tacitus, *Hist.* 2. 8; Dio 64. 9. 3.   [2] Dio 66. 19. 3b–c.
[3] Tacitus, *Hist.* 1. 2. 1; Suetonius, *Nero* 57. 3.
[4] Dio 58. 25. 1; Tac. *Ann.* 5. 10.   [5] Tac. *Ann.* 2. 39–40; Dio 57. 16. 3–4.

BIBLIOGRAPHY

SINCE this book touches on a fairly wide range of different subjects no useful purpose would be served by a combined list of all the books and articles cited in it. The bibliography is therefore divided under four headings: Dio, Historiography and other Historians, the Roman Empire in Dio's Time (including general works on the Empire), and the Greek East in the Roman Period. These are not bibliographies of the subjects concerned, but solely lists of the works to which explicit reference has been made. Standard works of reference are not included.

1. *Cassius Dio and the* Roman History

ADLER, M. 'Die Verschwörung des Cn. Cornelius Cinna bei Seneca und Cassius Dio', *Zeitschrift für die österreich. Gymnasien* 60 (1909), 193.

ANDERSEN, H. A. *Cassius Dio und die Begründung des Principates.* Neue deutsche Forschungen: Abteilung Alte Geschichte, 196 (Berlin, 1938).

BLEICKEN, J. 'Der politische Standpunkt Dios gegenüber der Monarchie', *Hermes* 90 (1962), 444.

BOISSEVAIN, U. P. 'Zonaras' Quelle für die römische Kaisergeschichte von Nerva bis Severus Alexander', *Hermes* 26 (1891), 440.

BÜTTNER-WOBST, Th. 'Die Abhängigkeit des Geschichtsschreibers Zonaras von den erhaltenen Quellen', *Commentationes Fleckeisenianae* (Leipzig, 1890), 121.

BUTTREY, T. F. 'Dio, Zonaras and the Value of the Roman Aureus', *JRS* 51 (1961), 40.

GABBA, E. 'Sulla "Storia romana" di Cassio Dione', *RSI* 67 (1955), 289.

—— 'Note sulla polemica anticiceroniana di Asinio Pollione', *RSI* 69 (1957), 317.

—— 'Storici greci dell'impero romano da Augusto ai Severi', *RSI* 71 (1959), 361.

—— 'Progetti di riforme economiche e fiscali in uno storico dell'età dei Severi', *Studi in onore di Amintore Fanfani* (Milan, 1962), 5.

GIANCOTTI, F. 'La consolazione di Seneca a Polibio in Cassio Dione, LXI, 10. 2', *RFIC* 34 (1956), 30.

GUTSCHMID, A. von. *Kleine Schriften*, 5 (Leipzig, 1894), 547–54.

HAMMOND, M. 'The Significance of the Speech of Maecenas in Dio Cassius Book LII', *TAPhA* 63 (1932), 88.

HARTMANN, K. 'Über das Verhältnis des Cassius Dio zur Parthergeschichte des Flavius Arrianus', *Philologus* 74 (1917), 73.

HAUPT, H. 'Jahresberichte: Dio Cassius', *Philologus* 39 (1880), 54; 40 (1881), 139; 41 (1882), 140; 43 (1884), 678; 44 (1885), 132, 557.

KLOTZ, A. 'Über die Stellung des Cassius Dio unter den Quellen zur Geschichte des zweiten punischen Krieges', *RhM* 85 (1936), 68.

KYHNITSZCH, E. *De contionibus, quas Cassius Dio historiae suae intexuit, cum Thucydideis comparatis* (Diss. Leipzig, 1894).

LEVI, M. A. 'Dopo Azio: Appunti sulle fonte augustee: Dione Cassio', *Athenaeum*, N.S. 15 (1937), 3.

LITSCH, E. *De Cassio Dione imitatore Thucydidis* (Diss. Freiburg, 1893).

MARX, F. A. 'Die Quellen der Germanenkriege bei Tacitus and Dio', *Klio* 26 (1933), 323.

—— 'Die Überlieferung der Germanenkriege besonders der augusteischen Zeit', *Klio* 29 (1936), 202.

MELBER, J. 'Dio Cassius über die letzten Kämpfe gegen Sextus Pompeius, 36 v. Chr.', *Abhandlungen W. Christ dargebracht* (Munich, 1891), 211.

MEYER, P. *De Maecenatis oratione a Dione ficta* (Diss. Berlin, 1891).

NIEMEYER, K. 'Zu Cassius Dion', *Jahrbücher für class. Philologie* 22 (1876), 583.

QUESTA, C. 'Tecnica biographica e tecnica annalistica nei libri LIII–LVIII di Cassio Dione', *Studi Urbinati* 31, N.S. B. 1–2 (1957), 37.

—— 'La morte di Augusto secondo Cassio Dione', *Parola del Passato* 64 (1959), 41.

ROOS, A. G. 'Über einige Fragmente des Cassius Dio', *Klio* 16 (1919), 75.

SCHWARTZ, E. 'Cassius' (40), *RE* 3, 1684–1722 = Schwartz, *Griechische Geschichtsschreiber* (Leipzig, 1957), 394–450.

SMITH, H. R. W. 'Problems Historical and Numismatic in the Reign of Augustus', *University of California Publications in Classical Archaeology* 2. 4 (1953), 133.

SNYDER, W. F. 'On Chronology in the Imperial Books of Cassius Dio's Roman History', *Klio* 33 (1940–1), 39.

STUART, D. R. 'The Attitude of Cassius Dio towards Epigraphic Sources', *University of Michigan Studies* 1 (1904), 101.

VRIND, G. *De Cassii Dionis vocabulis quae ad ius publicum pertinent* (Leiden, 1923).

—— 'De Cassii Dionis Historiis', *Mnemosyne* 54 (1926), 321.

WACHSMUTH, K. *Einleitung in das Studium der alten Geschichte* (Leipzig, 1895), 596–601.

2. *Historiography and Historians*

AVENARIUS, G. *Lukians Schrift zur Geschichtsschreibung* (Meisenheim-Glan, 1956).

BALSDON, J. P. V. D. 'Some Questions about Historical Writing in the Second Century B.C.', *CQ*, N.S. 3 (1953), 158.

BARBIERI, G. 'Mario Massimo', *RFIC* 32 (1954), 36, 262.

BRINK, C. O. 'Tragic History and Aristotle's School', *PCPhS* 186 (1960), 14.

GROSSO, F. 'La "Vita di Apollonio di Tiana" come fonte storica', *Acme* 7 (1954), 333.

HANELL, K. 'Zur Problematik der älteren römischen Geschichtsschreibung', *Fondation Hardt: Entretiens sur l'antiquité classique IV, Histoire et historiens dans l'antiquité* (Geneva, 1956), 147.

HEER, J. M. 'Der historische Wert der *Vita Commodi* in der Sammlung der scriptores historiae Augustae', *Philologus*, Supp.-Band 9 (1904), 1.

HOHL, E. 'Über die Glaubwürdigkeit der *Historia Augusta*', *SDAW* 1953, 2.

MARX, F. A. 'Aufidius Bassus', *Klio* 29 (1936), 94.

MOMIGLIANO, A. 'An Unsolved Problem of Historical Forgery: the *Scriptores Historiae Augustae*', *Journal of the Warburg and Courtauld Institutes* 17 (1954), 22.

PETER, H. *Die geschichtliche Literatur über die römische Kaiserzeit*, 1–2 (Leipzig, 1897).

SCHELLER, P. *De hellenistica historiae conscribendae arte* (Diss. Leipzig, 1911).

STEIN, F. J. *Dexippus et Herodianus rerum scriptores quatenus Thucydidem secuti sint* (Diss. Bonn, 1957).

SYME, R. *Tacitus*, 1–2 (Oxford, 1958).

—— 'Pseudo-Sallust', *MH* 15 (1958), 46.

—— 'Livy and Augustus', *HSCPh* 64 (1959), 27.

TILL, R. 'Sempronius Asellio', *Würzburger Jahrbücher* 4 (1949–50), 330.

TOWNEND, G. B. 'The Sources of the Greek in Suetonius', *Hermes* 88 (1960), 98.

VOSSIUS, G. I. *De Historicis Graecis*, ed. A. Westermann (Leipzig, 1838).

WALBANK, F. W. 'Tragic History: A Reconsideration', *BICS* 2 (1955), 4.

—— 'History and Tragedy', *Historia* 9 (1960), 216.

WALSH, P. G. *Livy: His Historical Aims and Methods* (Cambridge, 1961).

3. *The Roman Empire (A.D. 180–230)*

ALFÖLDY, G. 'Megjegyzések egy brigetiói szarkofágfelirathoz (*CIL* 3. 4327)', *Arch. Ért.* 86 (1959), 70.

BARBAGALLO, C. *Lo Stato e l'istruzione pubblica nell'Impero Romano* (Catania, 1911).

BARBIERI, G. *L'Albo senatorio da Settimio Severo a Carino (193–285)*: Studi pubblicati dall'Istituto Italiano per la Storia Antica, 6 (Rome, 1952).

—— 'Aspetti della politica di Settimio Severo', *Epigraphica* 15 (1952), 3.

BEAUJEU, J. *La Religion romaine à l'apogée de l'Empire I: la politique religieuse des Antonins (96–192)* (Paris, 1955).

BENARIO, H. W. 'Rome of the Severi', *Latomus* 17 (1958), 712.

BENOÎT, P. and SCHWARTZ, J. 'Caracalla et les troubles d'Alexandrie', *Études de Papyrologie* 7 (1948), 17.

BERCHEM, D. van. 'L'annone militaire dans l'Empire romain au IIIᵉ siècle', *MSNAF*, viiiᵉ sér. 10 (1937), 117.

BERSANETTI, G. M. 'P. Settimio Geta, fratello di Settimio Severo', *Epigraphica* 4 (1942), 105.

—— 'Gli auxilia di stanza nella Dalmazia nei secoli I–III', *Bulletino del Museo dell'Impero Romano* 12 (1941), 47.

BETZ, A. *Untersuchungen zur Militärgeschichte der römischen Provinz Dalmatien* (Baden bei Wien, 1939).

—— 'Zur Dislokation der Legionen vom Tode des Augustus bis zum Ende der Prinzipatsepoche', *Carnuntina*, ed. Swoboda (Graz–Köln, 1956), 17.

BIHLMEYER, K. *Die 'syrischen' Kaiser zu Rom (211–35) und das Christentum* (Rottenburg, 1916).

BIRLEY, E. 'The Governors of Numidia, A.D. 193–268', *JRS* 40 (1950), 60.

BRUNT, P. A. 'Pay and Superannuation in the Roman Army', *PBSR* 18 (1950), 50.

CHRISTENSEN, H. *L'Iran sous les Sassanides*[2] (Copenhagen, 1944).

CONDURACHI, E. 'La Costituzione Antoniniana e la sua applicazione nell'Impero Romano', *Dacia*, N.S. 2 (1958), 281.

CROOK, J. *Consilium Principis* (Cambridge, 1955).

DEBEVOISE, N. C. *A Political History of Parthia* (Chicago, 1938).

DOMASZEWSKI, H. von. 'Die Piraterie im Mittelmeere unter Severus Alexander', *RhM* 58 (1903), 382.

DREXLER, F. W. *Caracallas Zug nach dem Orient und der letzte Partherkrieg* (Diss. Halle, 1880).

FINK, HOEY, SNYDER. 'The Feriale Duranum', *YCS* 7 (1940), 1.

FITZ, J. 'Der Besuch des Septimius Severus in Pannonien im Jahre 202 u. Z.', *A. Arch. Hung.* 11 (1959), 237.

FREND, W. H. C. 'A Third-century Inscription relating to *Angareia* in Phrygia', *JRS* 46 (1956), 46.

GILLIAM, J. F. 'The Minimum Subject to the *Vicesima Hereditatium*', *AJPh* 73 (1952), 397.

—— 'The Governors of Syria Coele from Severus to Diocletian', *AJPh* 79 (1958), 225.

—— 'The Plague under Marcus Aurelius', *AJPh* 82 (1961), 225.

GUEY, J. 'Les éléphants de Caracalla (216 après J.-C.)', *REA* 49 (1947), 248.

—— 'Lepticana Septimiana VI', *Revue Africaine* 95 (1950), 51.

—— 'L'Inscription du grand-père de Septime-Sévère à Leptis Magna', *MSNAF* 82, N.S. 2 (1951), 161.

—— 'La date de naissance de l'empereur Septime-Sévère, d'après son horoscope', *BSNAF* 1956, 33.

HAMMOND, M. 'Septimius Severus, Roman Bureaucrat', *HSCPh* 51 (1940), 137.

—— 'The Composition of the Senate A.D. 68–235', *JRS* 47 (1957), 74.

—— *The Antonine Monarchy* (American Academy, Rome, 1959).

HANNESTAD, K. 'Septimius Severus in Egypt', *Classica et Mediaevalia* 6 (1944), 194.

HANSLIK, R. 'Prosopographische Bemerkungen', *JÖAI* 41 (1954), 159.

HASEBROEK, J. *Untersuchungen zur Geschichte des Kaisers Septimius Severus* (Heidelberg, 1921).

HEICHELHEIM, F. M. 'The Text of the *Constitutio Antoniniana* and three other Decrees of the Emperor Caracalla contained in Papyrus Gissensis 40', *JEA* 26 (1940), 10.

HIRSCHFELD, O. *'Die kaiserlichen Verwaltungsbeamten bis auf Diocletian*[2] (Berlin, 1905).

HOHL, E. 'Die Ermordung des Commodus', *Philologische Wochenschrift* 52 (1932), Poland-Festschrift, 191.

—— 'Das Ende Caracallas', *Miscellanea Academica Berolinensis*, 2/1 (Berlin, 1950), 276.

—— 'Kaiser Commodus und Herodian', *SDAW* 1954, 1.

—— 'Kaiser Pertinax und die Thronbesteigung seines Nachfolgers im Lichte der Herodiankritik', *SDAW* 1956, 2.

HOHL, E. 'Herodian und der Sturz Plautians', *SDAW* 1956, 2, 33 f.
HOWE, L. L. *The Praetorian Prefect from Commodus to Diocletian* (Chicago, 1942).
JAGENTEUFEL, W. *Die Statthalter der römischen Provinz Dalmatien von Augustus bis Diokletian*, Öst. Akad. der Wiss., Schr. der Balkankomm.: Antiqu. Abt. 12 (Wien, 1958).
KEIL, J. 'Kaiser Marcus und die Thronfolge', *Klio* 31 (1938), 293.
KUNKEL, W. *Herkunft und soziale Stellung der römischen Juristen*: Forschungen zum römischen Recht 4 (Weimar, 1952).
—— 'Der Prozess der Gohariener vor Caracalla', *Festschrift H. Lewald* (Basel, 1953), 81.
LAMBRECHTS, P. *La Composition du Sénat romain de l'accession au trône d'Hadrien à la mort de Commode (117–92)* (Antwerp, 1936).
LEDERER, Ph. 'A New Coin of Aquilia Severa of Alexandria', *NC*, 6th ser. 3 (1943), 487.
LEGLAY, M. 'Inscriptions de Lambèse sur les deux premiers légats de la province de Numidie', *CRAI* 1956, 294.
MACREA, M. 'Apărarea granitei de vest și nord-esta Daciei pe timpul împăratului Caracalla', *SCIV* 8 (1957), 215.
MARICQ, A. 'Les dernières années d'Hatra: l'alliance avec Rome', *Syria* 34 (1957), 289.
—— 'La chronologie des dernières années de Caracalla', *Syria* 34 (1957), 297.
MILLAR, F. 'The Date of the *Constitutio Antoniniana*', *JEA* 48 (1962), 124.
MORETTI, L. 'Due iscrizioni latine inedite di Roma', *RFIC* 38 (1960), 68.
MOUTERDE, R. 'Une dédicace d'Apamée de Syrie à l'approche de Caracalla et l'*Itinerarium Antonini*', *CRAI* 1952, 355.
MURPHY, G. J. *The Reign of the Emperor L. Septimius Severus from the Evidence of the Inscriptions* (Philadelphia, 1945).
MUSURILLO, H. A. *The Acts of the Pagan Martyrs* (Oxford, 1954).
OLIVA, P. *Pannonia and the Onset of Crisis in the Roman Empire* (Prague, 1962).
OLIVER, J. H. 'Three Attic Inscriptions concerning the Emperor Commodus', *AJPh* 71 (1950), 170.
—— *The Ruling Power: A Study of the Roman Empire in the Second Century after Christ through the Roman Oration of Aelius Aristides*. Transactions of the American Philological Association, n.s. 43. 4 (Philadelphia, 1953).
PASSERINI, A. *Le coorte pretorie* (Rome, 1939).
—— 'Gli aumenti del soldo militare da Commodo a Massimino', *Athenaeum* 24 (1946), 145.
PEKÁRY, T. 'Studien zur römischen Währungs- und Finanzgeschichte von 161 bis 235 n. Chr.', *Historia* 8 (1959), 443.
PETRIKOVITS, H. von. 'Die Chronologie der Regierung Macrins', *Klio* 31 (1938), 103.
PFLAUM, H. G. *Le Marbre de Thorigny*. Bibliothèque de l'École des Hautes-Études, 292 (Paris, 1948).
—— *Les Procurateurs équestres sous le Haut-Empire romain* (Paris, 1950).
—— 'Deux carrières équestres de Lambèse et de Zana (Diana Veteranorum)', *Libyca* 3 (1955), 123.

PFLAUM, H. G. 'La Carrière de C. Aufidius Victorinus, condisciple de Marc-Aurèle', *CRAI* 1956, 189.

—— 'A propos de la date de création de la province de Numidie', *Libyca* 5 (1957), 61.

—— 'Principes de l'administration romaine impériale', *Bulletin de la Faculté de Lettres de Strasbourg* 35 (1958), 179.

—— *Les Carrières procuratoriennes équestres sous le Haut-Empire romain*, 1–3: Institut français d'Archéologie de Beyrouth, Bibliothèque archéologique et historique, 57 (Paris, 1960–1).

—— and PICARD, G. CH. 'Notes d'épigraphie latine', *Karthago* 2 (1951), 89.

PIPPIDI, D. M. 'Beiträge zur römischen Prosopographie des dritten Jahrhunderts', *Philologus* 101 (1957), 148.

PLATNAUER, M. *The Life and Reign of the Emperor Lucius Septimius Severus* (Oxford, 1918).

PRÉAUX, C. 'Sur le déclin de l'Empire au IIIe siècle de notre ère: à propos du P. Fayum 20', *CE* 16 (1941), 123.

RAUBITSCHEK, A. E. 'Commodus and Athens', *Hesperia*, Suppl. 8 (1949), 279.

REIDINGER, W. *Die Statthalter des ungeteilten Pannoniens und Oberpannoniens von Augustus bis Diokletian*. Antiquitas: Abhandlungen zur alten Geschichte 2 (Bonn, 1956).

RICHMOND, I. A., ed. *Roman and Native in North Britain* (Edinburgh, 1958).

ROSTOVTZEFF, M. *Social and Economic History of the Roman Empire*,[2] ed. P. M. Fraser (Oxford, 1957).

SASSE, Chr. *Die Constitutio Antoniniana* (Wiesbaden, 1958).

SCHLEIERMACHER, W. 'Der obergermanische Limes und spätrömische Wehranlagen am Rhein', *33. Bericht der Röm-germ. Kommission, 1949–50* (1951), 133.

SCHWARTZ, J. 'Note sur le séjour de Caracalla en Égypte', *CE* 34 (1959), 120.

SORDI, M. 'L'epigrafe di un pantomimo recentemente scoperta a Roma', *Epigraphica* 15 (1953), 104.

STEIN, A. *Der römische Ritterstand*. Münchener Beiträge zur Papyrusforschung und antiker Rechtsgeschichte 10 (Munich, 1927).

—— *Die Legaten von Moesien*, Diss. Pann. I. 11 (Budapest, 1940).

—— *Die Praefekten von Ägypten* (Bern, 1950).

—— 'Le marbre de Thorigny', *Eunomia* 1 (1957), 1.

STOIAN, I. 'De nouveau sur la plainte des paysans du territoire d'Histria', *Dacia* 3 (1959), 369.

THOMASSON, B. E. *Die Statthalter der römischen Provinzen Nordafrikas von Augustus bis Diokletian*, 1–2 (Lund, 1960).

TOWNSEND, P. W. 'The Revolution of A.D. 238: the Leaders and their Aims', *YCS* 14 (1955), 49.

VITUCCI, G. *Ricerche sulla Praefectura Urbi in età imperiale* (Rome, 1956).

VOGT, J. 'Die Tochter des Großkönigs und Pausanias, Alexander, Caracalla', *Satura: Früchte aus der antiken Welt O. Weinreich . . . dargebracht* (Baden-Baden, 1952), 163.

WALTON, C. S. 'Oriental Senators in the Service of Rome', *JRS* 19 (1929), 38.

WELLES, C. B., FINK, R. O., GILLIAM, J. F. *The Excavations at Dura-Europos. Final Report, V. 1. The Parchments and Papyri* (New Haven, Mass., 1959).

WESTERMANN, W. L., and SCHILLER, A. A. *Apokrimata: Decisions of Septimius Severus on Legal Matters* (New York, 1954).

WILSON, D. R. 'Two Milestones from Pontus', *Anatolian Studies* 10 (1960), 133.

WIRTH, A. *Quaestiones Severianae* (Leipzig, 1888).

ZAWADZKI, T. 'Sur une inscription de Phrygie relative au *cursus publicus*', *REA* 62 (1960), 80.

4. *The Greek East in the Roman Period*

ARNIM, H. von. *Leben und Werke des Dio von Prusa* (Berlin, 1898).

BALDWIN, B. 'Lucian as a Social Satirist', *CQ* N.S. 11 (1961), 199.

BAYNES, N. H. 'The Hellenistic Civilization and East Rome', *Byzantine Studies and other Essays* (London, 1955), 1.

BOSCH, C. *Die kleinasiatischen Münzen der römischen Kaiserzeit, 2. 1. Bithynien I* (Stuttgart, 1935).

CHARANIS, P. 'Ethnic Changes in the Byzantine Empire in the Seventh Century', *Dumbarton Oaks Papers* 13 (1959), 23.

DÖRNER, F. K. *Bericht über eine Reise in Bithynien*. Öst. Akad. der Wiss., Phil.-hist. Kl. 75. 1 (1952).

DOWNEY, G. *A History of Antioch in Syria from Seleucus to the Arab Conquest* (Princeton, 1961).

FUCHS, H. *Der geistige Widerstand gegen Rom in der antiken Welt* (Berlin, 1920).

GEFFCKEN, J. *Der Ausgang des griechisch-römischen Heidentums* (Heidelberg, 1920).

GREN, E. *Kleinasien und der Ostbalkan in der wirtschaftlichen Entwicklung der römischen Kaiserzeit* (Uppsala, 1941).

HABICHT, Chr. 'Zwei neue Inschriften aus Pergamon', *Ist. Mitt.* 9–10 (1959–60), 109.

HAHN, L. *Rom und Romanismus im griechische-römischen Osten* (Leipzig, 1906).

HERRMANN, P. *Ergebnisse einer Reise in Nordostlydien*. Denkschriften der Öst. Akad. der Wiss., Phil.-hist. Kl. 80 (1962).

JONES, A. H. M. *Cities of the Eastern Roman Provinces* (Oxford 1937).

—— *The Greek City* (Oxford, 1940).

KEIL, J. 'Vertreter der zweiten Sophistik in Ephesos', *JÖAI* 40 (1953), 5.

—— 'Ein ephesischer Anwalt des dritten Jahrhunderts durchreist das Imperium Romanum', *SBAW* 1956, 3.

KÖRTE, A. 'Kleinasiatische Studien V: Inschriften aus Bithynien', *Ath. Mitt.* 24 (1879), 398.

MAGIE, D. *Roman Rule in Asia Minor to the End of the Third Century after Christ* (Princeton, 1950).

MENDEL, G. 'Inscriptions de Bithynie', *BCH* 24 (1900), 361.

—— 'Inscriptions de Bithynie', *BCH* 25 (1901), 5.

—— 'Inscriptions de Bithynie et de Paphlagonie', *BCH* 27 (1903), 314.

MILTNER, F. 'Vorläufiger Bericht über die Ausgrabungen in Ephesos', *JOAI* 44 (1959), Beiblatt, 243.

OLIVER, J. H. 'Two Athenian Poets', *Hesperia*, Suppl. 8 (1949), 243.

PALM, J. *Rom, Römertum und Imperium in der griechischen Literatur der Kaiserzeit* (Lund, 1959).

ROBERT, L. *Études Anatoliennes* (Paris, 1937).

—— *Les Gladiateurs dans l'Orient grec* (Paris, 1940).

—— *Hellenica* 1 (Paris, 1940), 5 (Paris, 1948), 9 (Paris, 1950).

SCHNEIDER, A. M. *Die römischen und byzantinischen Denkmäler von Iznik-Nicaea*: Istanbuler Forschungen 16 (Berlin, 1943).

—— and KARNAPP, W. *Die Stadtmauer von Iznik (Nicaea)*: Istanbuler Forschungen 9 (Berlin, 1938).

STEIN, A. 'Zur sozialen Stellung der provinzialen Oberpriester', *'Επιτύμβιον H. Swoboda* (Reichenberg, 1927), 300.

VITUCCI, G. *Il regno di Bitinia* (Rome, 1953).

INDEX OF PASSAGES IN DIO

This index is necessarily selective. It also omits the passages cited in Appendix IV, and almost all passages from chapters where substantial sections of Dio's text are discussed continuously.

INDEX

Emperors, authors, and legal writers are given under their conventional English names. Material from Appendix I (the Epitomes of Dio, Book 54) is not included.

133; has Commodus murdered, 133; goes to Pertinax, 134.

Legions, Dio's survey of, 93, 100, 212; naming of, 211.

I *Adiutrix*, transferred to Pannonia Inferior, 31, 210.

I *Parthica*, created by Severus, 210.

II *Parthica*, created by Severus, 210; in Syria in 218, 167.

III *Gallica*, in Syria in 211, 167.

III *Parthica*, created by Severus, 210.

III *Augusta*, in Numidia, 204; legate of, 207, 213.

XXII *Deiotariana*, lost under Hadrian, 69.

Lex Falcidia, 188, 212.

Lex Manilia, 48.

Lex Pedia, 58.

M. Cn. Licinius Rufinus, Greek senator, and jurist, 188.

Livia, dialogue with Augustus in Dio, 78–79.

P. Livius Larensis, 134.

Livy, referred to by Dio, 34; not source for speech of Cicero in Dio, 52; narrative of 44–42 B.C., 56; speech of Fabius Rullus in compared with that in Dio, 79; used by Dio on Augustus?, 84.

Lucian, on historians, 7; on contemporary historiography, 72.

Lucilius Priscillianus, senator, 164–5.

Ludi Palatini, 212.

Lycia, Brutus' campaign against, 59–60.

Lycia-Pamphylia, governed by Cassius Apronianus, 8; transferred to Senate, 69, n. 8.

Macrinus, Dio's account of reign, 160–8; *see* 30, 44; career, 161; *Praefectus praetorio*, legal knowledge, 115–16; in danger of execution by Caracalla, 159; letters to Senate, 22; appoints Dio *curator* of Pergamum and Smyrna, 23, 25; letter about rebellion of Elagabal, 23; removes titles of Pergamum, 23.

Q. Maecius Laetus, nominal consul *bis*, 209.

Magistri vicorum, 212.

Mallos, Dio examines votive tablet, 180.

Mansiones, 152, 216.

Marcia, concubine of Commodus, Christian, 126; warns Commodus to dispose of Cleander, 131; takes part in murder of Commodus, 133; killed with Didius Julianus, 125.

Marcius Agrippa, senator, career, 161; 172.

Q. Marcius Turbo, *Praefectus praetorio*, 70–71.

Marcomanni, treaty with Commodus, 124–5.

Marcus Aurelius, his freedman, Chryserus, 6; edict on senatorial property, 10; marriage of his daughters, 12; Dio's hearsay evidence for his reign, 36; accession, 39; transfers Lycia-Pamphylia to Senate, 69 n. 8.

Marcus, rhetor from Byzantium, 175.

Marcus Titianus, Lyciarch, descendants, 13.

Marius, his severity praised by Severus, 16–17, 142, 190; Dio's view of, 76.

Marius Maximus (L. Marius Maximus Perpetuus Aurelianus), imperial biographies of, 61; referred to by Dio as *Praefectus Urbi*, 61; Macrinus writes to as *Praef. Urbi*, 167; alleged source of Dio and *Historia Augusta*, 124; reports shouts of crowd after Commodus' death, 134; mentions execution of Laetus, 143.

Marius Secundus, Macrinus makes senator and *legatus* of Syria Phoenice, sends to Egypt, 163.

Mesopotamia, Severus' expedition to, 29, 141; governed by *eques*, 113.

Mob, Dio's view of political behaviour of, 76; political demonstrations in Rome, 137, 141, 145, 164.

Moesia, legions of, 25.

Monarchy, Dio's view of, 74–118 *passim*, esp. 74–76; in speeches, 79–81; in Maecenas' speech, 106.

Murena, conspirator, 88–90.

Narbonensis, 15, 67.

Native languages, survival of, 174.

Nero, confiscates property of Cassius Asclepiodotus, 8–9; appearances on stage, 43.

Nicaea, native city of Dio, 8; Cassii there, 9–11; Dio probably educated there, 13; pupil of rhetor Soter from there, 14; Dio goes there, 21, 23; retires there, 24; foundation, 176; absorbed by Bithynian kingdom, 176; Roman settlers there, 176, 185; rivalry with Nicomedia, 8; Hadrian's benefits to, 72.

Nicolaus of Damascus, historian, 7; life of Augustus, 46–47; possible source for Dio, 84–85.

Nicomedia, metropolis of Bithynia, 8; rivalry with Nicaea, 8; imperial Court there, 19, 20, 21, 23, 155–6, 168, 169; *agon* and temple gained by

Vandals, Caracalla negotiates with, 155.

Varius Marcellus, husband of Julia Soaemias, career, 166.

Vedii Antonini, leading family of Ephesus, 183, 185.

Velleius Paterculus, 5, 7.

L. Venuleius Apronianus Octavius, senator, 206.

Venus and Roma, temple of, 65.

Vespasian, adlections *inter praetorios*, 95; supported by Eastern communities, 187; abandons searching of guests, 213.

Vicesima hereditatium, 153.

Vicesima libertatis, 153.

Vigiles, 94, 212.

Vigintivirate, 97, 212.

Virgil, Dio's acquaintance with, 143.

Viri militares, careers of, 24.

Xenophon, Dio refers to in *consolatio* of Philiscus, 51.

Xiphilinus, Ioannes, his Epitome of Dio, 2–3; his Epitome of Dio Book 54 compared with Zonaras', 195–203; used by Zonaras, 3; had no text of Dio for reign of Antoninus Pius, 62, 72; major source for text of Dio on Hadrian, 63; omissions on Hadrian, 66, 67; full narrative of Hadrian's Jewish war, 68–69; brief reference to events in East under Hadrian, 69; adds reference to Christianity of Marcia, 123; compresses Dio's text, 125–6; inserted comment on destruction of Byzantium?, 140; inadequate on reign of Caracalla, 155; his text on reign of Severus Alexander, 170.

Zonaras, Ioannes, his Epitome and Dio, 2–3; Epitome of Dio Book 54 compared with Xiphilinus', 195–203; his reference to Severus Alexander, possibly from Dio, 170.

Zoticus of Smyrna, 169.